American Science Fiction Film and Television

Lincoln Geraghty

Oxford • New York

First published in 2009 by
Berg
Editorial offices:
1st Floor, Angel Court, 81 St Clements Street, Oxford, OX4 1AW, UK
175 Fifth Avenue, New York, NY 10010, USA

Berg is the imprint of Oxford International Publishers Ltd.

Library of Congress Cataloguing-in-Publication Data

A catalogue record for this book is available from the Library of Congress.

British Library Cataloguing-in-Publication Data

A catalogue record for this book is available from the British Library.

ISBN 978 184520 795 3 (Cloth)
ISBN 978 184520 796 0 (Paper)

Typeset by Apex CoVantage
Printed in Great Britain by the MPG Books Group, Bodmin and King's Lynn

www.bergpublishers.com

Contents

Acknowledgements

This book is the result of years spent in the cinema and in front of the television watching science fiction. From an early age I was captivated by the genre, indoctrinated by George Lucas's *Star Wars,* and inspired by Gene Roddenberry's *Star Trek.* Despite my first cinema memory, being carried out of a packed cinema in Calgary by my dad after watching only the first ten minutes of *E.T.* and crying my eyes out (yes, I found that loveable extraterrestrial scary!), I have been fascinated by science fiction on screen. The genre continues to attract audiences, its place in the American cultural psyche assured by wondrous and terrifying visions of the future, technology and the alien.

For that significant and lasting introduction to science fiction I thank my father (not forgetting all those *Star Wars* toys both he and my mum bought me) as without it I would not have been so captivated and intrigued to find out what makes science fiction so affective and influential. This book has come a long way from my first proposal, and there have been several people who have helped in its development. I would like to thank my editor, Tristan Palmer, who saw potential in my idea and had great patience when I kept pushing back the deadline. I must also thank Van Norris and John Caro, my valued friends and colleagues at the University of Portsmouth, with whom I spent many hours discussing the classics and moaning at the rubbish that continues to fill our cinema and television schedules. As ever, I thank my partner, Rebecca Janicker, who put up with me watching endless tapes and DVDs and tapping away at the keyboard late into the night for months.

Introduction
American Science Fiction Culture

This book stands as a critical history of late twentieth-century American science fiction film and television, offering a discussion of the cultural, industrial, political and social concerns of the popular genre on screen. While I cannot claim that it is exhaustive and inclusive of every film and TV series made in America from 1950 onwards, I would say that this work is an attempt to map themes and trends that have been common to both forms of mediated science fiction. It clearly indicates how the genre has influenced and been affected by the culture in which it is produced. This introduction is split into six sections: the first outlines notions of genre and how science fiction has been defined historically; the subsequent four sections then discuss in detail key historical events and science fiction texts that have had a major impact on the development of the genre and the films and television series we continue to watch today; the final section provides a breakdown of the texts and history discussed in each chapter, also offering an overview of the trends and themes important to a critical understanding of the science fiction genre in America.

Genre and Science Fiction

There have been numerous works that offer their own definitions of the genre, in both literary and visual form, and I do not wish to offer my own single definition here. However, it is important to consider how the genre has been talked about and critiqued at various times throughout its long history—indeed, being able to decide how far back we can trace the history of science fiction as a genre is a debate all unto itself. Generic terms are often ascribed to groups or cycles of texts such as films long after they have been made. Therefore we must be aware how genres are in a constant state of flux as the mechanisms through which media are produced, consumed and evaluated are themselves always changing. As will be discussed further in this introduction, Georges Méliès's silent classic, *Voyage dans La Lune,* is cited as a canonical science fiction film that represents one of the earliest examples of the genre. However, the term *science fiction* had not been invented in 1902, when the film was made. When Hugo Gernsback eventually coined the phrase in America during the 1920s, it was to promote the particular type of fiction that he published in the pulp magazine *Amazing Stories,* fiction that was genuinely opposed to the kinds of fantasy represented by Méliès's film work. So, while genres are fluid and can change over time, they are also historically specific since particular generic labels, canons and terminology give us insight into what cultural and industrial factors contributed to their construction in the first place: 'Genres, of course, are subject to history; that is to say that they are a product of particular societies at particular times' (Lacey 2000: 170).

Steve Neale, in his comprehensive and seminal work, *Genre and Hollywood* (2000), devotes only a few pages to the history of the science fiction genre—particularly, how attempts to define and critique particular film texts have helped to construct a canon of important examples of the genre and the major generic templates that have come to define it. Four of the most significant and culturally relevant templates in American science fiction are discussed here. Crucially, Neale (2000: 28) argues, as I have already summarised, 'that genre as a term has been used in different ways in different fields, and that many of its uses have been governed by the history of the term in these fields—and by the cultural factors at play within them—rather than by logic or conceptual consistency'. Therefore, it is not inconceivable that in talking about the science fiction genre one might easily compare and contrast Méliès with George Lucas, *Metropolis* (1926) with *Aeon Flux* (2005), or indeed a film such as *2001: A Space Odyssey* (1968) with the television series *Star Trek* (1966–1969). In fact, the main aim of this book is to analyse both film and television science fiction together, albeit in sections and boxed text, acknowledging that they differ in how they originated and continue to be made but also demonstrating how they are similar in the ways they have responded to and reflect important historical and political events in American life, and in the ways they have been consumed by audiences and fans.

That last point is crucial, I think, in trying to understand the particular focus of this book on America and the types of science fiction it produces for film and television. For sure, as the major media producer in the world, home to Hollywood and the largest network and cable TV companies, America dominates the genre and the kinds of science fiction that are made. However, as Scott Bukatman (1999: 265) has argued, one can see how science fiction is considered a 'deeply American genre' because of the constant attention paid to themes of science, technology, nature run amok, alien invasion, conspiracy, disaster and space exploration that correlate with particular moments in American history such as the development of nuclear weapons, the Cold War with the Soviet Union, the Space Race, the political and social unrest caused by Vietnam, the Civil Rights movement, the growth of the blockbuster and changes to the Hollywood film industry and the complete integration of computer technology in the network society. Furthermore, one can trace the anxieties built up around these events in late twentieth- and twenty-first-century America to their roots in literature, film and radio in the nineteenth and early twentieth century.

On a purely industrial level, genres historically were used by producers to create and maintain loyal audiences. Hollywood made genre films to help establish regular cinema attendance, attracting people who knew what the film was, what to expect and how it would normally end. Clearly, science fiction as a Hollywood construct had a recognisable audience which came back again and again to watch the latest film and, soon after, television series. There are obvious differences between film and television, none more so than in their production, style and exhibition; however, culturally the two media share a tremendous amount with regard to how contemporary America is depicted in both. Despite disparity between the more 'studio-bound setting of early television' and the bigger budgets afforded to film in terms of sets, location shooting and special effects, 'television has a track record of addressing moral, ethical, political and philosophical themes' just as much as film (Hockley 2008: 37). Indeed, as Jan Johnson-Smith (2005: 56–7) writes in response to one TV executive's statement that 'science fiction doesn't work on TV', 'the notion that the popularity of a genre holds clues to the ideological and cultural preoccupations of its producing society' helps us to recognise that notwithstanding the specific medium (film or TV) genre works in the same way so as to highlight cycles of production and their particular cultural contexts. Science fiction, using metaphorical disguises, reflects contemporary American society. The oscillation between the particular forms it takes is merely a sign of how the public choose to consume and interpret it.

Science fiction's relationship with American history will be explored in much further detail throughout this book; however, it is important to emphasise that as the genre changed along with historical events, so too did audience expectation. Rick Altman acknowledges the historical reception of genre in his book *Film/Genre* (1999) and states that despite the gap between the historical specificity of Cold War bug-eyed monster movies of the 1950s and more modern science fiction, typified by computer imagery and digital effects, people are able to recognise both as science fiction because the latter frequently refers back to the former:

> Whereas genres once served as a monument to real world configurations and concerns, today's genres have increasingly taken on what we might call a pseudo-memorial function. That is, they count on spectator memory to work their magic, but like the "Organization" in an increasing number of futuristic and spy films, they themselves implant in spectators the necessary memories, in the form of other genre films. Their minds filled with prepackaged memories provided by generic memory-masters, genre film spectators have become the true twentieth-century cyborgs. (Altman 1999: 191)

The following analyses of important early literary and media examples of science fiction are intended to highlight some of the consistently recurring themes in American culture that continue to be addressed in the films and television series discussed in the later chapters—that reappear, as Altman describes, as monuments to the genre's history. From Edward Bellamy's utopian novel that talks of a future American city, to the development of early film and its continued influence on spectacle and special effects technology in Hollywood, to the popularity and appeal of outer space and space flight in Hugo Gernsback's pulp magazines, and finally to Orson Welles's panic-inducing radio adaptation of *The War of the Worlds,* science fiction has been instrumental in representing and even instigating tremendous social and cultural change in American history.

Edward Bellamy's *Looking Backward* (1888)

In America during the nineteenth century those who believed that the nation no longer upheld their religious and social values, and that American society had strayed from the path of righteousness, began to form their own religious communities. These communal organisations saw themselves as agents for their own creation of utopia in America and often totally withdrew from normal life, setting up their own villages and communes based on their unique belief systems. Protestant communities in New York and New England, such as Rochester and Oneida, quickly sprung up and became characteristic of the nation's drive for religious and cultural reform: 'Utopia would be realized on earth, and it would be made by God with the active and united collaboration of His people' (Johnson 1978: 110). Utopia could be achieved through balancing the needs of the individual and the community. During this period of religious revival there were hundreds of utopias within America and each one was envisioned by a community dedicated to preserving and prolonging their own version of religious utopia in fulfilment of their divine mission. However, what these communities shared was 'a faith in the perfectibility of mankind and a belief that the millennium was at hand'. Whether these communities disavowed drinking or promoted free love, they all desired 'to bring heaven on earth' (Walters 1978: 39)—that heaven would be founded in America. Consequently, the utopian drive in American culture reached its peak in the late nineteenth and early twentieth century, resulting in the most famous example of American utopian literature, Edward Bellamy's *Looking Backward.*

Bellamy's famous utopian novel celebrates the march toward America's future. Written at a time when the Progressive Movement and religious groups aimed to reform urban American society by returning to community values of the small town, '*Looking Backward* anticipated the movement for reform not through the rousing rhetoric of revolution but by espousing rationalist principles and proposing a national bureaucracy and a disciplined industrial army as answers to "the labor problem"' (Tallack 1991: 12). The Progressive Era in American history can be defined as a largely city-based movement, focused on the reform of the social inequities of the nineteenth century looking forward to a new liberalism concerned for the working classes, wider social responsibility and the modernisation of the economy and industry. Much like the Puritan concern with the past and how it should influence the present, Bellamy (1888: 2) stressed in his preface that the American utopia was achievable through faith and hard work: 'Nowhere can we find more solid ground for daring anticipation of human development during the next one thousand years, than by "Looking Backward" upon the progress of the last one hundred.' The book provided social thinkers and architects with a stimulus for their redesigning of the nation's cities and social structures. Bellamy's main protagonist is Julian West, a time traveller who wakes up in Boston in the year 2000, and his description of a new and orderly city offered a prophetic vision of what would eventually become the architecture of the Chicago World's Fair in 1893:

> Miles of broad streets, shaded by trees and lined with fine buildings, for the most part not in continuous blocks but set in larger or smaller enclosures, stretched in every direction. Every quarter contained large open squares filled with trees, along which statues glistened and fountains flashed in the late-afternoon sun. Public buildings of a colossal size and architectural grandeur unparalleled in my day raised their stately piles on every side. Surely I had never seen this city nor one comparable to it before. (Bellamy 1888: 18)

This description of wide boulevards and tall skyscrapers clearly pre-empts the designs of futuristic cities seen in the science fiction films of the 20s and 30s. Yet it was not only the look of the future that interested Bellamy; he wanted to set out the plans for an alternative society based on city planning, social theory, national and economic reform, education and a new welfare system. Such changes would only be possible through the reordering of society and the incorporation of new theories such as Frederick Taylor's scientific management and the rationalisation of the labour system most famously employed by Henry Ford and the mass production of his Model T automobile. Assembly line production in the early twentieth century revolutionised the industrial workplace, and its effect on workers was critiqued in films such as Charlie Chaplin's *Modern Times* (1936). Scenes showing Chaplin being swallowed by the giant cogs of the machine driving the production line reflect contemporary concerns with industrialisation and the loss of individuality in American culture. Bellamy's novel may have offered a model for an American social utopia, but the means through which this could be achieved threatened the very things that such a utopia was meant to ensure: life, liberty and the pursuit of happiness.

Cities not only provide a physical backdrop but also 'the literal premises for the possibilities and trajectory of narrative action' (Sobchack 1999: 123). The urban science fiction experience as portrayed in film from the 1920s to the present day, according to Vivian Sobchack, offers a 'historical trajectory—one we can pick up at a generic moment that marks the failure of modernism's aspirations in images that speak of urban destruction and emptiness and that leads to more contemporary moments marked by urban exhaustion, postmodern exhilaration, and millennial vertigo' (Sobchack 1999: 124). Indeed, the ways we have imagined our fictional cities are clear indicators of how we continue to interact with the changing urban landscape. *Metropolis*'s city, its design inspired by Fritz Lang's visit to New York, is a mixture of modernist iconography, with its skyscrapers, airplanes and above street level highways, and dystopian decay, with its subterranean levels home to an enslaved underclass existing only to keep the city running for the elite class living above. This was the first fictional depiction of a future city. Less than ten years later the General Motors Futurama exhibit at the 1939 New York World's Fair showed what the real New York could look like in the not-too-distant future. The exhibit gave people 'the opportunity to enter the world of 1960. For Futurama [modelled by the industrial designer Norman Bel Geddes] culminated in a life-size intersection of a city of to-morrow, complete with advanced-model autos (and an auto showroom), an apartment house, a theater, and a department store' (Telotte 1999: 162). As J. P. Telotte surmises, those visitors to the exhibit must have felt as if they had walked onto the set of the latest science fiction film.

Metropolis's above ground city clearly predicts Bel Geddes's modernist vision as it emphasizes transport, entertainment, and consumption. We see inhabitants being marched through the city in ordered rows along mega highways and side-by-side with planes flying between skyscrapers, buildings in the nightclub district are covered in billboards advertising an extravagant lifestyle to the wealthy elite and beneath this all the workers toil to feed the vast furnaces that drive the city's power. *Metropolis,* like those cities in *Things to Come* (1936) and *Just Imagine* (1930), is an ordered hierarchy of capitalist activity, with the workers going to and from work and goods being shipped to the rich high up amongst the skyscrapers. The ground is largely missing from the film, except when the narrative takes the viewer to the scientist Rotwang's laboratory. Nevertheless, the high-up city, the city of skyscrapers presented in the opening sequences, mirrors the Futurist interpretations of modern urban life where artists such as Umberto Boccioni 'sought to capture the overall sensual cacophony of urban life and the way its varied forces interpenetrated one another' (Highmore 2005: 142). According to Douglas Tallack (2005: 84, italics mine), more than any other city, the real New York, as the template for the future city, has 'inspired an ambition to see it all and catch its essence'; the challenge to artists, photographers, filmmakers, and architects was to 'explore how, visually, *part* and *whole* relate or fail to relate when limited, local perspective on the city is chosen or accepted, and what to make of this relationship'.

Georges Méliès's *Voyage dans la Lune* (1902)

Voyage dans la Lune (Trip to the Moon) was Georges Méliès's first space opera, a parody of Jules Verne's and H. G. Wells's lunar novels, *From the Earth to Moon* (1865) and *The First Men in the Moon* (1901), respectively (Hammond 1974: 51). The film follows the voyage of a group of astronomers who use a giant cannon to shoot a rocket to the Moon, where they encounter mysterious sights, celestial bodies, and alien creatures called Selenites. Méliès's now iconic stop motion effect of the rocket approaching the face of the Moon and crashing into its eye is symbolic of his passion for camera trickery, fantasy and spectacle. An early originator of the genre, Méliès was a magician who used film as a source of wonderment and illusion rather than as a medium for narrative and story telling. His work is part of a period in early film history dubbed the 'cinema of attractions', and is representative of when film was an arena for technical experimentation and artistic expression. Méliès, like his contemporaries the Lumière brothers, used film to wow and astonish the audience. *Trip to the Moon* may have depicted space travel and extraterrestrial life, but what fascinated Méliès even more was the potential for the 'scenario' to act as 'pretext' for stage effects, tricks and a 'nicely arranged tableau' (Méliès cited in Gunning 1990: 57).

For Tom Gunning, the 'cinema of attractions' presented audiences with a series of views, and they were fascinated by the 'power' of 'magical illusion' (1990: 57). Film was not used merely to tell a story but to show off the creative, scientific and artistic talents of the filmmaker: 'the cinema of attractions directly solicits spectator attention, inciting visual curiosity, and supplying pleasure through an exciting spectacle—a unique event, whether fictional or documentary' (1990: 58). The history of early cinema had been constructed under a hegemonic bias toward narrative film, as that is the dominant form of filmmaking still produced today. The 'cinema of attractions' offers film historians and science fiction scholars an alternative framework through which they can interpret material produced by Méliès and others. After all he was a magician, so by nature his intention was to dazzle and grab the audience's attention rather than to construct a realistic and plausible world. Short films of this mode would be shown to audiences as part of a vaudeville program or magic show and would therefore sit disjointedly with other entertainment acts on the bill. Story and narrative were not the primary concern for those who made and watched these films. The 'cinema of attractions' would eventually give way to the dominance of narrative cinema; however, it has been described by some as still retaining its roots in the science fiction and fantasy films of George Lucas's and Steven Spielberg's 'cinema of effects' (Gunning 1990: 61).

Voyage à Travers l'Impossible (The Impossible Voyage) was another film made by Méliès that depicted space travel and interplanetary exploration. In this case, the surface of the Sun plays host to a group of scientists and gentlemen who travel there by steam train. Again, Méliès uses editing techniques, stop motion and camera trickery to offer audiences a picture of what it might be like in space and on the Sun, yet, of course, there is a clear suspension of disbelief involved when humans are able to set foot on the hot surface without burning up. Examples of such absurdist representations of the real are what separate Méliès's work from true science fiction for some scholars, yet it can be argued that his methods and the techniques he established for modern cinema making are by their very nature the stuff of science fiction and fantasy. As we know, the genre is often all about our relationship with technology and how it affects our daily life, so, for J. P. Telotte (2001: 25), it 'to a degree almost inevitably seems to be *about* the movies precisely because of the ways in which its reliance on special effects implicates both the technology of film and the typical concern of most popular narratives'. Trickery in fantasy films such as Méliès's not only calls attention to the illusion and deception but also to the very act of watching the movie. His films revelled in creating amazing effects and showing off new editing techniques, but they also reminded viewers of the cinema's new-found power to amaze audiences and imagine the previously unimaginable:

> In fact, we might say that it is precisely the tension between such seemingly magical effects and the desire to make those elements neatly "fit" into a reality illusion that is the core of his film's appeal—and, indeed, that of the entire science fiction genre. (Telotte 2001: 25)

Yet Méliès's films are jarring to the audience who watch them, actors disappear and reappear in clouds of smoke, objects change shape and appearance, the film itself jumps about—giving us a visual clue to the master's cutting and editing technique. The audience does not know what will happen next since the narrative does not follow a pattern of cause and effect. Viewers are in fact beholden to the filmmaker, and it is this relationship that most characterises Méliès's work. Gunning (1996: 82) says that this 'truly invokes the temporality of surprise, shock, and trauma, the sudden rupture of stability by the irruption of transformation or the curtailing of erotic promise'. Early cinema, then, as well as being about technological experimentation, was a medium that kept people on the edge of their seats, keeping them astonished long enough for them to be temporarily extracted from the reality of their lives and inserted into the realm of the filmmaker—a temporal experience of artistic practice. It is perhaps for this reason that Méliès can be seen as a progenitor of science fiction on screen because still today the genre has the ability to take audiences to the edge of their seats and show them the unimaginable.

Hugo Gernsback and the Pulps (1924)

The term *pulps* was used to describe a particular kind of story printed on cheap pulp paper and published for a small market of loyal readers. The types of stories produced ranged from westerns to crime fiction, romance to science fiction. Popular from the early twenties to around the middle of the twentieth century, pulps were part of a growing magazine industry (also including dime novels and comics) that targeted a large labour market that had more money to spend on leisure activities and cheap consumables. Largely dismissed by scholars as being aimed more at a juvenile audience—particularly since the most popular adventure stories were of the boy's-own variety—more recently, the pulps have been perceived as an integral part of the genre's history. The pulps 'appealed to an increasingly socially diverse readership: the emphasis was on eventful narrative, strong characters, a binary ethical code of good and evil, and (especially in SF Pulps) exotic and wonderful locales' (Roberts 2005: 174). A leading figure in the creation and development of science fiction pulps was editor Hugo Gernsback. His influence on the genre cannot be underestimated, and as such he is a figure that has attracted much attention from academics and enthusiasts. For some, he was the father of modern science fiction; for others, he was someone who stunted the genre's growth in the early part of the century. Either way, his impact can still be seen in the genre today—not least in the establishing of its name.

The term *science fiction* comes from Gernsback's first attempt in 1924 at producing a magazine devoted to what he called 'Scientifiction'. Stories from the likes of Jules Verne and H. G. Wells were up until this point termed *scientific romances,* and Gernsback wanted to publish magazines based on such fiction that would teach and entertain. His first publications were more practically minded: *Science and Invention* and *Modern Electrics* were two of his early attempts. These examples contained very technical stories, with large chunks of manual-like instruction for building new and wonderful pieces of electrical gadgets and machinery. Alongside these more factual narratives Gernsback included fiction of his own and republished more famous stories from authors such as Wells, Verne, and Edgar Allan Poe. His most famous magazine, *Amazing Stories* (first published in 1924), contained a mix of both the technical stories and the more fantastical. This combination seemingly added to the popularity of the genre, as Tim DeForest (2004: 64) notes: 'the illusion of scientific reality helped create the suspension of disbelief necessary to make the stories dramatically viable. In a world where impossible things like telephones and radio were becoming everyday items, steam-powered men and time machines didn't seem too unreasonable'.

Gernsback was a very competitive man, not least because he was in a very competitive industry. Millions of pulps were sold on newsstands and book stalls, and his magazines were just a few of the publications attracting readers. One could say that a defining trope of the science fiction genre is its enthusiasts' desire to continually define and redefine what is considered science fiction: whether it is Wells, Gernsback or even *Star Wars* (1977). Fascinatingly, as Gary Westfahl has uncovered, Gernsback was not only interested in defining the genre through the written word, but also through the use of a visual symbol—something that could be printed on the front of his magazines that would advertise: 'this is science fiction'. For Westfahl, this drive to find a symbol could be 'interpreted primarily as an expression of his desire for profit' (especially in a highly competitive market), but it also throws up some interesting questions around how we define concepts, and how very often our definitions are entirely verbal. Gernsback's search for a symbol for *Amazing Stories* may not have produced a lasting image for the genre, but pictorial representations did provide a 'potentially valid alternative approach to the problem of definition and might be usefully examined both for information about the attitudes towards science fiction of the people who created and used them and as possible influences on the attitudes of those people who regularly saw them' (Westfahl 2007: 45). The cover images used by Gernsback are perhaps the most remembered elements of the pulp phenomenon. Indeed, the comic strip clearly took inspiration from the visual designs of the pulp covers, offering the readers science fiction stories less scientific and more focussed on heroes and personalities. From the thirties onwards, comic book heroes such as Buck Rogers and Superman became important transition figures for science fiction's jump from the page to the screen.

Competing definitions aside, Gernsback was interested in publishing stories that taught his readers and also entertained them, so that they 'would be instructed through science fiction' (Ashley 2000: 50). As the pulp industry grew and Gernsback increased his sales through diversification, more and more people were reading and, indeed, writing. His magazines, as well as publishing established authors, offered the opportunity to aspiring science fiction writers to get their stories in print. One of Gernsback's most famous discoveries was E. E. "Doc" Smith. Whatever the focus and quality of the stories published in the pulps, it was clear that Gernsback had a dramatic impact on the perception of the genre. The greatest impact he had was to draw publishers, editors, writers and readers to science fiction: 'other publishers began defending the scientific value of their stories, writers started to include more scientific explanations in their stories, and readers wrote letters praising and analysing stories of this type' (Westfahl 1998: 27). A community grew up and around his and other publications, a community stimulated by the possibilities represented by the technologies described in the stories and fascinated with the idea that limitless invention and innovation could eventually take humans to other worlds. Still popular in the 1950s, Gernsback's brand of science fiction literature offered readers realistic visions of time travel, alien life and space exploration (Ashley 2005: 58). Of course, by that time what they were imaging from the pulp page was being literally shown to them on the big screen in the guise of UFOs, hideous alien blobs and charismatic all-American astronauts.

H. G. Wells and *The War of the Worlds* Radio Play (1938)

Wells's story is seen by many as the 'quintessential romance of interplanetary war', a critique of European, particularly British, imperialism and a story that raises 'questions about evolution and ethics, and about the boundary between humanity and animality' (Wagar 2004: 54). The book was published in 1898, but it was serialised before then. Simply put, Martians invade Earth; stepping foot in the south of England first, they intend to devour the planet's resources. Killing any human that stands in the way of their giant three-legged fighting machines, the aliens occupy London and force inhabitants to flee to the countryside. Advanced far beyond the level of current human technology (there is no weapon that can stop them), they arrive to colonise the planet, and the inferior human race is helpless. The Martians have evolved and they feed on human blood, yet for all their technological and biological superiority they are eventually found to be vulnerable to Earth's smallest of inhabitants: the germ. Disease germs, like the common cold, prove to be the Martian's downfall, and humanity is saved not by its own hand but by nature's own design.

The War of the Worlds has inspired multiple adaptations, remakes and homages, but what stands out as exemplar of its historical and cultural influence is the 1938 radio play, narrated by Orson Welles and scripted by Howard Koch. The impact of this radio adaptation is still discussed and analysed by mass media and communication scholars to this day, no doubt because it represents a moment in American history when reality gave way to fantasy and the power of the media was fully experienced for the first time. For Adam Roberts, the panic caused by Welles's radio broadcast 'expresses the truth that [science fiction], its assumptions and icons were now part of the mental furniture of most Americans. The decades to follow, known as the golden age of science fiction, were in no small part ushered in by the popularity and impact of Welles's *War of the Worlds*' (Roberts 2005: 193).

Radio as a medium drew the nation together during the first half of the twentieth century. It connected people's inner thoughts (as they thought silent thoughts throughout the day) with the voices of other people they never met. The multiple voices of singers, comedians, politicians, newsreaders, journalists, actors, and public officials reverberated through the radio. For Susan Douglas, this faceless relationship with new voices changed people's perception of the self and society: 'How one's inner voice resonated with these was now part of a new national dynamic. So was the process of imagining who was speaking, of visualizing what was happening and comparing your highly personal yet mediated imaginings with those of others' (Douglas 2004: 31). Being able to internalise and visualise what was being described, or not described, on the radio gave life to Welles's adaptation. People could, and did, imagine what the Martians looked like and what devastation they were causing—somehow filling in the gaps of invasion and ignoring the constant reminders that it was only a dramatization. Radio's capacity to bring the previously unknown and unfamiliar into people's homes proved to be the ultimate facilitator for the mass panic of *War of the Worlds* in 1938. It is clearly the first example of the modern day media event:

> Orson Welles, director and star of the program, had to hold a press conference the next day to apologize and insist he meant no harm. Dramatizations of simulated news bulletins became verboten. And the broadcast was taken, in many circles, as an indisputable demonstration of the "hypodermic needle" theory of radio's power to instantly inject an unsuspecting people with unchecked emotions that would produce irrational responses. (Douglas 2004: 165)

Originally selected by Welles to boost ratings for his weekly *Mercury Theater* show, *War of the Worlds* was broadcast during the week leading up to Halloween (DeForest

2004: 164). In Hadley Cantril's famous 1940 study of why the broadcast had such an effect on its listeners, he recorded that one million people believed the drama to be real, so real that they packed their bags and started to evacuate for fear of falling victim to the Martians. For five million other listeners, it was only a play; they had bothered to look out of the window or turn over to listen to another news channel. Often cited as evidence for the power of media effects, the fact that so many people did not fall for the drama highlights the fact that media, such as the radio, had a limited effect 'depending on key factors of audience selectivity, interpretation and social context' (Livingstone 2005: 30). Yet the constructed realism of the play, with its use of named speakers, real life locations in America (such as Times Square in New York) and the fact that it was being aired on the accepted medium for making important announcements, meant that its impact was still significant for those scholars concerned with the power of the media (Laughey 2007: 17–18). Indeed, mirroring Roberts's assertion that the broadcast helped inspire the genre's golden age, some media scholars have interpreted its impact as a dark foreboding of how a mass audience could be persuaded or coerced to believe in almost anything:

> [Welles's] announcement of Martian landings generated panic, but it could also be described by Dorothy Thompson as "the news story of the century", that made "a greater contribution to an understanding of Hitlerism, Mussolinism, Stalinism and all the other terrorisms of our time than all the words about them that have been written by reasonable men". (Briggs and Burke 2002: 216)

For this reason alone, H. G. Wells's science fiction story is truly a terrifying vision of humanity and the lengths to which it would go to survive.

Chapter Outline

The following chapters offer a broadly chronological social and cultural history of science fiction film and television in America. Taking into account important political and social trends that contributed to the growth and popularity of the genre, they highlight significant examples of what I would call America's science fiction culture. Having started this introduction with an overview of the genre's historical and cultural contexts, centred on the religious, film, media and literary roots of American science fiction film and television, I focus subsequent chapters on key moments in history from the Cold War to America's War on Terror, examining the growth and development of the genre through critical case studies of key films and television series. It is not my intention to compartmentalise cycles and periods of change both in the film and television industries and American history at large, even though it may seem so with chapters following a broad chronology of science fiction on the big and small screen. However, I must point out that where connections can be made and should be made between periods of production and cycles of films that begin and end in particular decades I will do so. This is not only so that we can recognise the difficulties inherent in categorising history and the media but also to show how intertextual and self-reflexive the genre has been and continues to be right up to today. Each chapter contains boxed texts that focus on specific films and television series that exemplify the particular social and historical moments discussed at length in the chapter. Covering basic plot points, as well analysing theme and style of the film or television show in question, the boxed texts are designed to also address specific academic and critical debates surrounding the particular text. For example, in the boxed text for *Battlestar Galactica* (2003–2009) not only are some of the episodes discussed in the contexts of post-9/11 American politics but so too are some of the cross media texts related to the series and its associated body of fans. Other boxed text examples discussed include *Invasion of the Body Snatchers* (1956), *2001: A Space Odyssey, Star Trek: The Next Generation* (1987–1994), *The X-Files* (1993–2002), and *Transformers* (2007).

Chapter 1—Conflict and Consensus: The Cold War and the Space Race

This chapter will contextualise the growth and popularity of science fiction film (predominantly the B-movie) within the cultural framework of the Cold War and America's changing post-WWII domestic situation—suburban growth, increased middle-class wealth, new technologies, and the Space Race. Commonly associated with the fear of the Red Menace, *Invasion of the Body Snatchers* will be examined within these new domestic contexts, offering alternative readings that see the film as a reaction to the loss of male identity as well as an allegory of the communist threat. Other films of the 1950s such as *The Day the Earth Stood Still* (1951), with its overtly antiwar message, representing the transition period between political consensus and international conflict will be discussed. These films are representative of American science fiction's ability to comment on the key social issues, offering audiences different perspectives on America's national agenda. While some films as mentioned were critical of America's nuclear proliferation and communist witch hunts, others such as *Destination Moon* (1950) can be seen as propaganda for America's fascination for reaching the Moon and winning the Space Race. The introduction and development of the new medium of television will be assessed, paying close attention to early science fiction serial series based on comics such as *Buck Rogers, Flash Gordon* and the original television series *Captain Video and His Video Rangers* (1949–1955), which paved the way for series such as *Star Trek, The Outer Limits* (1963–1965) and *The Twilight Zone* (1959–1964), whose episodes often dealt with prescient themes and tropes such as nuclear war, domestic conflict, threats from the Soviet Union, space travel and alien invasion. Television, although a relatively nonpolitical medium to start, clearly became a site for the same kinds of political debate as seen in science fiction film. The early serials glorified forms of space travel and colonisation, with comic book characters such as Flash Gordon serving as capable heroes for postwar America. However, as tensions rose towards the end of the 1950s and early 1960s, television science fiction responded by producing science fiction that not only critiqued the social climate of fear and ideological conflict but also offered the chance for viewers to see the consequences a nuclear war might have.

Chapter 2—Pushing the Frontiers of Reality:
Science Fiction and the Counterculture

Picking up from the previous chapter, the second chapter explores how science fiction of the late 1960s, both on television and on the big screen, offered more technologically advanced visions of America's future (Kubrick's *2001: A Space Odyssey* seen as the pinnacle of film special effects in this period) yet also highlighted the precarious position the country found itself in around the world (America's involvement in Vietnam often provided the critical and cultural contexts for many *Star Trek* episodes). From the release of *2001* onwards science fiction reflected a period of great change in the Hollywood industry as films such as *2001, Planet of the Apes* (1968) and *THX-1138* (1971) began to pick up on the warnings offered by television in the late 1950s and the emergent counterculture movement, showing the effects that nuclear war, racism and Nixon's conservative presidency were having on America. *Star Trek,* well-known for its didacticism, offered television audiences an equally dichotomous view of the future: if the era of Civil Rights and mass youth protest was not followed through, America would fail. Yet it also maintained that America's mission of global peace and national unity could still be brought about if Americans could learn from their mistakes and strive to achieve utopia sooner rather than later. Typical of much television in the 1960s, *Star Trek* represented a divided decade; the first two-thirds was filled with series such as *Voyage to the Bottom of the Sea* (1964–1968), *Lost in Space* (1965–1968), *The Time Tunnel* (1966–1967) and the more juvenile offerings like *My Favorite Martian* (1963–1966) and *The Jetsons* (1962–1963), which largely promoted space exploration in the run-up to the first Moon landing. As the decade drew to a close, however, neither *Star Trek* nor similar television shows could stem the tide of disinterest in American space exploration shown by science fiction film. Well into the 1970s, film was more concerned with domestic issues rather than interstellar travel.

Chapter 3—Unsettling Visions of America's Future Present:
Dystopian Science Fiction

Starting in 1971, with the release of Lucas's *THX-1138,* science fiction film and television was characterized by a sense of convergence. The negativity of the late

1960s continued, with science fiction films such as *Soylent Green* (1973), *Logan's Run* (1976) and *Silent Running* (1972) offering extremely bleak visions of the future where poverty, hunger, nuclear war and environmental disaster were taken to their natural ends, with humans having to survive on an Earth suffering from its mistakes of the past. Visions of space travel and alien contact were conspicuously absent from the big screen as Hollywood focused its attention on important domestic issues. Series on television such as the *Planet of the Apes* (1974–1975) spin-off continued to provide social commentary, originally initiated by *Star Trek,* focusing on ever-present issues such as America's continued involvement in Vietnam, political scandals like Watergate, and domestic social inequality. Reactions to Nixon's re-election and subsequent impeachment were ever-present in both media; however, films continued to be overtly pessimistic about the future and America's continued domestic and international problems. *Capricorn One* (1978) showed that Americans were no longer interested in space flight, and its use as a form of political propaganda could not deflect attention away from America's political failings at home and abroad. However, there was also a proliferation of science fiction series on the small screen, such as *Mork and Mindy* (1978–1982), *The Six Million Dollar Man* (1974–1978), *The Bionic Woman* (1976–1978) and *Battlestar Galactica* (1978–1980), which attracted audiences by combining humour and spectacular special effects to compete with their filmic counterparts. This decade also saw an influx of British science fiction series such as *Doctor Who* (1963–1989), *Blake's 7* (1978–1981), *UFO* (1970–1971), which showed American audiences that good science fiction did not have to rely on big budgets to be challenging and thought provoking. The final years of the 1970s, epitomized by Spielberg's *Close Encounters of the Third Kind* (1977) and Lucas's *Star Wars,* were a refreshing change to the nihilism of the period, yet they can also be seen as being critical of the national condition in their respective depictions of faceless, bureaucratic, and fascistic governments.

Chapter 4—Hopes and Fears: Aliens, Cyborgs and the Science Fiction Blockbuster

After a sustained period of negativity, science fiction after *Star Wars* returned to its roots, with films such as Spielberg's *E.T. The Extra-Terrestrial* (1982) and **batteries not included* (1987) offering light relief to the concerns of the 1970s. These films once again looked to the stars, offering visions of wonder and hope through the use of friendly and benevolent aliens. Whereas the films in the 1950s depicted aliens as a monstrous threat to America in the invasion narrative, Spielberg and Lucas harked back to the golden age of Flash Gordon and serial science fiction, showing that America could benefit from extraterrestrial life. While academic debate considers the films of the 50s, 60s and 70s as authentic in that they critically engaged with contemporary social issues—the nihilism of the 1970s seen as a positive thing compared with the overtly utopian visions of society and family life depicted in

1980s' science fiction—this chapter will show that, in fact, along with examples such as the *Alien* franchise's critique of Reaganite big business ethics, Spielberg's films warned of the threats posed by the increased division of society, the growing gap between rich and poor, and corporate attacks on the American family unit. The alien threat on the big screen rested with the monstrous feminine in space, exemplified by the *Alien* quadrilogy starting in 1979 (not including the two *Alien vs. Predator* films), where, allegorically, America's curiosity would be punished if it started to look elsewhere for profit and resources. The big-budget appeal of films such as *The Terminator* (1984) not only rested on the main star and lead character but also on the developing uses of special effects and film technology (science fiction was at last living up to expectations by making the unimaginable imaginable on screen). The intersection between the body and technology, as expressed in key cyberpunk texts of the 1980s such *Neuromancer* (1984) and *Blade Runner* (1982), was being realised in the hard body of the cyborg which would continue to play a major role in science fiction film and television through the late 1980s well into the 1990s (*RoboCop, Terminator 2,* etc.). On television, after a period of stagnation and little investment, science fiction returned with big budget appeal and special effects. Mini-series such as *V* (1984–1985), and revamped favourites such as *Star Trek: The Next Generation* (1987–1994), brought spectacle and wonder back to America's television audiences. Familiar tropes of alien invasion, time travel, intergalactic war, and utopia became popular again as these series continued to experiment and innovate within the genre. Continuing to serve as allegorical stories, these television series followed in tradition created by *The Twilight Zone* and *Star Trek* as described in previous chapters.

Chapter 5—Beyond Truth and Reason: Politics and Identity in Science Fiction

Influenced by a period of political uncertainty and mediocrity, science fiction in the early 1990s started to comment on the culture wars being fought in America as notions of individualism and national identity were challenged by historical revisionism, globalisation, technology and the powerful figure of the cyborg. Films such as *The Lawnmower Man* (1992), *Johnny Mnemonic* (1995) and *The Matrix* (1999) depicted computers and virtual reality as the next frontier of humanity. Notions of the cyborg began to influence not only contemporary science fiction but also science fact as developments in surgical enhancement allowed humans to push themselves harder and stretch the limits of the human body. The cyborg body in American culture at this time was personified by Arnold Schwarzenegger in the *Terminator* films, and the intellectual debate surrounding the potentials for human evolution centred on feminist Donna Haraway's concept of the human/cyborg hybrid. However, the body of the cyborg was changing as influences from the East and Japanese anime changed the cyborg from a masculine, body-built figure to a more feminine and sleek example of humanity's relationship with technology and the infinite potentials of jacking-in to a virtual reality environment. Human identity, as questioned in *The Matrix* trilogy, could no longer be purely based on notions of gender, sexuality and the body since all three can be done away with when creating and entering the realms of cyberspace. On television, the uncertainty and lack of confidence in the government present in American society, towards the end of the 1980s and early 1990s, clearly played a huge part in the popularity of series such as *The X-Files,* whose regular motto 'Trust No One' became a slogan for a generation. Familiar tropes such as alien invasion and abduction reappeared, only this time reflecting America's own self-doubt as the country headed toward the new millennium, unsure of its global position as the world's only remaining superpower. Even relatively conservative series like *Star Trek* followed suite with *Deep Space Nine* (1993–1999), alongside the rival *Babylon 5* (1994–1998), by offering allusions to increasingly complex political and religious issues affecting America at home and abroad such as genetic cloning, racial genocide in Rwanda and the Palestinian conflict. Successful series like these, as well as the long-running *Stargate SG-1* (1997–2007), were products of a significant change in the American television industry as the major networks looked for more bland and safe programming, thus forcing the more niche-market science fiction series onto cable and satellite. In its liberation from network television, science fiction could experiment with plot, narrative, and characterisation to offer multiple audiences and fan groups the sophisticated product they had longed for. However, the networks still enjoyed using science fiction motifs in sit-coms such as *3rd Rock from the Sun* (1996–2001) as integral parts of their primetime schedules.

Chapter 6—American Science Fiction Post-9/11

This final chapter will offer a survey of the most recent film and television science fiction but will also look ahead to what the future might have in store for the genre as America continues to struggle at home to cope with the aftermath of 9/11 and strive abroad in its almost divine mission to eradicate terrorism and establish world democracy based on American principles. The struggle at home is best represented by films such as Lucas's *Star Wars* prequels and *Sky Captain and the World of Tomorrow* (2004) that revisit familiar times in an effort to use nostalgia and history to recover from the wounds inflicted in 2001. Domestic issues are forgotten or overlooked science fiction film offering with elegiac visions of the future (ironically using state-of-the-art of computer technology and special effects) that seemingly return American audiences to better, more secure times. Another example of this can be seen in Hollywood's fascination with bringing back famous comic book characters like Batman, Superman, Spider-Man and so forth to the big screen—audiences clearly keen to see childhood heroes and adolescent memories reproduced and replayed in a period of national uncertainty. Alternatively, television series such as *Battlestar Galactica,* and, to a lesser extent, *Star Trek: Enterprise* (2001–2005) tackle more pressing problems in American culture such as the threat posed by international terrorism, the nation's position as global police force, religious fundamentalism and the loss of Earth's natural resources. These series continue to challenge the established cultural norms and conventions set by America's contemporary political leaders; following in the footsteps of science fiction television of the 1960s and 1970s, which also challenged the nation's audiences to think about the state of the country and its future in an ever-changing international context.

-1-

Conflict and Consensus
The Cold War and the Space Race

America in the 1950s was undergoing tremendous social and cultural change. Following the return of American soldiers from World War II there was huge population growth coupled with the suburban expansion of major cities. The 1944 G.I. Bill gave returning servicemen the means to buy their dream house and funded a return to college that would guarantee a better income. The Highways Act of 1956 linked work in the city with the sprawling suburban towns, making it easier for people to commute from their supposed domestic paradise. Fuelling these changes was the demand for more consumable products; the growth of consumer society meant a proliferation in goods such as cars, kitchen appliances, and other luxury items. Shopping malls became hubs for consumer buying and social interaction, replacing the city high street as a centre of commerce. Television became a window onto this new consumer world, with adverts promoting fashion, food, celebrities and a new American leisure lifestyle. The domestic model of masculinity became hegemonic. TV shows like *Father Knows Best* (1954–1962) and *Leave it to Beaver* (1957–1963) instructed middle-class suburban men how to live and behave in their new domestic environment.

For Martin Halliwell, the standardization of new corporate architecture and suburban developments in the 1950s—office blocks and white picket fenced houses—was keenly felt in popular literature, film and television of the time. Grey-suited men going off to work, waved goodbye to by their wives standing at the door, were images that even then were being satirized and questioned by cultural commentators (Halliwell 2007: 40). Indeed, the rigidity of the ascribed gender roles became subject of many films of the decade, with science fiction contributing to this cultural debate through *Invasion of the Body Snatchers* (1956) and *The Incredible Shrinking Man* (1957). However, the political consensus identified a more potent and visible threat to the stability of American life and society, namely communism. During the 1950s, the American public were convinced that what threatened their new domestic idyll was not the conformity imposed by the suburban dream but the external menace posed by the Soviet Union: 'The principal organs of government, the major political parties, the trade union movement, leading church spokesmen, and many public and private institutions across the land were agreed that Communists had no legitimate role in American society' (Heale 1990: 167). This anticommunist sentiment was brought to people's attention through blatant propaganda films such as *I Was a Communist for the FBI* (1951) and *I Married a Communist* (1950) where 'Communists were reduced to caricatures who saw human life as dispensable, had no room for private feeling, and were even in opposition to God and motherhood' (Quart and Auster 2002: 44). For many critics such anticommunist feeling is most apparent in the science fiction B-movie, specifically in the guise of a bug-eyed monster.

American science fiction films of the decade, this critical orthodoxy claims, demonised both the Soviet Union and any resistance to the status quo, ensuring that the institutions and authorities of the country were protected from the so-called Red Menace that was seen as permeating the nation (Jancovich 1996: 15). However, simply mapping the fear of the Soviet threat onto the fear of alien invasion ignored the subtexts of a genre which sought to locate the causes for American uncertainty internally rather than externally:

> It has often been pointed out that the qualities that identify the aliens with the Soviet Union are their lack of feelings and the absence of individual characteristics. It was certainly the case that during the 1950s many American critics claimed that in the Soviet Union people were all the same; that they were forced to deny personal feeling and characteristics, and to become functionaries of the social whole. It should also be noted, however, that…it was common in the 1950s for Americans to claim that the effects of scientific-technical rationality upon their own society was producing the same features within America itself. (Jancovich 1996: 26)

Paul Wells (1993: 181) substantiates this claim with his assertion that 'although these films were valuable in constructing metaphors around the nuclear threat or the fear of Communism, they also served as a distraction from the more mundane issues of the period'. People were more concerned with domestic and financial problems at home and in their local communities than they were with international affairs and the supposed reds hiding under their beds.

Aliens in America

The figure of the alien was a predominantly cinematic character in the 1950s. It was a mainstay of the B-movie science fiction/horror film that was presented in stark contrast to the human, and so challenged existing definitions of normality. Often this is read as simply presenting the alien as irredeemably other, with flying saucers, hideous alien blobs and mutant monsters operating to confirm American society as the rightful masters of the galaxy. However, as Mark Jancovich has pointed out, many of these aliens also challenged the status quo in other ways and operated to question established definitions of normality. In many films of this period, the threatening alien actually focused fears and anxiety about developments *within* American society—for

example in *Invasion of the Body Snatchers* (see boxed text)—while others presented
the alien as a persecuted figure oppressed by intolerance. It was this later trend that
was developed in Rod Serling's *The Twilight Zone* (1959–1964), a television series
that did not depict humanity as superior to the alien other, but instead turned its gaze
on humanity to challenge definitions of normality in Cold War America.

INVASION OF THE BODY SNATCHERS (1956)

As both a tale concerning invading alien pods and a stark critique of small-town America, *Invasion of the Body Snatchers* stands as a significant American film; whether it is considered merely a low-budget science fiction B-movie, a fantastic story that serves as an allegorical warning or an accurate portrayal of suburban life in the 1950s, the film continues to challenge modern audiences. *Invasion of the Body Snatchers* continues to stand the test of time both visually and in terms of narrative. Contesting accounts of the production budget put the film's price tag as low as $382,000 (LaValley 1989: 3), dead on $400,000 (Booker 2006: 64) and as high as $417,000 (Cornea 2007: 71). In an interview with Stuart Kaminsky (1976: 77), Don Siegel specifies $15,000 went on the special effects that produced the transforming pods and replica corpses. Although these figures appear insignificant compared to other more special effects orientated science fiction films of the decade they do draw attention to the understated nature of the film's production and the important role this plays in the construction of a believable and, at first glance, normal small-town setting.

The film is a taut mixture of conspiracy narrative and contemporary fears; a film noir tale (Booker 2006: 59), as told by its main protagonist, Dr. Miles Bennell, of the outsider as threat to a supposed tranquil American idyll. David Seed rightly places the film within its cultural contexts, stating that, 'A cluster of films from the mid-fifties demonstrates a consistent paradigm of such invasion-as-conspiracy where the battle for the nation's mind is played out in Smalltown USA.' In *Invasion* and these other contemporary films,

> The instrumentality of threat comes from outside (creatures from Mars or Venus, pods from outer space) but the real power of these films is carried by their transformation of humans rather than the crude 'monstrous' devices, their fracturing of the nuclear family or local community. (Seed 1999: 132–3)

The last point is crucial, since the family and community were seen by many politicians, including those involved with the communist witch hunts of Senator Joseph McCarthy and the House Un-American Activities Committee (HUAC), as important weapons in the fight against communism and the socialist threat to American capitalism. *Invasion*'s significance partly lies in its role as a social barometer for America in the 1950s but also in the fact that it dared to compare the imaginary invading other with the then largely unrecognised danger posed by America's consumerist ideology.

As highlighted in this chapter already, Mark Jancovich points out that most critics of the decade's invasion narratives see them as being inextricably linked to Cold War ideology. Americans had two choices: either support America or be seen as a communist sympathiser—in *Invasion* this distinction is clearly represented between Miles and the residents of Santa Mira as they try to persuade him to become a pod person. This distinction meant that there was a clear line between right and wrong, America and the alien other. Leonard Quart and Albert Auster, in their examination of American film after 1945, recognise and then quickly dismiss the film's reading as a comment on conformity: 'In another, more probable interpretation, the pods could be seen as communists, the omnipresent aliens of the fifties, who are everywhere conspiring to turn people into robots' (2002: 51). However, as both Jancovich and this chapter contend, American culture was itself going through a sort of identity crisis as men returned from war to face changes in the work and domestic spheres. The so-called suburban dream was little more than a cover for a loss of individual identity, the threat posed by the communist as alien was not as pressing as the threat posed by the push to conform: men having to go to work in the city dressed in grey flannel suits and return home to idealised, yet all too similar, modern suburban homes. The technological advancement of consumer culture that had promised so much was instead stifling Americans' own self-worth.

Despite the contradictory reasons for America's feeling of vulnerability in the 1950s, the fact remains that the alien, its desire to conquer Earth and technological pre-eminence, were common themes in films of that decade. *Invasion* took that external threat and made it a discernibly internal one by focusing on the invasion of the human body by an alien force (Hendershot 1998: 26). Yet, what makes this film stand out is its constant ability to contradict itself, to offer the audience competing definitions of what might be the most attractive lifestyle to have. In Miles the audience has an ideal role model, a successful professional man loved by the local community. His race to prevent the pods from spreading to the rest of the west coast and perhaps the entire country is a heroic representation of American masculinity. At that time, such masculinity was valorised as part of the nation's communist containment strategy: 'The decade's focus on rigid gender roles, respect for authority, patriotism, and hygiene was part of a larger fear that [America] might unravel from within' (Caputi 2005: 142).

For Elaine Tyler May (1999), the communist threat could be contained by a return to the family values of a pre–World War II America where men went to work and women stayed at home. However, with the disruption that the war brought, husbands were displaced in both the home and at work by their wives; this led to a sense of masculinity in crisis as the traditional male breadwinning role became increasingly obsolete. Thus, like the male protagonists of popular books such as Sloan Wilson's *The Man in the Gray Flannel Suit* (1955) and William Whyte's *The Organization Man* (1956), Miles is a man caught in a suburban nightmare, unable to escape the encroaching conformity symbolized by the white picket fences and mundane daily routine of work and family responsibility (see Castronovo 2004). The kiss between Miles and Becky Driscoll towards the end of the film, and his revulsion as he realizes she has become a pod person, has been read as an indicator of emasculating femininity and symbolic of Miles's latent homosexuality—a common theme in science fiction films of this period (Benshoff 1997). Christine Cornea, for example, links the role of women in the film to the then contemporary theory that domineering mothers who smothered their teenage male offspring posed a threat to the patriarchal status quo (2007: 43–4). However, what really appears to be at stake here is the notion that America's changing society is the threat to Miles; neither the pods as communism nor Becky as the feminine are as critical as the choice he has to make between becoming a pod person or continually running from the conformity that a pod society ultimately represents.

When Miles and Becky are confronted by the pod versions of Jack Belicec and Dan Kaufman they are offered the choice to become pod people. The complicated emotions of modern life such as love, desire, ambition and faith would be destroyed and life simplified; since the pod people have no need for these human traits their society would be one without conflict and pain—Miles and Becky would be reborn into an untroubled world. This scene is an important signifier of the social contradictions at the heart of 1950s America: conformity to the status quo would offer a safe society in which to bring up the nuclear family—free from a communist threat and wealthy enough to participate in a consumer lifestyle; yet conformity also signals an end to the individualist ethos of American culture—the business ethos of the period was creating a society of clones with no individual creativity. What is truly horrific and unnerving in this exchange and underlies the tensions beneath the film's narrative is that both choices are attractive:

> Amid all this critical activity, one might also note that there is a definite emotional appeal to the idea of being 'taken over' which goes beyond the inherent attractions presented by the pod-psychiatrist in *Invasion of the Body Snatchers* . . . That added emotional attraction is 'no more responsibility'. Being 'taken over' can be likened to being drafted, to having to follow orders. 'Taken over', we cannot be held accountable for our crimes—passionate or passionless. (Sobchack 1998: 123)

It is the mundane appeal of conformity, the normality and familiarity of small-town life, which the film makes out to be threatening. The look and feel of the film underscores the contradictions in individual identity; the audience becomes vigilant in watching for anything that looks out of the ordinary. The low-budget mise en scéne, black and white colourisation, and flat characterisation contribute to painting a picture of domestic drudgery that was both desired and despised: 'What is visually fascinating and disturbing . . . is the way in which the secure and familiar are twisted into something subtly dangerous and slyly perverted' (Sobchack 1998: 124). Humans in this film are dehumanised in such a way that we can neither tell them apart nor perhaps want to differ from them.

Along with *Invasion of the Body Snatchers,* films such as *The Day the Earth Stood Still* (1951), *The Thing from Another World* (1951), *War of the Worlds* (1953), *Invaders from Mars* (1953), *It Came from Outer Space* (1953) and *This Island Earth* (1955) presented America and the world in the grip of emergencies—emergencies 'that jeopardized the future of the race; they were not national, nor even international, but planetary' (Biskind 2000: 102). The format of many B-movies allowed for the narrative to be introduced at the beginning by an off-screen narrator, giving the film a pseudoscientific feeling that served to underscore the possible emergency and real life threat the alien invader might pose. This clearly played on cultural fears first made obvious by the *War of the Worlds* radio broadcast as discussed in the introduction. At the opening of *Invaders from Mars,* the narrator intones 'known facts about the universe and questions applicable to those facts' with a haunting voice. For Errol Vieth (2001: 174), 'The function of science here is to answer globally significant questions. Even through science has not answered those questions in the past, that is not a reason to stop the process.' The 1956 film *Forbidden Planet* went further in questioning the secrets of the universe through its tale of Dr. Morbius discovering and harnessing the technology of a long lost alien race on Altair-4. The first big-budget Hollywood studio science fiction movie of the decade, *Forbidden Planet* used the familiar extraterrestrial motif to interrogate the human impulse for death and destruction. A colourful example of the type of film prevalent in the 1950s, its story illustrated the precarious position humanity held 'on the cusp of destruction or development—a position of obvious relevance during the Cold War tensions of the year' (Grant 2005: 175).

Nuclear Horror and Science Gone Mad

The postwar boom in scientific progress is clearly reflected in the abundance of films that portrayed advanced technology and the scientists that used and invented it. In the 1940s science and scientists were represented in the popular media as saviours; after all, it was nuclear power that brought an end to the war with Japan. Although the devastating effects of the bomb in Hiroshima and Nagasaki were seen by the whole world, the potentials for atomic power to help improve people's lives were also made very apparent in the American media. The first steps to actual space flight were taken when Chuck Yeager broke the sound barrier in 1947 using the Bell X-1 jet aircraft. America was at the cutting edge of science as it entered the 1950s so it was little wonder the nation expected to win the race to be the first country in space when the Mercury Project was started in 1959. Nuclear power symbolised America's dominance, and even though it had many dangerous consequences responsible use could bring about a potential utopia: 'The Manhattan Project may have been a secret, and Hiroshima a shock, but Americans of 1945 were prepared in a general way for news of atomic breakthroughs that would transform their lives' (Boyer 1994: 109). Inevitably, science fiction film picked up on these contradictory themes and began to question America's faith in the atom and its willingness to ignore the dangers of harnessing nuclear power. Many films in the 1950s, from those featuring mad scientists to marauding mutant monsters, offered a darker view of what might happen if humans went too far in their pursuit of a scientific utopia.

The first film to really caution against the use of nuclear weapons and critique America's Cold War with the Soviet Union was *The Day the Earth Stood Still*. Robert Wise's contribution to the oeuvre was inspired by American fascination with UFOs and is considered one of the best of the saucer films alongside *Earth vs. the Flying Saucers* (1956). In the film an alien ship lands in Washington, DC, and the pilot, called Klaatu, has come to Earth to offer a warning that humanity's drive to make more and more nuclear weapons is attracting attention from Earth's extraterrestrial neighbours. Petty human squabbles could bring about the planet's destruction as the aliens are willing to attack so as to stop the threat humans pose to intergalactic peace. Mocking human idiosyncrasies, the film portrays America's faith in firepower as insignificant compared to the superiority of alien technology.

Gort, Klaatu's giant robot protector, has a laser beam weapon that can dissolve matter, and it is put to use immediately after first contact in defending the ship and Klaatu from overzealous soldiers. Klaatu, under the name of Carpenter, goes undercover and befriends a mother and her son. He attempts to bring together the world's scientific community so he can explain how humanity no longer needs nuclear weapons and can instead devote time and energy in developing fuel and ships that will take them to the stars. On finding out that Klaatu has been living as a human in Washington, people panic and the army track him down and shoot him. His temporary resurrection from death at the end of the film clearly parallels Christ's return from the dead; Klaatu (Carpenter) acts as sacrificial lamb to point out Earth's sins. On the one hand this film is seen by some as a positive idea during the 1950s; Klaatu's message to humanity at the close emphasises 'Humanity is now free to discover its true self with respect to the powers and forces that run through the cosmos' (Lucanio 1987: 45). However, on the other hand, the film's overall message is fascistic in that it suggests that 'what the Earth needs is to be policed by aliens to control mankind's worst instincts and save the Universe from destruction' (Humphries 2002: 57). Furthermore, the fact that Klaatu chose to land in Washington and pass on his message to Americans intimates that America will be the Earth's police force and that only its values and ideologies will help serve to unlock humanity's potentials in the future.

The dangers of nuclear power also appeared in feature films that depicted mutants and monsters created by the leaking or exploding of radioactive elements: Joyce A. Evans (1998: 93) describes this as the 'radiation-produced monster' genre. Popular examples of the subgenre include *The Beast from 20,000 Fathoms* (1953), the American version of Japan's *Godzilla, King of the Monsters* (1956) and *Them!* (1954). For Jerome F. Shapiro (2002: 112), these films were inspired and energised by real life events in the South Pacific as the superpowers upped their commitment to developing and testing hydrogen bombs during the mid-1950s. The swarm of giant ants in *Them!* not only functions as a warning on scientific failure but also taps into the other latent fear in American culture previously discussed: communism. The ants 'act as a metaphor for invading communist hoards' (Evans 1998: 102). However, these films provided perfect comment on the threat of nuclear devastation, genetic mutation, environmental disaster, and fears of the monstrous other. The various mutated beasts created as a result of science gone wrong 'typically seem drawn to our modern cities, where they proceed to carry out nature's revenge on a reckless, environmentally heedless human culture' (Telotte 2001: 98). Labelled by Susan Sontag (2004: 41) as films that depict the 'imagination of disaster', they are 'concerned with the aesthetics of destruction, with the peculiar beauties to be found in wreaking havoc, making a mess'. However, the scientists that cause these monstrous mutations rarely escape. They are usually disfigured or destroyed by their invention/creation and therefore punished for their misdeeds in trying to overcome nature.

For Andrew Tudor (1989: 133), mad scientists in the science fiction genre 'devotedly and misguidedly seek knowledge purely for its own sake' and often 'want no more than to rule the world'. They are driven and entirely 'volitional' in their actions. The archetypal mad scientist would be the evil genius Rotwang from *Metropolis*, whose efforts to wreak revenge on the city he helped to create leads him to create the female robot Maria. More often than not, the scientist figure in science fiction film is determined to outdo God by way of inventing or creating new life, yet this typically results in the scientist being punished for his delusions of god-hood. The appearance of such figures usually offers visual clues of the extreme lengths to which they are prepared to go to fulfil their ambitions. Rotwang has a metal hand for example, presumably a replacement for his real hand lost during a dangerous experiment. Physical disability or disfigurement signifies the warped nature of both the scientist and his plans: 'Rotwang's physical appearance is an outward and visible challenge to the moral of [*Metropolis*] ... The evil genius's understanding comes from somewhere else. Not from the harmony and balance between head, heart and hand. His house faces the cathedral, but it has no windows so he cannot see it' (Frayling 2005: 62).

Tarantula (1955), as the singularity of the title implies, is about a giant tarantula that escapes and starts to terrorise the inhabitants of a small desert town. The result of a scientific group's eagerness to experiment with an enlarging formula on live animals, the giant arachnid kills indiscriminately. Both *Them!* and *Tarantula* have female scientists battling to reverse the results of scientific misadventure. While these films follow science fiction's trend in visualising nuclear fear through giant insects, Bonnie Noonan (2005: 73) asserts that these two films, along with *The Deadly Mantis* (1957), 'exteriorize the gender-related tensions' that other films of the decade elide. The 'bulbous, throbbing, truculent insects function as floating signifiers, a phantasmagoria of resistance, fear, complicity, and confusion as society attempts to adapt to women's new opportunities'. The gigantism and miniaturisation narratives of 1950s science fiction proved interesting conduits for the nation's anxieties over changing gender roles induced by the war effort. Extreme examples of the fear of women include *The Attack of the 50 Foot Woman* (1958), which magnified the perceived threat of women's increasing sexual freedoms and domestic authority through the enlarging of a woman. The reverse could be said of *The Incredible Shrinking Man* in its interpretation of the changing definitions of 1950s masculinity. In this film Robert Carey is exposed to a radioactive cloud that causes him to start shrinking, eventually reducing to the size of a microscopic atom. His inability to fulfil the traditional gender role of male bread winner forces him to withdraw from normal society, literally emasculated by his shrinking size and the fact he has to live in a doll's house. M. Keith Booker (2001: 156) stresses that while the film 'partakes of the 1950s fear of both radioactive and chemical contamination' it also 'allegorizes various 1950s anxieties about gender roles'. As such, *The Incredible Shrinking Man* follows *Invasion of the Body Snatchers* in its representation of males' suburban nightmare, with their masculinity being symbolically stifled by work, family responsibilities and domestic conformity.

Television Grows Up

Film was able to take on ambitious projects showing humanity at the brink of destruction using 'Technicolor, Cinemascope, and 3D technologies' (Telotte 2001: 95). As a result, the threat of the alien was intensified on the big screen during the 1950s, and television's contribution to the genre was largely postponed until the beginning of the 1960s. What the small screen did offer were cinema-like serials from the

1940s such as *Captain Video and His Video Rangers* (1949–1955), *Rocky Jones, Space Ranger* (1954), *Space Patrol* (1950–1955) and *Tom Corbett, Space Cadet* (1950–1955). These series, although generally deficient in technical brilliance, created a space for the science fiction television series. However lacking they were in adult storytelling or complex character development, these series showed that television was a suitable medium through which the alien, usually men with face paint, and the human, albeit idealised visualisations of the human male, could be shown in a futuristic setting. As Rick Worland (1996: 104) points out, these series were considered to be 'aimed at children,' yet the fact that they appeared on television showed just how much the medium was affected by 'a repressive political climate that obstructed presentation of any ideas outside the commonplace'.

Moreover, these television programs were themselves informed by the technological innovations and increased production of consumable goods resulting from the battle between America and the Soviet Union in the Space Race and Cold War. Advances in domestic appliance technology, kitchens controlled by computers, automobiles and home intercom systems became important symbols of American dominance in science and technology. The so-called Kitchen Debate in 1959, when Vice President Richard Nixon travelled to Moscow to meet Nikita Khrushchev at the American Exhibition, symbolised America's drive to outdo Russia on all technological fronts, both planetary and domestic: 'the latest in kitchen consumerism stood for the basic tenets of the American way of life. Freedom. Freedom from drudgery for the housewife. And democracy, the opportunity to choose' (Marling 1994: 243). New technologies, whether the simple electric can opener or the most advanced space rocket, were a sign of national and human achievement and symptomatic of America's drive to produce more consumable goods than the Soviet Union, a drive described by sociologist David Riesman as 'Operation Abundance': 'In 1951, he argued that Americans should conduct a "Nylon War" with the Soviet Union, in which its citizen comrades would be bombarded with consumer goods rather than weaponry' (Crowley 2008a: 30). The future depicted in both film and television at this time not only acknowledges this domestic reality through the abundance of spaceships, scientific inventions and a multitude of labour-saving devices and robots, but it also illustrates a certain mirroring effect where the aesthetics of technological innovation and visualizations of the future were brought from screen to the suburbs.

The spaceships and interstellar rockets seen in *Tom Corbett, Rocky Jones, Captain Video* and films such as *Destination Moon* (1950), alongside their real life counterparts in NASA's Mercury Project, provided graphic inspiration for the architects, inventors and designers involved in America's Cold War with Russia (see Holloway 2008). Cars in the 1950s, with their sleek outlines and exaggerated tail fins were expressions of motion through design, symbols of the technological optimism of the Space Age, where automobiles stood in as suburban replicas of the rockets that shot into space. Phallic symbols of technology, cars were representations of what Karal Ann Marling terms 'autoeroticism', whereby America's love for the automobile, its convenience and style, were hailed as aspirational consumables. Every home had to have one, 'as the purchaser of an automobile was no longer paying for a mere piece of machinery. He (and, increasingly, she) was buying a brand new life. High style. Sex. Social standing. A rocket to the moon' (Marling 1994: 136–7). A visual trope of the science fiction genre, dating back to Georges Méliès's 1902 silent classic, *Trip to the Moon* (*Voyage dans La Lune*), the space rocket, and the influx of cinematic and televisual spacecraft that were to follow, symbolise both the genre's fascination for technical gadgetry and special effects and also Western culture's fetishisation of technological consumption: 'Spaceships are the emblems of the technology that produces them; a technology of cultural reproduction, rather than science' (Roberts 2000: 154).

Wheeler Winston Dixon acknowledges the child-centric nature of television at this time, positing that the space opera motif 'by design inculcated cold war values into their young viewers', yet he says they may also be credited for setting 'the stage for a counterrebellion in the 1960s' when anthology series promoted a more mature outlook on society and American culture through science fiction, fantasy and horror narratives (Dixon 2008: 94). His overview of the space opera format, exemplified by series such as *Tom Corbett* and *Space Patrol,* is a valuable reappraisal of a cycle of science fiction television that can all too often be dismissed. These series, after all, were made at a time when the country's involvement and investment in the Space Race with the Soviet Union demanded total devotion to the promises of space travel and interstellar exploration. These series are barometers for the social climate which at that time was being dictated by ideological consensus: America must be first into space; it must win the Cold War for fear of 'imperilling our national freedom' (Dixon 2008: 93). Space operas directed at children may have relied overly on archetypal characters, tired generic tropes and the same plot structures, but they also offer an insight into how television was reflecting back and responding to the Cold War psyche.

The fascination for all things space worked in conjunction with the wonderment of having new domestic technologies there in living rooms and kitchens. Television as an icon of American technological progress was a powerful symbol and is part of the reason for science fiction's huge popularity in the 1950s: 'With such fantastic devices right in their living rooms, Americans were ready to believe anything was possible through science and technology' (Lucanio and Coville 1998: 1). Seeing outer space on the screen only fuelled the nation's passion and drive to win the Space Race. Patrick Lucanio and Gary Coville's study of 1950s science fiction television again stresses the importance of not discounting this period as simple childish hokum. Indeed, *Tales of Tomorrow* (1951–1953) is considered to be the first adult-orientated anthology series, the antecedent of *Science Fiction Theatre* (1955–1957) and *The Twilight Zone,* and is representative of the shift in television production to more mature programming.

Tales of Tomorrow, a series of live half-hour broadcasts, was aired on the ABC network and followed many years of popularity and success for radio and live broadcast drama in America—note for example the impact of Orson Welles's *War of the*

Worlds radio adaptation. The series' format was based on combining presentations of classic and new science fiction stories, in many respects the television version of Hugo Gernsback's approach to science fiction magazine publishing, and as such the series adapted stories from established authors but also encouraged new writers to pitch ideas. As a sign of its adult-orientated ethos writers were told to avoid certain science fiction clichés of the time such as the bug-eyed monster and set the action for the drama in mostly contemporary settings—although this can clearly be ascribed to the tight budgets of production rather than to the serious nature of its storytelling. Some critics objected to what they saw as the condescending of classics to the television medium, with adaptations of Wells, Verne and Mary Shelley coming under particular scorn. However, the series' ability to work within the bounds of television production as it stood in the early 1950s showed just how much networks had faith in the literary roots of the genre and how audiences continued to consume science fiction at a time of heightened national interest in science, technology and the future. Moreover, the 1952 adaptation of *Frankenstein,* starring Lon Chaney Jr as the monster, indicates the close relationship television had with its filmic forebears in that movie stars from the big screen wanted to appear in what was deemed serious TV drama: '*Tales of Tomorrow* clearly demonstrated that science fiction and fantasy, if presented in the proper framework, held a viable appeal for mom and dad as well as for junior members of the family' (Lucanio and Coville 1998: 208).

The development of anthology series such as *The Twilight Zone* (see boxed text) and *The Outer Limits* (1963–1965), with their more critical take on the political and ideological struggle between American and the Soviet Union, signalled an attempt on behalf of writers such as Rod Serling and Leslie Stevens to comment on the very conservativism that had pushed the Cold War into the suburbs and had driven the television networks to produce uncritical and problematic representations of America's race to dominate outer space.

THE TWILIGHT ZONE (1959–1964)

Unable to discuss politics directly, *The Twilight Zone* used futuristic settings and the alien body as metaphors through which to participate in current debates. As Rod Serling recounted about his work prior to making the series, 'I was not permitted to have Senators discuss any current or pressing problem . . . In retrospect, I probably would have had a much more adult play had I made it science fiction, put it in the year 2057, and peopled the Senate with robots' (quoted in Engelhardt 1998: 153). Just as Gene Roddenberry managed to address issues such as Civil Rights, Vietnam, and sexual inequality on *Star Trek* by setting it in the future, so too could Serling by using the generic tropes and signifiers of fantasy, horror and science fiction. This attempt to create morally informed storylines was emphasised by *The Twilight Zone*'s anthology series format—half-hour episodes introduced and concluded by Serling's short verbal commentary that summarised the lessons learnt in the drama (Worland 1996: 104)—and the use of 'science fiction to question the conformist values of post-war suburbia as well as the rising paranoia of Cold War confrontation' (Sconce 1997: 1454).

The Twilight Zone's power to subvert notions of reality and human identity was mainly revealed through the use of mind games, the plot twist at the end which jolted the audience's perception about what is right and real. Format, settings and even the title portray the series as a 'place of shadows, of vision that is clouded, a place that may be penetrated by light and understanding or cast into darkness and confusion' (Ziegler 1987: 33). The human body was central to the series' sense of things not being what they seem, yet rarely was the body shown as looking anything other than normal. In episodes such as 'I Shot an Arrow into the Air' (1960) human astronauts are the central characters—after crash landing on a desert planet, the crew of the *Arrow* are forced to fight and kill each other for what supplies are left in the hot and arid environment. Humans are perceived as being nasty, savage creatures that resort to murder so that the individual can survive. The ironic twist at the end, where the surviving astronaut realises that they had actually crash landed in Nevada and were only a few miles from water and civilisation, serves to underscore the savage potentials that lie beneath the façade of humanity—the real monsters that came from space are human. Likewise, in the episode 'The Invaders' (1961), we are introduced to a shabby looking house were a women is being terrorised by small and technologically advanced humanoid invaders—the two images of civilisation contrast sharply so as to make us think that the woman living alone is the alien. However, as we find out after a series of encounters between the giant and the humans, the little invaders are actually from Earth and have travelled to the giant's planet in the name of conquest and exploration. When they mistake the woman's attempts at defending herself from attack as aggressive posturing, the humans return to Earth under the impression that the planet is too dangerous to be explored. What is clear from this ironic twist, using body size to emphasise humanity's galactic insignificance, is that humans are the aggressors, not the alien giant—the bodily harm and psychological trauma suffered by the woman is proof of human cruelty. For most of this episode, there is no dialogue, which 'deflates our self-importance visually' and codes the miniature humans as the invaders (Wolfe 1996: 135). 'Such reversals', according to M. Keith Booker, 'were highly effective at a moment in American history when many traditional "Us vs. Them" boundaries were being challenged' (2004: 14). As America entered a new age as a world leader and nuclear power, Americans were coming into contact with new cultures and peoples that forced them to reconsider their own self-identity.

In instances when the alien threatened humans on Earth, its physical presence was more often implied in the actions and reactions of humans. The visually distinctive and monstrous alien body was rarely seen, and humanity was presented as monstrous, particularly in its tendency to turn on each other when threatened by the outsider. For Matt Hills, *The Twilight Zone* favoured 'the subtle approach, arriving at horrifying images through unsettling its audience rather than aiming for a "gross-out" moment' (2004: 220). In 'The Monsters Are Due on Maple Street' (1960), humanity is presented as problematic when a fear of alien invasion causes a local community to turn upon itself in a hunt for alien intruders. In the process, this story emphasises the human potential for cruelty and intolerance, as the friendly neighbours turn into an angry mob whose fear of the other leads them to persecute those who display supposedly alien qualities such as reading comic books and astronomy—signifiers of people who exist outside perceived normal social behaviour. Most interestingly, visions of the extraterrestrial are notoriously absent from this episode until the concluding twist, when it is revealed that the aliens are actually watching Earth from above. They do not need to invade the Earth because human ignorance, prejudice and fear destroy society from within. Similarly, in 'Will the Real Martian Please Stand Up?' (1961), a group of stranded commuters in a diner discuss the rumour that a UFO might have landed nearby and, in so doing, start to suspect that the inevitable alien could be one of them. Questioning notions of what is human—who is the real American?—Serling presents a broad range of characters from different racial and ethnic backgrounds among the stranded travellers. Again fear of the alien reveals a wide range of prejudices and intolerances, and again the twist at the end shows that humans are fallible: they not only fail to identify the alien, but it is even revealed that there were actually two aliens in their midst, one of whom is a Martian with a third arm under his trench coat and one of whom is a Venusian with a third eye under his hat.

Like the invasion narratives of the previous decade, both these episodes conform to Vivian Sobchack's observation that science fiction films' 'flat angles, uninspired camera movements, and downright unimaginative cinematography seem finally purposeful in creating mise en scéne in which a drumming insistence on the ordinary creates extraordinary tension' (Sobchack 1998: 125). The emphasis on the mundane mise en scéne—a diner, a quiet street—heightens the potential threat posed by a group of stranded passengers and acquainted neighbours. Dressing humans and aliens in normal attire not only recreates the contemporary look of Cold War America—thus locating the paranoia within a realistic setting—but also serves to underscore *The Twilight Zone*'s ability to make much from the limited budget and costuming.

Rick Worland sees the revelation at the end of 'The Monsters Are Due on Maple Street' as a signal to the Cold War conservatism inherent in 1960s television programming—despite Serling's attempts at questioning the orthodoxy of American politics. The twist showing that aliens really do exist reveals 'Maple Street's fears to be anything but delusional'; in some senses the fact that the neighbours were reduced to paranoia and social panic is justified considering the threat that does linger on the outside. The Soviet Union coded as alien, a potential threat to an idyllic American suburb, confirms that if Americans do not act—however much in a frenzy—then the country will be forced to fight the Cold War closer to home rather than abroad (Worland 1996: 107). However, it is possible to see these two episodes somewhat differently. In both episodes, the aliens have 'outperformed their human counterparts' (Wolfe 1996: 136), either by subtly changing their physical appearance or, more pointedly, not even coming down to Earth at all. The physical differentiation between human and alien body merely comes down to having an extra limb or eye, but the gulf between species is shown as insurmountable.

Pushing the Limits

If *The Twilight Zone* rarely used make-up to present that alien, then the deformed, mutated, monstrous and totally inhuman body was central to the storytelling of Joseph Stefano and Leslie Stevens's science fiction series, *The Outer Limits*. However, like *The Twilight Zone*, these alien creatures were not simply monstrous others but frequently acted to relativise established definitions of normality. If they were visually different, to the human, these differences were defined as alternative rather than inferior. As the show's creators put it, they wanted to present the audience with 'new worlds beyond reality; sights and sounds never before experienced; adventures of the innermost mind, the farthest galaxies, and all that lies between' (quoted in Schow 1998: 2).

As a result, the aliens were not just painted men in jumpsuits; rather, the production team showed great imagination in the make-up and costuming departments as the producers tried to imagine creatures completely different from their human counterparts, creatures such as Empyrians, Ebonites, Zanti, Helosians and Kyben. Such diversity worked to displace humanity from the centre of the Universe. The aliens were not simply humanoids or monstrous others, and their sheer diversity as creatures presented humanity as simply one species among many. Furthermore, many of the episodes concerned the threat of science going wrong or with humans destroying themselves with nuclear warfare, radiation poisoning and genetic mutation—all of which were fears directly relevant to its period, which was one of the Cold War and the nuclear arms race (Boyer 1994: 354). In this context, the alien was not simply a figure of suspicion and fear, but was often a potential saviour—so long as humans could learn to live with a being that looked so different from themselves.

The pilot episode 'The Galaxy Being' (1963), originally titled 'Please Stand By', emphasised the eerie nature of the Control Voice's now famous opening monologue and showed how the series would come to view the human and alien body throughout the first season—visually distinctive yet perhaps ideologically linked. Lowly radio station owner and inventor Allan Maxwell (Cliff Robertson) struggles to prove to his wife that the time that he has spent on research have not been wasted, although others see his search for alien life in the galaxy as an infantile project. Instead of using his radio equipment solely to provide advertising and entertainment, Maxwell would rather use it in an attempt to contact extraterrestrial life. When his wife asks him, 'What makes you think you can discover anything? Who are you?', Maxwell replies, 'Nobody. Nobody at all. But the secrets of the universe don't mind.' His response to the wife's antagonistic question serves to accentuate the alienation felt by Maxwell as he struggles to continue his work. Becoming more and more of a loner, the inventor would rather spend time with his machinery than go out with his wife, and his desire is rewarded when an alien replies to Maxwell's communications. The eponymous Galaxy Being, a resident from the Andromeda system, appears to Maxwell as a strange yet friendly figure. The dark brown costuming of the creature was enhanced by reversing the negative so that the original wetsuit became bright white in the actual finished version on screen. As well as using traditional make-up effects to create this alien creature, staff working on the suit added slippery rubber and stuck on large-pupiled eyes to accentuate the exotic nature of the being (Schow 1998: 37). Combined with the technical wizardry of simple negative reversal, the Galaxy Being had two layers of alienating features: not only did the costume make the alien imposing to humans but so did his radioactive glow.

Significantly, Maxwell's first words to the alien are 'Who are you?'—effectively repeating his wife's original question to him but with a different meaning. Furthermore, like Maxwell, the Galaxy Being is a loner. Both are solitary beings that are willing to risk isolation from their respective cultures in pursuit of a passion for the unknown, a passion that is only matched by their ingenuity in using radio waves to cross the galactic expanse. The Galaxy Being tells Maxwell that he was not allowed to use his equipment to explore space, just as Maxwell was often criticised for draining the radio station's power to pursue his quest. The two beings, although physically alien to one another, are kinsmen in spirit: both are struggling to discover something beyond their own experience and escape the limitations of their respective societies.

The contrast between bodies is obviated by the similarities between their social sur-roundings. Only when the Galaxy Being is mistaken for an aggressor toward the end of the episode is there a potential for death and destruction, but here it is the humans who are the real threat, and they are presented as small-minded beings that use vio-lence when confronted with the unfamiliar. Perhaps more significantly, unlike the differences between altered human and alien bodies in *The Twilight Zone,* the simi-larities between Maxwell and the Galaxy Being's philosophy serve to illustrate the polemical tone of the Control Voice at the end of the episode:

> The planet Earth is a speck of dust, remote and alone in the void. There are powers in the universe inscrutable and profound. Fear cannot save us. Rage cannot help us. We must see the stranger in a new light—the light of understanding. And to achieve this, we must begin to understand ourselves and each other. (quoted in Schow 1998: 7)

As the series began its second and final season, it was felt by some that too much time was being spent on the 'usual monster bullshit…funny rubber masks, and basi-cally silly ideas' (Harlan Ellison quoted in Schow 1998: 249). With such sentiments being expressed by key writers working on new scripts, there was a clear shift in nar-rative emphasis in the later episodes. From the sense of general human insignificance seen in 'The Galaxy Being', stories from the second season started to expound upon humanity's more positive traits: the main one being humanity's endless thirst for knowledge. Instead of being portrayed as an immature, savage and technologically backward race, humans were forgiven for these indiscretions because their overall raison d'être was a noble one—if innocent people and aliens were harmed in the process of gathering knowledge, then it was a small price to pay.

The episode 'Demon with a Glass Hand' (1964) typifies *The Outer Limits'* more utilitarian mantra. In this story Robert Culp plays Trent, the last human alive, on the run through time from a humanoid species called the Kyben. In stark contrast to the bug-eyed monsters typical of the first season, the only physical feature that distinguishes the Kyben from the human is their thick black eye make-up. Dressed in dark sweat pants and tops, with a gold medallion around the neck, they look more like burglars or bank robbers than an intergalactic army. Indeed, the episode's writer, Harlan Ellison, whilst critical of the series' over-the-top alien costumes criticised the make-up and wardrobe, asking, 'And why the black circles around the Kyben's eyes? Some of them look like human beings; some of them look like weirdos with cheesecloth over their faces' (quoted in Schow 1998: 287). The shock twist at the end of this story is that Trent is actually a robot that has been created by humans of the future to protect humanity from the Kyben. His body houses a copper wire that contains the essence of every human in electrical form; the entire knowledge of the human species is contained in his metal body. His glass hand holds the key to un-locking this power but he must remain the lone guardian of humanity for eons, until sufficient time has passed and it is safe for humanity to return to the Earth. Trent's body becomes the embodiment of technical achievement, through which humanity is able to outwit the Kyben and use an artificial body to contain their real human form. The closing monologue intimates that although Trent looks human, and even literally contains the essence of humanity within himself, he cannot feel love or pain and therefore he must wait out his years in isolation. While he looks human, he is unable to experience human emotion, and it is the technological appendages to his body—the copper wire and the glass hand—that embody humanity.

Television began to supersede film as the dominant form of mass media in the late 1950s and early 1960s, but science fiction remained popular. As an icon of science fiction itself, J. P. Telotte (2008b: 37) notes that 'Before becoming a fixture in American homes and a purveyor of its own brand of science fiction', television was more familiar to audiences who grew up watching classics such as *Metropolis, Things to Come* and *Modern Times*. These films represented the new medium 'optimistically, as a kind of ultimate communication device, but also more darkly, as a means of surveillance, a tool of deception, even a potentially deadly force' (37–38). Television was clearly trying to attract a different kind of audience—perceived as a more adult audience—and therefore film had to change in order to cope with the drop-off in box office receipts. Television not only competed as the dominant media form, it also 'changed the shape and physical dimensions of domestic settings' such as the home living room (Gray 2002: 104). According to Lynn Spigel, the 1950s domestic space took on qualities previously associated with the movie theatre as new televisions became the centre of individual and family entertainment. There was no need to go to the cinema when 'the ideal home theatre was precisely "the room" that one need never leave, a perfectly controlled environment of mechanized pleasures' (Spigel 1992: 108).

David Marc and Robert J. Thompson (2005: 76) state that 'By 1960 TV use had soared to some five daily hours per household', and as a result other forms of media, such as radio and the cinema, 'had to redefine themselves to fit the new communications regime'. At the same time that Hollywood was facing this competition from television, the studio system was breaking up and undergoing significant changes in how movies were funded, produced and distributed. According to Leonard Quart and Albert Auster (2002: 102), 'the industry was a chronic invalid, with the studios losing a combined aggregate of $500 million between 1969 and 1972'. This period in the history of Hollywood in the 1960s and 1970s is termed New Hollywood and was characterised by the rise of auteur filmmakers and 'the media conglomeration of the film industry' (Wyatt 1994: 8). As will be discussed in the following chapter, New Hollywood's influences on science fiction film would have huge repercussions for the genre for many years to come. Both film and television's production of the genre changed thematically as the cultural landscape evolved from the ideological consensus of the Cold War and developed into a more fragmented and rebellious reaction to America's political establishment fuelled by increasing civil unrest, calls for social and economic change and opposition to the country's mounting involvement in international affairs and overseas conflict.

–2–

Pushing the Frontiers of Reality
Science Fiction and the Counterculture

Following the plethora of bug-eyed alien, nuclear mutation films seen in the 1950s, science fiction in the 1960s turned away from its B-movie roots and started to focus on the more political aspects of nuclear proliferation and technological advancement. Two strands began to emerge in the genre: one continued to use the potential threat and consequences of nuclear war as a backdrop to its stories, including *On the Beach* (1959) and *Fail Safe* (1964), and the other has been identified by John Brosnan (1978: 139) as 'a small trend in satirical [science fiction] films', including *Dr. Strangelove, Or How I Learned to Stop Worrying and Love the Bomb* (1964) and *Barbarella* (1968). However, *Dr. Strangelove* clearly combined elements of the nuclear theme and satirical form, offering audiences different perspectives on America's national agenda. Strangely, for a period in American history that is most characterised by social conflict, war and suffering, science fiction films largely neglected the more extreme visions of contemporary and future society (Baxter 1972: 140); instead, the genre can perhaps be viewed as being in a state of flux as it struggled to attract audiences tired of alien invasion narratives and more impressed with the colourful action adventure serials now appearing on television. Like most genres in Hollywood, science fiction was experiencing the changes and uncertainties brought about by the industrial shake-up in Hollywood: the period starting in the late 1960s and stretching to the mid-1970s known as New Hollywood.

New Hollywood and Science Fiction

Christine Cornea sees the effects of New Hollywood on the industry—the influence of European cinema, growth in art cinema, new directors, revisionist interpretations of history and established genres—as vital within science fiction. Stanley Kubrick's *2001: A Space Odyssey* (1968) is representative of what she terms the 'new art' cycle of science fiction films, 'marked by the simultaneous display of the creative energies and sensibilities associated with the counter-cultural movements of the 1960s/1970s and the industry's efforts to engage with a new and younger audience' (Cornea 2007: 82). *2001*'s influence and impact (see boxed text) has long been debated and defended within academia, yet other films in this New Hollywood period deserve further exploration. Indeed, if Hollywood was struggling to maintain audience appeal by experimenting with form and style, it was also still producing more traditional genre features that relied on special effects and B-movie themes. For example, *Fantastic Voyage* (1966) depicts humans achieving miniaturisation and entering the human body using the latest in effects technology. Hollywood also returned attention to the literary classics, providing adaptations of Jules Verne and H. G. Wells. *Journey to the Center of the Earth* (1959), *Mysterious Island* (1961) and *The Time Machine* (1960) are evidence of the industry's fascination with adapting established authors and stories, only these versions carried the hallmarks of studios willing to splurge money on effects and sets to help guarantee high box office returns. The 1960 adaptation of Arthur Conan Doyle's *The Lost World* (1912), directed by Irwin Allen, may have been described by some as 'appallingly juvenile' (Brosnan 1978: 140), but it was surely a sign of greater things to come for the genre, especially with regard to Allen's work soon to be seen on television.

2001: A SPACE ODYSSEY (1968)

No discussion of science fiction is complete without consideration of the genre's most landmark film, Stanley Kubrick's *2001: A Space Odyssey*. Still seen by many as the archetypal science fiction movie, *2001* is one of the most analysed and critiqued texts in film studies. This point is alluded to by George Zebrowski (2009: 60) in his rather short analysis of science fiction on film, where he asserts that it 'showed what scientific accuracy combined with visual realism could do for written [science fiction]'. This statement reveals the tension between those who defend the literary form of the genre over the visual, and indeed Zebrowski begins his summary by outlining the prejudice against film from those who deem it incapable of containing the ideas that stimulate readers. However, *2001* is often accepted as part of the literary canon (not least because it is a book) because Kubrick's ingenuity gave the film depth and elicited 'thought in the viewer' (Zebrowski 2009: 57).

Another reason for its seminal status is that it literally redefined the genre after a period of relative stagnation. As the alien invasion and nuclear monster movies of the 1950s lost favour and died out, they were replaced by films less informed by a sense of Cold War paranoia and rather more receptive to the changing technological landscape and the real life space exploits of the astronauts and cosmonauts battling to win the Space Race. In effect, one might have asked oneself in this period, 'Why go see a movie about space suited astronauts and interstellar travel when you could turn on the TV and watch the real thing as it happened?' The perception that real science was taking over from the science fiction once popular with kids and young audiences was being created by NASA to help sustain a public relations campaign designed to put pressure on the government to continue funding research and building for the Space Race: 'there were televised reports and official photographs of the missions undertaken. As early as 1962 close-up photographs of the moon were taken from Ranger 4 and in 1964 television pictures of Mars (recorded from Mariner 4) were available. The exploration of space was truly a spectacular media event' (Cornea 2007: 76).

As we shall see later in this chapter with reference to television in the 1960s, science fiction did still attract an audience, with numerous series charting the voyages of space and time travellers becoming ever more popular with children and adults alike. What such media and television coverage created, according to Howard E. McCurdy (1997: 110), was a sense of 'cultural anticipation' whereby the fictional images of space and space travel spurred scientists to realize such potentials sooner, and in turn their achievements prompted people to wonder what, if anything, could hold them back from finding out the secrets of the universe. The American civilian space program tapped into the cultural fascination for exploring the unknown and debating the potentials of there being extraterrestrial life, and by 1968 (the same year as *2001*'s cinema release) 'public support for NASA space flights reached a peaked [sic]' (McCurdy 1997: 102). The optimism felt for NASA's continuing Apollo missions and the multitude of mediated images of the Moon, space and space flight ensured a receptive audience for Kubrick's film. Yet, interestingly, *2001* would not be quite the science fiction film such anticipation demanded. The film would certainly be visually spectacular, but its message would in fact be less affirmative about humanity's technological and scientific achievements to date.

J. P. Telotte (2001: 100–1) suggests that the film followed the documentary style of *Destination Moon* (1950) and *The Conquest of Space* (1955), offering a visual experience coupled with the promise and wonder of science fiction. Kubrick wanted more than to simply chart the meteoric rise of human achievement; he wanted 'to develop a larger story of human evolution'. With this, the film is split into three distinct narrative segments that chart such evolution over the course of our pre-, current and future history. The first segment, titled 'The Dawn of Man', shows our simian ancestors surviving on the plains of ancient Africa; the only preoccupations for the ape men are to survive being eaten by feline predators and protect the waterhole which gives them life. The first of the four appearances of a mysterious large black monolith (its appearance each time provides the impetus for the next stage in human evolution and the film's narrative progression) seemingly prompts the ape men to realise the use of bones as primitive tools for protecting themselves from other apes and to kill large animals for food. In the act of killing, the alpha male of the group throws his bone high into the sky where, through the use of the most famous match cut in film history, it becomes an orbiting spaceship floating in the open vastness of space. It is at this point that the audience is thrust four million years into the future, from primitive Earth to 2001, where humans have mastered space travel and we now inhabit large space stations and the Moon. America and the Soviet Union still maintain their Cold War in this 2001, yet in their attempts to achieve technological superiority all sense of human instinct and emotion have been lost. For Mark Crispin Miller, this part of the film emphasises Kubrick's use of antimyth, where human technological achievement has served only to stifle and suffocate the evolutionary process instigated by the first black monolith: 'In 2001, in other words, there is *too much* science, *too much* made, the all-pervasive product now degrading us almost as nature used to do' (Miller 1994: 19).

So, far from being a film that celebrates human triumphs, *2001* is a philosophical denunciation of humanity's overreliance on science and technology. The famous match shot emphasises that humans are no longer on the rise but are instead on a descent; we are being reduced by the very tools we have created to help ourselves. The second segment, titled 'Jupiter Mission', is prompted by another encounter with a black monolith found underneath the surface of the Moon—technology has allowed humans to reach the Moon, and the second slab will set humans on the next course of evolution further into space. This next chapter in evolution, however, is tempered by perhaps the genre's most notorious representation of technology gone bad: the HAL 9000 computer. Following a signal emanating from the moon, Earth sends the spaceship Discovery to Jupiter to discover the origin of the monolith. Five astronauts, three of whom remain in hibernation for the voyage, are the only human members of the crew. The ship is largely maintained by a HAL 9000, the advanced supercomputer on board. To keep themselves occupied, the two supervising astronauts play chess with HAL, watch TV, and exercise. After a HAL makes a minor error in anticipating a fault with the communications unit, the two astronauts, David Bowman and Frank Poole, contact Earth to inform them of HAL's mistake. HAL 9000s do not make mistakes, so the potential dangers of maintaining a faulty computer force Dave and Frank into having a private conference in one of the space pods. Unbeknownst to them, HAL is watching them, reading their lips; it discovers that it may be switched off before the mission is complete. In an act of self-preservation, HAL turns off the life support to the hibernating astronauts and kills Poole by cutting loose his air hose while he is outside replacing the communication equipment. Bowman realises that HAL must be disconnected so that the mission can continue and he can survive, although HAL is equally determined to continue the mission without human interference. Clearly, this segment of the film serves as a blatant 'Frankensteinian cautionary tale, a representation of our disquiet over the cybernetic blurring of the human, of our fear of an evolutionary showdown with increasingly autonomous technologies' (Mateas 2006: 105), yet for many critics it functioned as padding, a conflict between good and evil more familiar to traditional Hollywood movie audiences (Palmer 2006: 19).

After Bowman kills HAL he discovers the third monolith of the film in orbit around Jupiter. The last segment of *2001,* titled 'Jupiter and Beyond the Infinite', begins when Bowman approaches the monolith in his pod. Entering what is referred to as the Stargate, both Bowman and the audience are confronted by psychedelic images, lights and colours. At this point, 'the film shifts from a relatively comprehensible [science fiction] narrative and into a mode of avant-garde art cinema' (Booker 2006: 79) where the next stage in human evolution is envisaged. An older Bowman discovers the pod has appeared in a period style suite, and upon getting out of the pod he encounters an older version of himself eating at a table. Through a series of jump cuts, an increasingly aging Bowman continues to meet older versions until he is bed ridden. At the foot of the bed stands the fourth monolith, and as Bowman reaches out to touch it the scene cuts to show the now famous image of the Star Child suspended in space, the foetus representing humanity being reborn and ready to embark on the next stage of evolution. Many critics have discussed these closing scenes with reference to the concurrent counterculture movement and the taking of mind-altering drugs. Telotte (2001: 102) describes the Stargate as a 'drug-inspired hallucinatory vision' and Christine Cornea (2007: 82–5) links the film and contemporary science fiction literature to the psychedelic art movement, which at the time was experimenting with marijuana and LSD. Whatever the reading, *2001*'s ending is clearly emblematic of the period's fascination with social change and resisting the status quo. A film that still influences the genre, both visually and thematically, *2001* serves to ignite thought and challenge preconceptions. However, as inspiration to the films and popular culture that followed, Kubrick's film has fallen victim to its 'satiric prophecy' (Miller 1994: 25), whereby the ships and corporate logos used to satirise our then ordered and stagnated reality have become symbols of what the future will look like. With that, the next step in human evolution may not be possible.

As Hollywood started to revise its attitudes toward and methods of filmmaking, America too was going through some deep-seated changes. Society was starting to break apart as the nation's youth began to drift from the more conservative politics shared by their parents and demand social and political change. In a reactionary move away from the consensus of the 1950s, this counterculture movement was shared across the globe—running parallel with the spread of socialism and communism in Eastern Europe and the Cultural Revolution in China. Students and young people were demanding changes to the social structures they saw as impinging on personal freedoms. Feminism, drugs, sex and racial and sexual equality were at the forefront of what critics have called the culture wars, the battle between liberal and conservative, younger and older generations, over who could shape the nation's ideologies and values after World War II. This break away from the old is clearly visualised in the decade's fascination for the new: fashion, art, music and film all stressed novelty. New Hollywood is part of this counterculture movement because of its newness and because of what Jeremy Black (2006: 107) calls the 'specific rejection of conventional social and cultural assumptions'. Challenging the established norms of the previous decade and generation led to the culture wars and a renewed focus on particular forms of youth culture such as film—bearing in mind it had long been seen as a medium that attracted young audiences. Yet whether or not film was for a younger generation, science fiction continued to be used by some writers and directors as a means to offer political comment and critique during this tumultuous time of social change.

The Nuclear Threat

Kubrick's *Dr. Strangelove* was one of the many films to highlight and criticise American and human excessive reliance on technology and the so-called need for nuclear weapons. The Cuban Missile Crisis of 1962 not only renewed fears of the bomb first brought to attention in the mutant monster movies of the late 1950s but also reminded people of the fine line between life and death that America and the Soviet Union straddled during the Cold War. One simple press of the button and the whole world could be obliterated by nuclear warheads. Science fiction tapped into this nascent fear of nuclear holocaust by continuing to depict scientists and engineers as Faustian figures, corrupted by technology and an ever-present God complex. Indeed, as America and the Soviet Union continued the Space Race and nuclear arms proliferation, the first James Bond feature, *Dr. No* (1962), wowed audiences with stylish set design, technical gadgets and devices. Bond's mission to stop Dr. No from sabotaging American space rockets launched from Cape Canaveral, thus causing America to blame the Soviets and start a war, had realistic undertones as the Space Race continued to attract attention after the launch of *Sputnik 1* in 1957. The location of Dr. No's secret base in the Caribbean offered a direct parallel to the threat posed to American soil by the Soviet presence in Cuba during the Missile Crisis and clearly associates Bond with its Cold War contexts. Whether the first few Bond features of the 1960s can be seen as real science fiction is open to debate— Brosnan (1978: 150) describes *Dr. No* as an influence on the genre's spread to a wider audience—however, elements such as plot, characterisation and visual tropes do mirror those genre conventions established in the previous decades. The fact that the Bond 'films were deliberately de-politicised and detached from the Cold War background of the novels' (Chapman 1999: 76), with SPECTRE as enemy and not the Soviet Union, did not prevent audiences from associating Dr. No's plans with contemporary reality.

Clearly following in the tradition of science fiction's mad scientist, the epony-mous Dr. Strangelove, played by Peter Sellers, offers a comic interpretation of the 1960s scientist and humanity's faith in governmental technocrats. Like Dr. No, Dr. Strangelove is deformed—his mechanical hand is evidence of his physical corrup-tion and transformation brought about by an insane devotion to scientific experimen-tation. Towards the end of the film, Strangelove leaps from his wheelchair raising his mechanical arm in a Nazi like salute to the American president while exclaiming 'Mein Führer!' This scene provides a direct commentary on America's determination to win the Cold War and Space Race by employing the knowledge and skills of real life ex-Nazi scientists such as Wernher von Braun, who had helped develop the Ger-man V-2 Rocket and subsequently NASA's Mercury Rocket.

Kubrick wanted to show the absolute absurdity of the Cold War and the super-powers' policy on nuclear weapons and MAD (mutually assured destruction). For David Seed (1999: 147), the film's 'treatment of fears of extinction and mutation ex-emplify how black humour feigns to deprioritise subjects presumed to carry weight', and thus the ultimate fear of nuclear destruction is reduced to absurdity through the inaction of principal characters and the coincidental events that bring about an American B-52 bomber dropping its nuclear payload on Soviet Russia. Scenes in the war room offer the most satirical bite, as the generals and politicians squabble over who should be blamed for the accidental launch of America's missiles. Acting like spoilt children, the fight between the Soviet Ambassador and General Turgidson on the floor of the war room is emblematic of Kubrick's perception of war being point-less; the irony of Sellers, as the American president, shouting, 'Gentlemen, you can't fight in here, this is the War Room!', obliquely sums up the futility and absurdity of the superpowers' tussle for world domination. Yet, also, 'the realism of the settings and the machinery, particularly the interior of the B52, gives an added impact to the horrifying absurdity of the action and characters' (Brosnan 1978: 157). Likewise, the juxtaposition of images of nuclear mushroom clouds with Vera Lynn songs at the end of the film disturbs the audience's perception of reality (Baxter 1970: 168). Should we be celebrating the use of nuclear weapons? Can they ensure the right side will win? Will humanity survive the fallout?

Such questions are perhaps answered by the nuclear film cycle's most signifi-cant feature, *Planet of the Apes* (1968). Based on Pierre Boulle's 1963 *La Planètes des singes,* the film sees astronaut George Taylor, played by Charlton Heston, crash land on a planet he believes to be alien. Injured and unable to talk, he is captured by a civilisation of apes who can walk, talk and use guns. The apes deem humans to be vermin-like savages and kill them for sport. Split into three classes or strata of ape society, the chimps are pacifists and scientists, the gorillas are soldiers and aggressors, and the orang-utans are the politicians and philosophers. Before the scientists can experiment on Taylor, he escapes, finally blurting out the words "Get your hands stinking paws off me, you damned dirty ape!" which prove to all apes that some humans are intelligent. Fleeing for his life, Taylor and female compatriot

Nova look for evidence of the civilisation that existed on the planet before the apes evolved. Taylor's discovery at the end of the film is one of science fiction's, indeed cinema's, most shocking twists. On a secluded beach Taylor and Nova find the remains of the Statue of Liberty buried in the sand, thus confirming that he did not crash land on an alien world but in fact had travelled thousands of years into the future and landed back on a postapocalyptic Earth; humans had destroyed themselves with their nuclear weapons, and the apes evolved to become the dominant species.

Eric Greene (1998: 48), ties the desolate landscape of postapocalypse Earth to Charlton Heston as an icon of 'Western imperial privilege'. He links Heston's role has white male hero in *Planet of the Apes* to some of his previous leading roles, stating that 'Heston seemed to be perpetually fighting a "last stand" battle to defend a fort or outpost of Western "civilisation" against the onslaught of hordes of non-Western, dark-skinned "barbarians"' (Greene 1998: 41). Comparisons with the then contemporary war in Vietnam, where American soldiers identified their enemies as savage 'gooks' and 'Charlies', cannot be overstated here. Furthermore, Greene (1998: 45) goes on to extrapolate that the film is an inversion of the Western myth by 'denying the Western hero both victory and the mythological gesture of martyrdom'. This can be seen in the dystopian ending when Taylor discovers that the ape planet is in fact Earth in the future. Whereas traditionally the space of the mythical West in previous incarnations of Western and science fiction films implied positive rebirth, here it has become a counterculture wasteland of death and destruction. The frontier myth is no longer relevant or positive for an American society undergoing tremendous social and cultural change while the nation struggles to fight a needless war in South East Asia.

The story was continued in four sequels and a short-lived television series in the mid-1970s. In *Beneath the Planet of the Apes* (1970), we see the crumbling ruins of New York beneath the planet's surface; this destroyed city is inhabited by human mutants who worship an unexploded nuclear bomb. The apes, led by the gorilla soldiers, attack the mutants, thus triggering a second nuclear holocaust as the bomb explodes at the end of the film. The franchise's treatment of controversial issues of the time, such as the Civil Rights movement's fight for racial equality and America's continued involvement in Vietnam, became more obvious in later sequels: *Escape from the Planet of the Apes* (1971), *Conquest of the Planet of the Apes* (1972) and *Battle for the Planet of the Apes* (1973). As dystopian visions of a future earth, 'The *Apes* films arose during a time of perceived crisis, or perhaps more precisely a time of perceived heightened crisis, and such conditions are fertile ground for apocalyptic responses' (Greene 1998: 23–4). Like Kubrick's *2001,* these films showed radical change through extreme breaks between past and present. Films of this period stood out as bleak warnings from the counterculture that continuing down the path of nuclear proliferation and social injustice would ultimately lead to America's and humanity's destruction.

Alternative Views

The success of series like *The Twilight Zone* and *The Outer Limits* in the late 1950s and early 1960s showed that audiences and television networks were just as keen to experiment with thought-provoking stories on the small screen as well as in the cinema. As we learned in the previous chapter, science fiction on television matured as programming changed narrative emphasis from ray guns and rocket ships in the serials to political allegory and moral lessons in *The Twilight Zone*. Networks on the whole saw huge potential for the genre as a money spinner, guaranteeing large audiences for their sponsors, but so too did writers and producers who believed the genre capable of stimulating viewers tired of the typical mix of quiz shows, sitcoms and chat shows. It was true that networks were keen to fill air time with anything they could as more and more people bought and watched television, therefore leading to a multitude of short-lived and dreary series that never took off. Yet the space in the schedules for science fiction did grow, thereby giving writers and producers such as Serling, Stevens, and Gene Roddenberry the chance to test the boundaries and offer intellectual genre programming. Such programming reached its zenith in the 1960s, one might argue, with *Star Trek* (1966–1969), but its contemporaries should not be simply dismissed because they did not garner the same level of critical and cultural attention. In fact, as shall be discussed later, without the success and influence of Irwin Allen's more juvenile adventures or camp series like *The Man from U.N.C.L.E.* (1964–1968), there may never have been an audience for *Star Trek* (see boxed text) in the first place.

Until the late 1950s the types of programming on the three American television networks—NBC, CBS and ABC—were largely dictated by companies that controlled the content of the particular shows they sponsored. Entire series or individual shows would clearly be associated with one sponsor, a result of the system of sponsorship on radio being transferred to TV, which saw soap operas named as such because they would be sponsored by specific detergent companies. Only after the quiz show scandals in the late 1950s did things start to change, with more programming power being given back to the networks through the use of multiple advertisers. The most famous quiz show scandal revolved around NBC's popular *Twenty-One* in 1957. Instructed by the network, who wanted to increase ratings by building in drama, long-time but unpopular champion Herbert Stempel had to purposely forget an answer so that the intellectual and good looking Charles Van Doren could take his quiz show crown. The network bowed to sponsorship and audience pressure to ensure that the ex-G.I. Stempel would be replaced by the privileged PhD student Van Doren in a tense quiz face-off—as Van Doren's face and demeanour was deemed more appropriate. When the scandal finally hit the newsstands, it showed that American values and ideals were not under threat from communism but rather from the overt consumerism that drove television and its sponsors to lie. For Stephen J. Whitfield (1996: 176), these sorts of scandals during the Cold War 'provoked considerable soul-searching, a fear that the nation that thought of itself as goodness incarnate had gone astray'.

Having ad breaks that brought many different consumer products to the attention of viewers instead of only having one soap manufacturer or chocolate company associated with the show meant that advertisers could not dictate or influence television production theme or content (Hilmes 2007: 171). Networks controlled most of the primetime and daytime production companies, thus they began to regulate affiliate stations and their content across the country. However, in an attempt to differentiate themselves from each other, as they juggled to fit popular shows around their competitors, the networks were willing to take more risks with programming, and therefore genre series were one potential method of securing an audience: science fiction could perhaps guarantee a niche.

Contrary to academic accounts of the how the Nielsen ratings eventually gave way to the use of demographics by the networks from 1970, Mark Alvey (2007: 16–17) asserts that during the 1960s networks experimented with television by targeting specific groups with 'diverse, interesting and aesthetically rich' programmes as well as continuing to attract existing audiences with the more conservative and familiar sitcom format. Political and social issues were coming to the fore in series, inspired by American news reporting, that dramatised 'the various social revolutions of the decade—the Civil rights movement, black radicalism, women's liberation, youth unrest, opposition to the Vietnam War, and so on' (Alvey 2007: 17). The counterculture found a space on 1960s television, and through the displacement of the contemporary onto the future settings of alien planets and spaceships, series like *Star Trek* were able to tackle divisive topics without attracting too much attention from censors and network bosses. In fact, the political and social climate had changed so much that networks felt that they had a duty to at least look like they were making an effort. The rise and popularity of colour television literally exposed the nation to the inherent racial discrimination in society as few nonwhite faces appeared on screen early in television history. Increasing the production of programmes for different audiences meant that networks had to make shows that reflected the nation's social, racial and ethnic diversity. This change was important as the networks vied for larger shares in key demographics, and they could not ignore the significant growth in minority groups who also symbolised new potential markets to whom advertisers could sell their products:

> By the mid-1960s, it was clear that American network television faced dramatic social, technical, and business changes. Civil rights groups' agitation highlighted the need for firm commitments on hiring minorities, at all levels, and eliminating racial stereotypes. Color television and videotape emerged from network research laboratories, where they had languished for years, to reshape the medium. (Pounds 1999: 31)

Science fiction series offered networks a chance to experiment, gambling with the bigger budgets needed for special effects and large sets and using colour to attract new audiences. *Star Trek* was clearly a product of these cultural and industrial contexts.

STAR TREK (1966–1969)

Gene Roddenberry's *Star Trek* was a symbol of JFK's progressive and liberal New Frontier politics, with its metanarrative now being as famous as the iconic ships, uniforms, and actors that populated the fictional worlds of the Federation's future: 'Kennedy was elected on his promise to "get the country moving again" and his vision of a "New Frontier"' (Quart and Auster 2002: 68). For all those who explored space, from the original series (1966–1969) to the retrospectively historical crew on *Star Trek: Enterprise* (2001–2005), their voyages to places unknown in which they meet with aliens both hostile and friendly were a constant education. Freed from the past turmoil of an Earth wracked by war, poverty and inequality, *Star Trek* was able to depict a future where humans could fulfil their true potential. Humanity was on a constant voyage of discovery where it could learn from mistakes of the past and continue to improve and achieve the utopia first conceived by Roddenberry in 1964. The multicultural crew that sat aboard the Enterprise was representative of all that America should live up to: Women would be able to assume positions of responsibility equal to men, African, Asian, and Euro Americans would be able to live in harmony after overcoming the divisions of race and racism, and nations once at war with each other could overcome their petty squabbles for the benefit of humankind. While 'The decade was ushered in with a growing sense of possibility for political change,' JFK symbolised a youthful energy to combat the overt militarism of the previous decade (Quart and Auster 2002: 68). Therefore, the physical image of the President stood as a symbol for America's renewed efforts to achieve its mission of peace through the American way. Consequently, the physical body in *Star Trek,* specifically the relationship between human and alien bodies, became vitally important in visualising the American project of multiculturalism and education: 'In this sense *Star Trek* [acted] much like a Jeremiad, as a moral guide to humanity's progress in life, making obvious what [needed] to be done but not providing its audience with all of the answers' (Geraghty 2003b: 235).

The first episode to be aired, 'The Man Trap' (1966), was heavily inspired by *The Twilight Zone* and *The Outer Limits* in that the plot involved a mind game in which things are not what they appear to be. In this story Captain Kirk and his crew are called to planet M-113 on a routine supply mission when people start to die from extreme salt deprivation, due to a monster that is not only able to create the illusion of being human but requires salt for its survival. As the story progresses the Salt Monster has to change appearance several times in order to get more salt from its helpless victims, and finally attempts to kill McCoy in the guise of a past lover. In other words, the monster mimics femininity to seduce McCoy before she strikes and, when Kirk interrupts this encounter, McCoy is forced to kill the image of the women that he once loved. This episode also reveals the tension within the show. On the one hand, the alien is portrayed as a relatively sympathetic being in this episode, the last survivor of a lost civilization, and yet it is also seen as a dangerous threat hat kills without remorse. Furthermore, the image of beauty that it shows to Kirk and McCoy hides a hideous alien body and treacherous alien motivations. Its frequent association with femininity is also significant, and it saps the life from its male victims much like the monstrous feminine described in Barbara Creed's classic study of horror (see Creed 1993). As a result, it could be argued the episode suggests that femininity threatens to distract heroic masculinity from its five-year mission, to convert the male explorer into a domesticated conformist.

Certainly, *Star Trek* used the alien body and the idea of physical difference to explore contemporary political and social issues. For example, Roddenberry used the alien to explore issues of civil rights, and its politics here were often fairly radical for the period. Episodes like the 'The Enemy Within' (1966) used the doppelganger motif to point out humanity's capability of committing acts of violence. When Kirk is caught in a transporter accident, his personality is split between two identical versions of himself: one that inherited his good traits such as compassion and caution, the other inheriting his more evil traits such as deception, lust and violent aggression. Throughout this episode Kirk's body is depicted in abject ways: the good side is weak and feeble without the more stronger, vicious Kirk, and the evil side shows signs of madness and physical instability without the calming influences of the compassionate Kirk. Mike Hertenstein sees this treatment of humanity's multiplicity as typical *Star Trek;* in this case the weak and strong body of the captain represents human duality often seen in myth and legend as the centaur—half man, half beast—part of nature yet also an outsider (1998: 8). The moral of the story is that people need both halves to live; allowing one to take over the other means that we will destroy each other. In order to survive, humanity must learn to be inclusive: the individual must learn to accept the different parts of itself, and the society as a whole must learn to accept the different elements from which it is composed: 'To *integrate* is to combine elements to form an inter-related, unified whole. *Trek* certainly has always prided itself on inclusiveness' (Hertenstein 1998: 10).

Similarly, *Star Trek*'s 'Let That Be Your Last Battlefield' (1969) 'addresses the meaning of race with telling self-consciousness' by showing two aliens unable to forget their bigotry (Bernardi 1998: 3). However, Daniel Bernardi suggests that this episode, although intending to highlight America's inher-ent racism and social segregation based on colour, confirms *Star Trek*'s liberal humanist intent through dialogue and alien make-up (the aliens differ in that while both have bodies that are black on one side of their face and white on the other, one alien is white on his left side and the other on his right side). Using the aliens' bodies as an allegory for America's problems, the series implies that humanity will have integrated and progressed beyond racial bigotry in the far future. Nonetheless, at the same time, the series also implies that the future will be one where whites 'are morally, politically, and innately superior, and both colored humans and colored aliens are either servants, threats, or objects of exotic desire' (68). The predominantly white crew of the *Enterprise* see the warring pair of painted aliens as primitive because they have not progressed like humans—however, what this sentiment underscores is that the notion of the racial other is still a sensitive subject in the twenty-third century, particularly when the Federation is run by young, white men. Hertenstein's notion of inclusivity discussed in rela-tion to the evil twin comes true only if the racial minority submits to the ideology of the majority.

As a result, there are clear contradictions within *Star Trek* vision of the future, yet there is also evidence of a strong desire to visualise difference, both physical and cultural, in ways that challenge the audience to make up their minds for themselves. Part of the polemical nature of the series is reflected in what Catherine Johnson calls the 'regulated innovation' of *Star Trek* (2005: 75). The series clearly conformed to generic tropes of science fiction, but within a heavily regulated television industry and under the constraints of small budgets and artistic practice it had to be innovative yet familiar in order to attract and maintain an audience: 'Far from being merely a "cloak" within which to disguise the treatment of contemporary issues, [*Star Trek*] actually works at the service of the action-adventure format within the demands of 1960s network television production' (Johnson 2005: 92). This is best exemplified in the series' use of colour (NBC was set on making colour one of its unique selling points to advertisers and consumers) in that imaging new worlds week in and week out could best be achieved by using and reusing sets and make-up techniques in the representation of alien worlds and creatures (84). Bold colours and outrageous alien costumes were just a small part of the particular look the production crew was trying to establish. Such an aesthetic is identifiable in the epi-sodes discussed here: for example, the boldly contrasted face paint of the warring aliens in 'Let That Be Your Last Battlefield' not only stood in for the race debate that waged during the Civil Rights years but also represented *Star Trek*'s desire for innovation in the use of vivid colours and costuming of the alien characters. Production in this case is clearly influenced by Roddenberry's personal politics, NBC's desire to please sponsors, and the production staff's talent for visual design. Moreover, *Star Trek*'s use of the body as site for innovation and regulation through make-up and production design is symptomatic of the 'representational strategies' employed to fulfil 'the network's desire to represent racial minorities without alienating certain audience demographics' (Johnson 2005: 89). The alien body in *Star Trek* was more than just a site for encountering the unfamiliar; it served to visualise the developing relationship between the science fiction genre and America's television networks.

Television Thinks Big

In service to network demands for more product, science fiction series dotted the TV schedules. Ranging from espionage and spy series like *The Man from U.N.C.L.E.* and *Get Smart* (1965–1970) to action adventures such as Allen's *Voyage to the Bottom of the Sea* (1964–1968), the diversity in science fiction output was extraordinary. Even children's television was being given a futuristic revamp with animated sitcoms like *The Jetsons* (1962–1963) bridging the gap between Saturday morning and prime time. The network grab for audiences ensured a healthy turnaround of science fiction that would appeal to the most discerning fans. Not content with garish and colourful yarns produced by the likes of Irwin Allen, viewers could still watch stories written and inspired by established science fiction authors in the anthology series *The Twilight Zone* and *The Outer Limits*. Inspired by the success of prime time anicoms such as *The Flintstones* (1960–1966), networks also saw potential for targeting both adults and children in the animated series market. In what is described as 'television's first animation boom' ABC introduced *The Jetsons* to American audiences (Mittell 2003: 46). Animated series, or anicoms, like *The Flintstones* and *The Jetsons,* differed from their feature-length and seven-minute progenitors 'in their employment of live-action narrative conventions commonly associated with sitcom series' (Dobson 2003: 85). This mixing of genres was intended so that a wider audience could be reached; however, critics immediately lampooned these series for their perceived limited attraction to only children.

Produced by Hanna-Barbera, *The Jetsons* was a thirty-minute, family-orientated anicom about the Jetson family and their life in the twenty-first century. While both *The Jetsons* and *The Flintstones* projected contemporary American culture and lifestyles onto different time periods, these series can clearly be read as traditional sitcoms with a domesticated settings, strong family structures and emphasis on daily life and routine. The Jetson family lived in a future utopia, where humans benefited from every elaborate robotic and technological device writers and animators could think of. Parodying the suburban nightmare of the 1950s, with George Jetson feeling trapped by his three-hour, three-days-a-week office job and tyrannical boss, Mr. Spacely, the series used established science fiction and sitcom clichés to emphasise the absurdity of human reliance on technology to make their lives easier. The family clearly live a perfect life, depicted in what we read now as a retro aesthetic, yet they often complained about the hardships they endured such as going to work or doing the occasional spot of housekeeping. Although ultimately unsuccessful, being dropped from prime time to Saturday mornings (Hilton-Morrow and McMahan 2003: 76), the series can be seen as a direct influence on contemporary anicoms such as *Futurama* (1999–2003) which become popular when networks returned to animation to provide prime time viewing.

Parody proved popular in Bond-inspired spy series such as *Mission: Impossible* (1966–1973), *The Man from U.N.C.L.E.* and *Get Smart.* Like their big screen brethren

Dr. No, these series combined gadgets and futuristic technology with traditional espionage and Cold War narratives—pitting the masculine and stylish heroes against evil foes usually from the Eastern Soviet bloc. Not only influenced by the British Bond franchise, these series followed in the footsteps of a pioneering television from the UK called *Danger Man* (1960–1962 and 1964–1968), broadcast in America as *Secret Agent* (1965–1966). Characterised by an intense and cynical 'realism and seriousness' *Danger Man* has attracted critical and popular praise (Chapman 2002: 16). As both British and American television benefited from bigger budgets, realism was sacrificed for more fantastic and parodic espionage narratives, foregrounding guns and gadgets used by the agents rather than characterisation and plot. Yet the popularity of the many spy series in the 1960s indicates the mutability of science fiction across different television genres and allows us to see such series as important contributors to the history of the genre on the small screen. The continued fascination for spying also highlights their Cold War contexts.

Whereas Agents 86 and 99 in *Get Smart* worked for CONTROL, an overtly American government secret spy agency, Napoleon Solo and Illya Kuryakin in *The Man from U.N.C.L.E.* worked for U.N.C.L.E., a neutral organisation more aligned with the United Nations than any specific country. Ignoring national rivalries, the series was pitched as a glimpse of a post-Cold War world—an interesting idea since it was first broadcast two years after the Cuban Missile Crisis threatened nuclear Armageddon. The series implied that an organisation like U.N.C.L.E. could exist in the present day, therefore making the extraordinary feats of James Bond and fellow television spies appear more realistic. Weapons and technical gadgets like the super car again alluded to Bond, but the sheer amount of technology used to help the agents get out of sticky situations or travel the globe overloaded the series, eventually appearing more mundane and run-of-the-mill. Not appearing wholly implausible, the gadgets did provide a temporal break between the contemporary timing of the series and the slightly futuristic aesthetic, something which did not happen with Bond films in the 1960s as they were explicitly tied to a British imperial and colonial agenda. Without a doubt, as M. Keith Booker (2002: 46) describes, *U.N.C.L.E.* 'tended much more toward the ludic, displaying a superficial (or even campy) interest in style that marked [it] as far more distinctively postmodern than' the UK's James Bond or *Danger Man.*

Jon Abbott's (2006: 8) following description of Irwin Allen appears blunt and yet is a statement with which many would find hard to disagree: 'Allen was no storyteller...he was into spectacle.' The creator of the renowned 1960s pulp science fiction television shows *Voyage to the Bottom of the Sea, Lost in Space* (1965–1968), *The Time Tunnel* (1966–1967) and *Land of the Giants* (1968–1970) is seen by some critics as an aberration, someone always keen to aim for the fantasy and kid's TV audience rather than the perceived 'serious and highbrow' audience who might have watched *The Twilight Zone, The Outer Limits* and *Star Trek.* Yet Abbott points out there was space for both in the TV schedules, that audiences could handle political science fiction and colourful spectacle: 'But when we need to escape from the misery of the news broadcasts, or the tyranny of historical or scientific fact, that is when the door to the wacky worlds of Irwin Allen and his colleagues in sheer, unadulterated fantasy seems so inviting' (4). Oscar De Los Santos offers a helpful discussion of Allen's series, bringing attention to the debates surrounding more juvenile science fiction television and its more sophisticated counterparts. He delineates between science fiction and what he calls 'sci-fi', positing that science fiction in literature and visual media uses 'scientific principles and exponentiates them to concoct its "what if?" scenarios'. On the other hand, 'Sci-fi' is a 'sketch that doesn't work very hard if at all—to explain its science and technology', and is concerned more with 'dazzling the audience with spectacle than credible ideas'. Indeed, according to De Los Santos (2009: 26), 'Sci-fi is closer kin to the fantasy genre.' In terms of the Allen series, this is a plausible framework through which to understand their popularity with audiences of all ages and the television networks keen to cash in on the genre. However, looking at the genre in this way does tend to replicate debates first raised around earlier visual examples such as Flash Gordon which positioned the science fiction serial as childish in orientation, with little concern for the genre's potential to offer social critique.

Voyage to the Bottom of the Sea, the first of Allen's series, saw him return to familiar ground by adapting his own 1961 film of the same name. Sea-based films and TV proved popular in the 1950s and 1960s, and Allen was keen to cash in on this trend. The story followed the adventures of the *Seaview,* a super submarine, and its crew, who explored the ocean, running into various villains and sea creatures that posed a threat to the Earth and the peace that existed between the superpowers. Familiar espionage stories from contemporaries like *Get Smart* often crept into the series, no doubt influenced by the tense political situation created by the Missile Crisis, and the submarine was often dispatched by the American government to broker deals and offer military muscle to prevent new conflicts. However, in an effort to stimulate audiences and create spectacle Allen introduced garish and colourful sea creatures and aliens from the second season onward, thus giving the show a somewhat undeserved reputation as only offering parades of monsters rather than detailed characterisation and political intrigue. The series did also highlight Allen's penchant for recycling footage, props and sets from his previous projects, therefore confirming to critics that he was merely concerned with the look of his shows. Nevertheless, Gerald Duchovnay (2008: 73) argues that the recycling of his own material, taking footage from the film version of *Voyage* and reusing scenes already shown in previous episodes, excited viewers and network executives because 'Allen had brought his filmic sense to television by combining that already proven adventure plot with the aesthetic experience of wonder that marked the best science fiction cinema'.

Reworking formula and recycling footage would continue in his follow-up series. *Lost in Space,* a *Swiss Family Robinson* (1812) in space, had over-the-top alien creatures attack the young Will Robinson, Dr. Smith and Robot week after week. Some of the monsters even made the leap from deep sea to outer space, with Allen using the same sea creature costumes for his extraterrestrials. Of course, the space-exploring format tied in neatly with the decade's fascination for rockets, astronauts and space travel, and Allen was keen to tap into the Space Race craze in America at that time. However, the bizarre monsters and fantastical stories eventually wore thin, and Allen moved onto his third and fourth series, *The Time Tunnel* and *Land of the Giants,* which differed from the man-in-a-monster-costume look of the first two.

The Time Tunnel harked back to the popular science fiction theme of time travel, with H. G. Wells being the most familiar proponent of such stories, and fitted in with Allen's filmmaking background as he had already directed adaptations of classic science fiction literature. The series' premise was basic, with two scientists travelling back in time using a secret government time machine, and the ability to use 20th Century Fox's back lots and sets to produce his show meant its budget was kept under control. With the time travellers going back and forth between different periods in Earth history, the sets could be easily dressed with existing props, and stock footage from different films from the studio's archive could be used to offer historical contexts. Seemingly cutting corners to save money, Allen's decision to reuse and recycle again gave his series a cinematic quality, just as cinema was about to astound audiences with *2001.* The expansive merits of Allen's creative work would be fully realised in *The Land of the Giants,* with audiences once more revelling in seeing the juxtaposition between gigantism and miniaturisation popular in B-movies of the 1950s. Similar to the plot of *Planet of the Apes,* a mixed crew of scientists and military personnel veer off course and crash land on a planet that resembles Earth. However, the planet is populated by a race of gigantic humans who see the tiny humans as a threat—ironically positioning the characters with whom the audience sympathise as the invading alien aggressor. Appearances were not to be trusted, and the line between right and wrong was blurred; such lessons were typical of science fiction during the 1960s, and Allen did not hold back on visualising this through large sets and colourful costumes.

It is true that the genre has allowed space for both story and spectacle; Jon Abbott (2006: 1) sees the work of Georges Méliès (as we have seen, one of the first filmmakers to experiment with screen science fiction) as an example of how the genre could be presented as a work of 'showmanship and special effects.' However, many critics have dismissed so-called childish science fiction, *Buck Rogers, Flash Gordon, Captain Video,* Allen's series and so forth, as pure fantasy, products of an unscrupulous Hollywood industry that cared only for profits not politics. Yet what these criticisms often forget is that science fiction of this type filled a specific need and had a particular role in the survival and development of the science fiction genre on both the big and small screens. Without *Flash Gordon* serials in the 1940s, which enticed audiences to go to the cinema regularly, the genre may have died out and we might not have seen the classic films of the 1950s such as *Invaders from Mars* or *Forbidden Planet*. Without *Captain Video* and the like on television in the early 1950s, which carved out a permanent place for science fiction in people's homes, we may never have felt the need or got the go-ahead to produce *The Twilight Zone* and its progeny. Likewise, without the Allen productions regularly featuring in 1960s television schedules, the genre may have receded into relative obscurity with only cerebral series such as *Star Trek* attracting a determined but marginalised audience.

–3–

Unsettling Visions of
America's Future Present
Dystopian Science Fiction

In 1978 Joan F. Dean examined the state of the science fiction film and the commercial failure of many productions between the release of Kubrick's *2001: A Space Odyssey* and George Lucas's *Star Wars* (1977). According to Dean, despite the promising start provided by *2001,* the failure of many 1970s science fiction films was due to their focus on the conflicts arising from America's escalating social and political problems and the continued resentment of military involvement in Vietnam. These issues were often reflected in dystopian visions of the future in films such as *Westworld* (1973), *Zardoz* (1973), Lucas's own *THX-1138* (1971), *Soylent Green* (1973), *Rollerball* (1975), *Logan's Run* (1976), *A Boy and His Dog* (1975), *Beneath the Planet of the Apes* (1970) and *Silent Running* (1972). Furthermore, she argues that, as a result of these concerns, there was also a corresponding lack of interest in the perennial favourite icon of American science fiction: the alien. This situation was particularly ironic given that the period was framed by two of the most identifiably extraterrestrial movies in the history of science fiction film: *2001* and *Alien* (1979).

Furthermore, Dean claims, films that did deal with the possibilities of extraterrestrial life, such as *The Andromeda Strain* (1971), *The Man Who Fell to Earth* (1976), *Slaughterhouse-Five* (1972) and *The Rocky Horror Picture Show* (1975), displayed a 'developing neo-isolationism' and did little to broaden the genre's comprehension of anything beyond America's domestic and foreign interests (Dean 1978: 36). In effect, Dean claims, 'all that the science fiction films of the early seventies offer in the way of extra-terrestrial life were bacteria, David Bowie, an Invisible civilization, and a few perverts' (37). Dean's harsh analysis of the genre is by no means unconvincing, but we must not underestimate the influence that the state of both the nation and Hollywood had on science fiction and its audiences at this time. The prophetic impulse of *2001* and *Star Trek* was a false dawn, as their glittering visions of interstellar space travel, alien life and super technology appeared tarnished by America's economic recession, impending defeat in Vietnam, the Watergate scandal and increasing social division and unrest. One can agree that 'The unknown and subliminal messages of the 60's science fiction became overt, aided by increasingly monumental displays of special effects' (Anderson 1985: 11); however, those overt messages were unceasingly downbeat, with films such as *No Blade of Grass* (1970), *The Omega Man* (1971), *Soylent Green* (see boxed text), *Silent Running* and *Logan's Run* showing Earth on the brink of ecological disaster. This eternal precipice, the overarching sense of impending doom, was envisaged so regularly and with aplomb in films of this period that it is hard to imagine that they could and would give way to the more upbeat science fiction blockbusters of Lucas and Spielberg.

The overarching theme of this period in science fiction on screen was dystopia: the negative of utopia, a place or society depicted as worse or indeed a potential future of the contemporary world in which we live. A common trope in the literary form of the genre, dystopias in the twentieth century are more often critical dystopias in that they neither celebrate the possibility of utopia nor entirely reduce the narrative to total despair. For Graham J. Murphy (2009), the critical dystopia explores ways in which those marginalised by the corrupt or totalitarian regime can fight and change the system and perhaps move forward, thus offering a sense of hope as well as a vision of hopelessness. What is more, dystopias offer social critique alongside pessimistic presentation: 'The typical narrative structure of the dystopia (with its presentation of an alienated character's refusal) facilitates this politically and formally flexible stance' (Baccolini and Moylan 2003: 6). This particular facet of the critical dystopia is most obvious in the decade's representation of the lone individual fighting the corrupt forces above him (as the protagonist is usually a man) and offers an interesting twist on the American narrative of the self-made man who succeeds through individual endeavour and enterprise. The films discussed in the following section not only position the refusing individual as central to the narrative, but it is through these characters that the audience is given a glimmer of hope even if the protagonist ultimately fails to evoke social change. The critical dystopia portrayed in film during the 1970s transferred to the small screen in the 1990s, the most obvious example being seen in *Babylon 5* (1994–1998).

To the Death

From barbaric death matches to testing trials of humanity, sports and games in 1970s science fiction played an important part in constructing a believable and often shocking vision of the future. Frequently used to emphasise the futility of existence in a dystopian world, sports and games represented the baser elements of a civil society: violence, conflict, intolerance and dishonesty. For example, the future worlds of *Rollerball* and *Death Race 2000* (1975) are divided into massive continental corporations and global superpowers. International diplomacy and war are not carried out by politicians or the military but by sporting heroes, champions of the blood sports Rollerball and Auto Racing. Violent sport in both these films stands as metaphor for human contest and international conflict: *Rollerball*'s tagline reads, 'In the not-too-distant future, wars will no longer exist. But there will be Rollerball!'

In *Rollerball,* James Caan's Jonathan E. is the world's greatest Rollerballer, a hero of the people who tune in to watch their teams, sponsored by large global corporations, play to the death on giant TV screens. The dominance of Rollerball and the medium of television help to maintain the ideological status quo, wherein the big corporations profit from giving their citizens what they want; keeping them subjugated and focussed on the game, the corporations avoid revolution by offering legitimate bloodletting vicariously through the television screen. When Jonathan E. refuses to retire after the final match (the sport's bosses feel he is becoming too powerful, a dangerous icon for the people) he subverts the hegemonic system by being the last man standing, thus showing that the individual can triumph over the corporate body. For Fred Mason (2007: 131), the film 'is clearly reminiscent of the Roman coliseum, as players are injured and die for the amusement of the spectators and the underlying purposes of the corporate overlords' and 'is meant to be a critique of the increasing tide of violence in sport', yet it failed to convince at the box office as critics saw it as a spectacular glorification of violence rather than a moralistic and critical tale.

Not dissimilar to Jonathan E., in *Dear Race 2000,* where millions tune in to see the world's greatest racing drivers compete in a transcontinental road race, gaining extra points by running over pedestrians, champion driver Frankenstein represents the disaffected hero who wants to overturn the system. The media is shown to be the dangerous instigator of violence, with the world's population glued to their television sets, revelling in the exploitative sport contest. Jokingly, the film's tagline reads, 'In the Year 2000 Hit and Run Driving Is No Longer a Felony. It's the National Sport!' However, the somewhat tongue-in-cheek undertones of this film serve to highlight and critique the notion that sport will become the violent opiate of the masses. Again, for Mason, 'gratuitous violence... serves as spectacle, but this is diffused by the film's refusal to take it seriously... The conscious self-parody in *Death Race 2000* stresses the serious points lying more deeply' (2007: 132). Whether one prefers *Rollerball* or *Death Race*'s critique of sport, government and the media both films are emblematic of how the genre had become just as concerned with politics as with spectacle. For Bryan Senn (2006: 209), the 1970s was a period of transition 'moving away from the hopeful brotherly love mentality of the 1960s toward the unapologetic greed-is-good corporate mindset of the 1980s', and both films ably managed to communicate such concerns for the future using violence and humour. No doubt these and many films of this period show how 'the science fiction genre had pointedly become a popular and effective vehicle for addressing important cultural concerns, even ones that, in various ways, offered a subversive view of the status quo' (Telotte 2001: 104).

The science fiction sports feature highlighted the decade's fears and paranoia. America was going through significant social and political changes; what is more, these changes were being broadcast day after day in the nation's media: 'For the first time in American history public opinion polls reported that the American people were no longer optimistic about the nation's future' (Quart and Auster 2002: 101). President Jimmy Carter went so far as to say that America was suffering from a 'crisis of confidence'. Such mediated angst was characteristic of what William Graebner sees as a 'nation in existential despair'. His thesis maintains that the events of the decade served to 'deflate' and 'mock' the hopes and dreams of America's white middle classes. They developed a siege mentality, seeing themselves as survivors. Defeat in Vietnam had signalled a decline in heroism, and life seemed meaningless: 'At bottom, they perceived and talked about themselves as bored—not bored with the little things, or minimally bored, but bored big time. They were bored by what they saw as the collapse of meaning and values' (Graebner 2004: 158–9). Graebner's argument is particularly compelling when he takes into consideration Hollywood films being made during this period, which he describes as reflective of the inner turmoil middle America was experiencing. Irwin Allen disaster movies such as *The Poseidon Adventure* (1972) and *The Towering Inferno* (1974), along with George Romero's zombie films, showed Americans going through the motions of living without really appreciating life. People in these narratives were merely surviving, trying to live without pain, trauma or dying.

Certainly these films share similarities with the texts already discussed in this chapter, yet it is a surprise that Graebner does not mention any of the decade's science fiction movies. Perhaps what marks out his chosen films as different is their contemporary locality—they were films set in the present day. *Rollerball, Death Race* and *Soylent Green* for example were set in the future, not in the audience's present, and it is the forward-looking aspect of these Hollywood features which truly serves to underscore their dystopian theme. If *Poseidon* or *Dawn of the Dead* (1978) showed possible hope for the few remaining survivors at the end of each film, then science fiction emphasised the fact that all hope in the future had vanished. One man could not make a difference, and society was not worthy of being saved. With any luck, surviving, or just getting by, would be the best humans could wish for.

SOYLENT GREEN (1973)

Already a Hollywood icon thanks to his leading roles in epic films such as *The Ten Commandments* (1956), *Ben Hur* (1959), *El Cid* (1961) and the polemical science fiction of *Planet of the Apes* and *The Omega Man*, Charlton Heston's character in *Soylent Green* perhaps most of all assured him the status of the genre's augur. The final twist, closing scenes, and his last words in the film sum up the decade's nihilistic and dystopian prediction for what the world will become in the not too distant future. The film's tagline, 'It's the year 2022 . . . People are the same. They'll do anything to get what they need. And they need Soylent Green' only hinted at the macabre depths to which humans would stoop to survive.

In the film, based on Harry Harrison's novel *Make Room! Make Room!* (1966), Heston plays Detective Thorn, a New York City policeman who lives with elderly roommate, Sol Roth, played by Edward G. Robinson, in a cluttered apartment in an overcrowded tenement block. The city has a population of over 40 million; people live in the streets, gutters, hallways and doorways of dilapidated buildings. The city is divided into the haves and the have-nots; those that can afford to live in luxury do so in tall skyscrapers separated from the ghetto by high fences and deep trenches. These power-ful city elite can afford to buy overpriced and rare food such as meat and fresh vegetables, while the poor can only hope to survive on food provided by the Soylent Company: Soylent Green being the latest wafer-like protein product made available. Thorn and Roth eke out a meagre existence, scrap-ing together enough luxuries such as the odd vegetable or half bottle of alcohol. Roth is a scholar and helps Thorn with his detective work using an assortment of books and papers collected over the years. Roth's roll as archivist is made more prominent as he can remember the Earth before it became overpopulated and ruined by pollution, telling stories of what it was like to eat an apple for example. The men are companions, each adding value to their dingy subsistence, yet both yearn for a better life— for Roth this is his past life, for Thorn it is one he feels life owes him.

The plot revolves around Thorn's investigation of the murder of one of the city's powerbrokers. Digging deeper into the case, Thorn uncovers connections to the Soylent Company and their new food product, Soylent Green. During the investigation, Thorn becomes involved with Shirl, the female assigned as so-called furniture to the dead politician's luxury apartment, and through her he experi-ences the pleasures of running hot water and soap. Such is the rarity of meat, vegetables and luxury products made from fossil fuels, when they are encountered they are treated as completely alien to established reality. 'The presence of food' in science fiction features of this period, where 'the familiar and the strange, past, present, and future all collide lends materiality to the answers being worked out on screen' (Retzinger 2008: 372). Part of the genre's ability to depict different spaces is to make the familiar unfamiliar, what Vivian Sobchack (1998: 133) sees in films like *The Incredible Shrinking Man* (1957) as the 'transformation of the absolutely familiar into the absolutely alien'. So while films in the 1970s like *Soylent Green* ignore the extraterrestrial alien, they do still visualise the alien through the estrangement of everyday objects and routines: 'Thorn (Charlton Heston), is so entranced with the taken-for-granted sensual pleasures of a middle class bathroom that it is impos-sible for us to look at the bathroom in the film as a familiar place' (Sobchack 1998: 132). Turning the tap and rinsing his hands with soap is the most alien of experience for Thorn, as human life has been reduced to mere survival. Estrangement plays a vital role in the science fiction genre, as it juxtaposes what seems normal and everyday with the alien and otherworldly. In *Soylent Green* we are provided a vision of a city familiar to us, New York, yet in the film's depiction of poverty and what constitutes luxury the audience is offered a bleak outlook on the possible future of civilised society. Icons of human achievement, the simple bar of soap or running water, become at the same time signifiers of human folly. As Sobchack further underlines, 'It is the very plasticity of objects and settings in [sci-ence fiction] films which help define them as science fiction, and not their consistency' (1998: 87).

For Pat Brereton, Thorn acts as the moral centre to the film, the detective that stands up for the individual against the faceless forces of the government and company, yet, his relationship with Shirl (he uses her for sex and to get luxuries he feels the city owes him) legitimises 'the commodification and objectification of women described as "furniture", bought and sold within the dominant patriar-chal environment' (Brereton 2005: 168). When Shirl is assigned to a new resident of the apartment Thorn is relatively unmoved; the only relationship he truly values is with Roth. This is emphasized near the end of the film when Roth commits suicide. Roth's voluntary euthanasia acts as trigger to Thorn's eventual demise. Both men can no longer stand to live in the overcrowded city, yet this is particularly vital for Thorn when he finds out the real process by which Soylent Green is made. Following the truck that takes Roth's body to be disposed of (death brings no ceremony in New York as bodies have to be cremated to save space), Thorn finds that all the city's dead are being brought to the Soylent factory where, instead of being incinerated, the bodies are being dumped on conveyer belts and turned into the raw material which makes Soylent Green. The shocking realisation that Soylent Green is people tips Thorn over the edge, and he heads back to the city determined to expose the truth. Chased by factory guards, Thorn is shot and injured, forcing him to take refuge in an overcrowded church. Unable to escape he is eventually carried out, shouting out to any survivors the true meaning of Soylent Green.

In a sense, the shocking truth comes as no surprise to the audience, as we have already seen how humanity has regressed to the lowest level of existence. Daily food riots, disease, starvation and poverty are all that people have to live for, and the food situation is so grim that humans have resorted to feeding dead people to those who survive. Nature no longer exists in this future world; crops and animals have long since died out. Death in fact has become the better option for those surviving in the ghetto. For Roth, death brings a peaceful end, and it is a better alternative. The Soylent Company runs huge euthanasia facilities that tempt Roth and others to give up their lives in exchange for one last glimpse of how the Earth used to be. On his death bed Roth is bombarded with images of nature, from blue skies and green fields to flowing rivers and wild animals; the pastoral symphony acts as musical companion on Roth's final transcendent journey. Thorn can only look on as Roth is freed from the grim realities of life, and it is at this moment that he also desires a return to paradise—not yet knowing that there is no escaping from humanity's self-created dystopia:

> This evocation of nature is emblematic of the transformative power of light producing new life through photosynthesis. On a narrative causal/effect level, however, the potency of such evocative representation of nature is tainted since the price that has to be paid for exposure is extermination. (Brereton 2005: 169)

The underlying ecological message of *Soylent Green* largely parallels contemporary moves by pressure groups and lobbyists in the 1970s to bring about environmental change before Earth could no longer sustain human life. Similar visual commentaries on the dangers of wasting energy and nuclear war were channelled through poster art inspired by American architect Richard Buckminster Fuller, which depicted central Manhattan under a giant transparent dome. Originally envisioned by Fuller in 1961 as a way of conserving energy and creating community in New York, the image was recycled and used in 1971 on a poster crying out 'Save Our Planet!' For David Crowley, 'Fuller's remarkable image was conscripted to provide a powerful symbol of the dark future facing the planet in the event of nuclear war or rampant industrialization' (2008a: 42). Yet one might also mention its immediate influence on science fiction films of the decade which, for example in *Logan's Run*, depicted small pockets of humanity living under giant biodomes surrounded by a postapocalyptic landscape. In turn, such a landscape was a recurrent subject of architects in the 1960s and 1970s, who imagined 'a new scale of architecture for environments that had hitherto been overlooked or dismissed as inhospitable to mankind' (Crowley 2008b: 253–4).

It would appear today that we have not progressed much beyond these fears, as countries continue to work out how we can save the planet before it is too late. Again, science fiction film acts as a warning to us that all life is precious and we are more likely than any other exterior force (alien or otherwise) to bring about our own destruction. Poignantly, *Soylent Green*'s prognosis for the future is that in finding a possible solution to our problems we will lose all sense of morality.

Technological Nightmares

Despite the overly pessimistic tones of many films in the 1970s America still had confidence in one area of society: technology. As we know, science fiction has continually offered up technology as the driving force behind human progress. 'The promise of the future', for Wheeler Winston Dixon (2006: 159), 'is that of infinite change, in which one technology is replaced by another in a relentless parade of invention and improvement'. Americans in the 1970s still had faith in the potentials of technology, computers and the machine, yet this was tempered by the genre's warnings against technological overreliance. Interestingly, Timothy Moy (2004) contends that although the decade was characterised by malaise, corruption and social turmoil, the nation's scientists and engineers had embarked on a technological drive that would have America dominate international technological innovation and see Americans developing a new relationship with their domestic and public technologies.

Such an evaluation of American attitudes to technology differs markedly from how technology has been repeatedly depicted in science fiction film: as a threat. Indeed, *The Stepford Wives* (1974) and *Demon Seed* (1977) would appear to follow the genre's traditional slant on technology in that both caution against the development of cyber technology and supercomputers to help improve human society. In the first film, replacing the women of Stepford with beautiful cyborg copies poses a threat to notions of American individuality and female independence, and, in the second, the hybrid offspring of a supercomputer wanting to procreate serves as a warning that we may one day become obsolete and be replaced by the technologies we created to serve us. However, both these films use technology as a device to critique patriarchal society. For example, Anna Krugovoy Silver (2002: 109) sees *The Stepford Wives* as 'a feminist allegory that stems from the ideological and political concerns of feminists' such as Betty Friedan and Pat Mainardi. The film draws attention to the insidious nature of the very same things that Second Wave Feminism and the Women's Liberation Movement critiqued and fought against in the late 1960s and early 1970s: namely sexism and inequality in the workplace and the ideologies of female beautification, domesticity and the nuclear family.

The contradictory nature of *The Stepford Wives'* popular reception in the mid-1970s gives us a little insight into how science fiction film at this time was being used as a form of political discourse. The story of the plucky and independent Joanna's eventual replacement by a subservient and overtly sexualised robot lookalike was taken by some as dark parody of the domestic situation for women in America, bringing to the attention of its audience the inequalities of a patriarchal society and acting as a political manifesto for the feminist movement. Yet, for some critics, the film was nothing more than a confirmation that women would never be freed of their domestic prison since Joanna becomes a victim of the town's plans to make all the wives submissive and obedient Barbie dolls. For Elyce Rae Helford (2003: 25), critics of the film felt it merely fell in line with contemporary male representations of the feminist movement, rendering 'women's efforts to attain equality and justice as both comedy and horror'. Betty Friedan and others saw it as a 'rip-off of the women's movement' that failed to offer an alternative to the patriarchal system which had corrupted the men of Stepford to make perfect robot replacements for their 'imperfect' wives. To an extent, this damning appraisal of the film is justified, yet, taking into account contemporary science fiction films being released during this period (the likes of which have been discussed in this chapter already), positive endings were not the fashion, and as such *The Stepford Wives* merely serves to underscore the innate negativity of the genre. Where *Soylent Green* or *Death Race 2000* denied audiences a happy ending, since there appeared to be no similar happy ending in sight to the economic and social problems affecting the country, *The Stepford Wives* shows that change is impossible as there was seemingly no viable challenge to patriarchy.

Demon Seed is equally negative in its representation of women and technology, as it shows Julie Christie's character bring about the possible end of humanity in her embracing of computers to help run the family home. The sentient computer traps her in the domestic prison, rapes her and impregnates her so that it can produce its own progeny to take over Earth and ensure its survival. J. P. Telotte (2001: 103) describes this ending as 'a very specific sort of technophobic vision that has become far more dominant in the American science fiction film in recent years as it has continued to respond to the impact of the computer and artificial intelligence on our lives'. However, I would also argue that films like *Demon Seed* follow in the footsteps of *Metropolis* by locating a specific technological threat within the female body and the boundaries of femininity, thus displacing and projecting fears of technology onto patriarchal fears of female sexuality. In *Metropolis* the female android is created by Rotwang to destroy the city using her sexuality to hypnotize the male elite and her passion to incite the male slaves to rise up and revolt. Subsequently, technology has been regularly eroticised and coded as female, thus the threat posed by new technologies to the freedom of humanity also becomes female (Short 2005: 7–8). So, while America was benefiting from its burgeoning superiority in the global technology industries, science fiction film was continuing to envision the various positive and negative effects technology has on society.

Science Fiction's New Hope

Star Wars, subtitled *A New Hope,* which only cost $11 million to make, 'began as a summer movie, ran continuously into 1978, and was re-released in 1979'. It earned 'over $190 million in U.S. rentals and about $250 million worldwide, on total ticket sales of over $500 million' (Thompson and Bordwell 2003: 522). Justin Wyatt (1994) sees *Star Wars* as a high concept franchise, the first to really approach merchandising with vigour, and, as a result, increase its market appeal. For Wyatt, the high concept movie was an important part of the New Hollywood film industry. High concept films are those that are conceived as highly marketable, and therefore highly profitable, as well as being visually striking and stylistically innovative. Such films, for example *Star Wars,* are different through their 'emphasis on style in production and through the integration of the film with its marketing' (20). We can describe them as high concept since they are composed of what Wyatt labels 'the look, the hook, and the book': 'The look of the images, the marketing hooks, and the reduced narratives' (22). The fictional world of *Star Wars* that had kept young and old engrossed for two hours also had underlying marketing advantages: 'The film's novel environment and characters have been so striking that Kenner Toys has been able to go beyond the figures in the film by adding new characters to the *Star Wars* line in keeping with the film's mythological world' (Wyatt 1994: 153). The infinite potential for expansion kept the figures and toys popular throughout the 1970s and 1980s as children continued to watch and rewatch the movies and play with their own make-believe worlds. While *Star Wars* was influencing children playing, it was also having a profound effect on American politics.

Star Wars has always held close links with contemporary American politics, and, as Peter Krämer points out, we can thank Ronald Reagan's 23 March 1983 televised speech asking support for the proposed increase to the defence budget for prompting people to associate the two. However, it was not Reagan who first used *Star Wars* to paint a picture of America's Strategic Defense Initiative (SDI): 'When Senator Edward Kennedy first attached the "Star Wars" label to the President's vision in comments made on the floor of the Senate the day after the speech, it was to accuse Reagan of "misleading Red Scare tactics and reckless *Star Wars* schemes"' (Krämer 2000: 46). Right wing Cold War politics were indelibly etched onto the characters and back story that informed the *Star Wars* universe: heroic rebels versus the evil empire became America against the Soviet Union. Intriguingly, for those opposed to the SDI, the rebellion in *Star Wars* could be seen as a metaphor for the left's struggle against Reaganism and the politics of big business. The blockbuster films that followed were clearly influenced by *Star Wars'* nostalgic visioning of fantasy and science fiction, and these will be discussed in more detail in the next chapter.

However, it important to point out that *Star Wars* is indicative of a cultural engagement with nostalgia so intimate and impervious that, as postmodern theorist Fredric Jameson (1983: 117) has pointed out, 'we are unable today to focus on our own present, as though we have become incapable of achieving aesthetic representations of our current experience'. J. P. Telotte describes *Star Wars* as 'homage to a great number of films and film types—the western, war films, Japanese samurai films—all of which have contributed to Lucas's vision' (2001: 105). *Star Wars'* use of nostalgia to convey the heroism of the past is an illustration of an American yearning to return to more innocent times: for example the films and Saturday afternoon TV serials such as *Buck Rogers* and *Flash Gordon* (Jameson 1983: 116). Tom Engelhardt (1998) recognizes this yearning in the creation and development of the Kenner action figures of 1978, and argues that Lucas reconstituted 'war play as a feel-good activity for children' (268). His new franchise reversed the feeling of loss after Vietnam and literally replaced it with *A New Hope*. The concerns over national politics, overpopulation and energy shortages that had once weighed heavily on the films of the early 1970s had been forgotten as George Lucas and Steven Spielberg took moviegoers to another place. Their films rejected the pessimism of the earlier period and suggested that the social problems of the decade could be solved. Many conveyed a vision of hope, in which the future might become a technological para-dise complete with world peace. As a result, while *Star Wars* has been criticised for its affirmative visions, which have often been associated with a conservative shift to Reaganite cinema, it is possible to view the film differently.

The science fiction films of the early 1970s were unable to imagine the possibility of redemption and viewed humanity as simply doomed. Thus, while they have been seen as radical, they were also profoundly nihilistic, providing no alternative to the decadent order of things. In contrast, *Star Wars* was concerned with the exact op-posite, an attempt to imagine an alternative and establish a sense of hope. Kenner's decision to make the figures pocket size meant that children could carry these repre-sentations of a fictional, future universe around and create their own make-believe world wherever they played. As we have seen, throughout American history, tech-nology has stood as a symbol of progress. For example, as America became more industrialized in the eighteenth century, the notion of technological improvement became important to national identity (Marx 1964: 197). Therefore, the futuristic-looking aliens, creatures and humans with a superior command of technology, both on screen and in toy form, reassured adults and children alike that America was on the right track. Representation of technology on TV would follow in a similar positive vein.

Going Round in Circles

A similar kind of filmic homage, *Star Wars*' nod to the Western myth and classic Hollywood genres for example was transferred to television as networks demanded more science fiction programming. As we saw with the Irwin Allen series, largely based on or taken from his previous big screen productions in the early 1960s, adapting genre films was one method of filling the schedules. Television adapta-tions of *Planet of the Apes* and *Logan's Run* were commissioned in an attempt to repeat the big screen success of science fiction. However, according to J. P. Telotte (2008a: 16), 'many American science fiction series of the 1970s would prove ephem-eral, drawing a comparatively modest viewership and hinting that genre might ap-peal largely to a niche audience'. By turning to cinema as inspiration, networks were looking for a quick fix but were in fact alienating large portions of the television audience who were perhaps unfamiliar with the premise and narrative of the original films.

Planet of the Apes (1974–1975), produced by Herbert Hirschman and starring Roddy McDowall from the previous *Ape* features, was expected to repeat the winning formula of the film franchise. Again set on a future ape planet, human astronauts crash land and encounter the stratified simian society. Befriended by McDowall's Galen, the humans escape the clutches of the aggressive military gorillas and embark on several adventures throughout the short-lived season run. Through thinly veiled metaphor, the *Apes* TV series and final film, *Battle for the Planet of the Apes* (1973), used contemporary political events as inspiration for its stories: 'Military coups in Afghanistan and Chile provided grounding for the metaphors of government instability and corruption in the control of the armed forces…where civil war threatens and a military takeover is in play' (Gateward 2007: 100). *Logan's Run* (1977–1978) also stuck close to the format of its progenitor, following Logan and Jessica on the run on a futuristic dystopian Earth. The series only lasted for one season, a common occurrence for these sorts of adaptations. However, Gerald Duchovnay maintains that the tight budgets were not to blame for the short-lived nature of the small screen series; instead they could not live up to the coherent narratives offered by the big screen texts. The nature of television writing meant that there were multiple writers, and therefore multiple viewpoints, working on each episode out of the many that would make up a whole series. Consistency was harder to sustain on television as writers brought different ideas to the table. The film versions of these kinds of series, on the other hand, benefited from the fact they were typically created, gestated and realised by one or two writers who had time to consult and decide on plot and characterisation. This sort of luxury, influenced by time and working towards an achievable deadline, was not afforded to the writing staff for TV series, who could be making and working on one or two hour-long episodes every week: 'Even if there is a solid premise and consensus on a show's narrative arc, if the group consists of very different egos and ideas, the final product will probably be marked by inconsistency' (Duchovnay 2008: 82).

The other way networks could use science fiction to attract an audience was to combine it with other television formats such as the sitcom. As we saw with series like *The Jetsons* in the 1960s, science fiction could reach a far wider audience by offering comic variations on typical generic tropes and settings such as aliens and the future. *Mork and Mindy* (1978–1982), having similar ratings success as the earlier *My Favorite Martian* (1963–1966), traded on the huge popularity of 1950s nostalgia sitcom *Happy Days* (1974–1984) and the fresh-faced appeal of comedian Robin Williams. The premise of the series, whereby Mork crash lands in small town America and befriends wholesome all-American Mindy, gave writers enormous leeway in the types of stories they could have and comic situations they could write. Episodes could either centre on the alienness of Mork, where he struggles to fit into normal suburban life, or they could focus more on his extraterrestrial background and thus make jokes out of the fantastical nature of the science fiction genre; in other words, the series offered something for everyone in a notoriously difficult prime time orientated television industry.

Rebuilding America's Body Politic

The relative failure of adapted science fiction series was offset by the success of more original programming such as *The Six Million Dollar Man* (1974–1978) and *The Bionic Woman* (1976–1978). Focussing on the potentials of biotechnology, these series returned to recurring science fiction concerns of technology and its relationship to society and the human body. *The Six Million Dollar Man* (see boxed text) also tapped into the increasingly important toy and merchandising market highlighted by the *Star Wars* phenomenon, releasing dolls and accessories that gave children the opportunity to experiment with identity construction and role play. Television continued to offer legitimate science fiction hero figures that stood out as role models for the younger audience—following the escapades of 1940s icons Flash Gordon and Buck Rogers or caped adventures of superheroes like Superman. Compared to the more nihilistic visions of humanity on the big screen, this was a huge deviation from the norm, yet it would prove to be an important part in the genre's continued existence on television through the 1980s.

Like film, with its representations of the technological body which reflected 'our increasingly troubled sense of identity by exploring how we might be enhanced, reconfigured, and ultimately even replaced by the product of our science' (Telotte, 2001: 103), television also offered audiences glimpses of how notions of the corporeal were changing in American society. With the human body being literally rebuilt with cybernetic implants in *The Six Million Dollar Man* and *The Bionic Woman,* there was clearly a concern about the limitations and fragility of the human body. This national anxiety can most clearly be seen in the aftermath of the Vietnam War, where the harrowing aspects of the conflict such as physical injury and psychological trauma affected thousands of veterans on their immediate return and many years following the withdrawal from Saigon in 1975. Soldiers who fought and civilians who watched it unfold on television felt deeply traumatised in confronting their own mortality for the first time—conceding that America's self-image was not invincible. According to Fred Turner (1996: 81), the war had taught Americans that 'the ties that held them together as a nation, ties that many Americans had long taken for granted as permanent and strong, could be cut'. Vietnam, more than any other war, 'had demonstrated that the body politic could be dismembered' (80). To recover from the loss in South East Asia notions of the national hero had to be rebuilt, like the bodies of many returning G.I.s who had lost limbs and other body parts; therefore it is not hard to see why these biotechnology series were accepted by television audiences.

Other more interstellar series, influenced by the blockbuster *Star Wars,* such as *Battlestar Galactica* (1978–1980) and *Buck Rogers in the 25th Century* (1979–1981) drew upon space exploration as a narrative template for expounding on the potentials for human improvement. Ironically this was at a time when America was losing interest in celestial ventures after originally striving to become the predominant superpower in the Space Race during the previous two decades. However, these

THE SIX MILLION DOLLAR MAN (1974–1978)

Steve Austin, astronaut, a man barely alive. Gentlemen, we can rebuild him, we have the technology. We have the capability to make the world's first bionic man. Steve Austin will be that man. Better than he was before. Better. Stronger. Faster.

The opening monologue to *The Six Million Dollar Man* (above) was symptomatic of a time where engineers and 'techies' 'were emboldened with the political and social vision of transformative, appropriate technology'. Learning from the lessons and social critiques revealed through the counterculture, the work of these techies allowed, for a brief moment, the realisation of a 'technological utopianism not prevalent since the beginning of the twentieth century' (Moy 2004: 211). Plainly, *The Six Million Dollar Man* envisions a time when human life would not be limited—Steve Austin could be rebuilt with modern technology and therefore no longer confined by the physical limitations his body bestowed upon him. The cybernetic implants and appendages used to give Austin new life and new powers were not seen as a threat to human freedoms and individuality, as shown in the films of this period, but rather they were seen as the inevitable positive outcome of our continued experimentation and mastery over technology.

The fascination with biotechnology as exemplified in the series, and its spin-off *The Bionic Woman* (1976–1978), mirrored the contemporary reality of the 'real-world context, marked by the corresponding headlines scientists were then beginning to make by producing such real prostheses as the first artificial heart' (Telotte 2008a: 17). As we have seen, science fiction series in this period were largely based on films, so the fact that *The Six Million Dollar Man* took a different direction added to its audience appeal. It was set on Earth, its plot centred on real people, and the plausibility of seeing humans benefiting from real biotechnology allowed for a certain amount of what-if thinking. Steve Austin, and his female counterpart Jaime Sommers, were 'realistic versions of comic book superheroes' (Telotte 2008a: 16), endowed with powers made possible through human ingenuity; they used these powers to stand up for the vulnerable, defeat crime and expose corruption.

The series was based on the 1972 novel *Cyborg* by Martin Caidin, and a made-for-TV movie was produced with Lee Majors starring as Steve Austin in 1973. The series quickly followed after another two films were made and the Austin character and backstory were fleshed out to emphasise his down-to-earth, self-made man persona. The survivor of an air crash, former astronaut Austin was rebuilt—his right arm, legs and left eye were replaced by bionic implants that enhanced strength, speed, and vision. A member of the Office of Scientific Intelligence (OSI), Austin was sent on numerous perilous missions such as to retrieve stolen money, rescue military personnel, protect diplomats and prevent a nuclear meltdown. Clearly inspired by the then current Cold War and espionage thrillers, *The Six Million Dollar Man* was just as much a crime or detective series as a science fiction drama. Budgetary constraints, as well as the limitations of visual and special effects techniques at the time, ensured that the series never just relied on the visual attraction of seeing Austin perform his superpowers. For sure, the series was known for the slow-motion action sequences and sound effects which highlighted the use of his powers, but these often took a backseat to the mystery and intrigue of the plot and Austin's weekly secret missions. Nevertheless, it was not adverse to using politically sensitive topics as inspiration for storylines: The episode 'Outrage in Balinderry' (1975) blatantly alluded to the religious and political troubles in Northern Ireland at that time, with Austin sent to rescue the wife of the U.S. Ambassador kidnapped by freedom fighters claiming independence for their nation Balinderry (evidently a amalgamation of Ballymena and Londonderry).

Elements of the series clearly paralleled how the James Bond movie franchise was developing in the mid-1970s. For example, the Bond film *The Spy Who Loved Me* (1977) upped the ante in the representation of counter-espionage technology and Bond's reliance on new gadgets to get him out of tight situations: 'There [was] also an emphasis on ever more elaborate and visually exciting technological gadgetry, ranging from Bond's rocket-firing ski-stick to his sleek Lotus Esprit sports car which transforms into a submersible' (Chapman 1999: 182). As Bond's missions became ever more critical, racing against the clock to save the world from nuclear Armageddon, the range and capabilities of his techno-gadgets increased. Austin, as the world's first bionic man, simply took this a step further by physically merging the human secret agent with the tools required to do his job. Interestingly, the similarities to British spy drama do not stop there; indeed, James Chapman sees *The Six Million Dollar Man* as a techno-orientated extension of the British spy television series *The Champions* (1969–1970).

Part of a group of spy series to come from ITV in the 1960s and 1970s, *The Champions* followed the missions of a trio of secret agents who had returned from Tibet imbued with special powers. These powers were of supernatural origin, thus clearly marking the series out as different from its contemporaries (Bond for example), yet its position as 'generic forerunner' of *The Six Million Dollar Man* and other American science fiction series in the 1970s is referenced by James Chapman (2002: 188): 'These series endowed their protagonists with certain super-human powers and sent them to work for secret organisations fighting against sabotage and subversion . . . There are obvious parallels with *The Champions*.' Austin, of course, gets his abilities from the nuclear-powered bionic implants and prostheses, but in both series the superhumans are noticeably sensitive to the burden of responsibility in having such powers. As well as *The Six Million Dollar Man* and *The Bionic Woman*, Chapman sees *The Champions'* influence in series such as *The Gemini Man* (1976), *The Invisible Man* (1975–1976) and *The Man from Atlantis* (1977–1978).

The premise for *The Six Million Dollar Man* is indicative of what J. P. Telotte calls the 'double vision' of the science fiction genre. By this he refers to the genre's 'tendency to accept but also draw back from the alluring technological imagery that empowers the science fiction film and that finds specific embodiment in every robot' (Telotte 1995: 126). As film began to imagine and visualise the possible merging of humans and machines for the benefit of mankind, audiences were both fascinated and horrified by the notion that by becoming more like a robot all sense of human individuality and soul would be lost. Telotte continues his analysis with discussions centred on the ultimate masculine representation of human artifice seen in *Westworld* and its sequel *Futureworld* (1976). Yul Brynner as the android gunslinger on a killing spree reflects 'our increasingly troubled sense of identity' and fears of becoming obsolete or replaced by our own technological innovations (Telotte 2001: 103). Yet, on TV, Steve Austin was still a man. Capable of feeling emotion, being injured, and even coming close to death, he remained human. His technological appendages did not prevent him from leading a normal life (when he wasn't fighting crime of course). His relationship with Jaime Sommers testifies to the fact that being a bionic man did not stop him from being a married man. Technology is venerated so much in the series that Austin makes his superiors perform the same operation on Sommers (thus making her a bionic woman) so that she can still live. He clearly continues to feel and act human even if most of his body is more machine. A series that recognised the changing cultural attitudes towards technology, it did not fully portray them in a negative light. More attuned to the potentials of the revolution happening in biomedical science and information technology, it emphasised the possibilities of science over its risks. The more recent yet short-lived *Bionic Woman* (2007–2008), a reimagining of *The Bionic Women*, clearly indicates television's continued fascination with science fiction's 'double vision'.

aspirations did not grow purely from the need to outdo the Soviet Union; rather they were 'rooted in cultural traditions as forceful as the terrestrial exploration saga and the myth of the frontier' (McCurdy 1997: 2). Television shows such as *Star Trek* and its gung-ho, high-budget counterparts replayed these traditional aspirations on the new frontier of space. As the frontier inspired generations of Americans to dream of making it big, these television space operas transferred the myths of the old west onto the frontier of outer space and used it as an allegorical device for explaining the nation's history. Or, as Howard McCurdy (1997: 2) observed in his examination of space and the American imagination, 'Space exploration is as much a re-creation of the past as a vision of the future.'

Examining American science fiction's frontier legacy also highlights how much the genre relies on familiar themes of the Puritan Errand and the belief in a divine mission. According to Mark Siegel, as well as trying to replicate the fast-paced action and special effects of *Star Wars, Battlestar Galactica*'s main theme clearly implied '[a science fiction] solution to the old puzzle of creation, with Adama leading his fallen legions to Earth after being driven from a technological Eden by Lucifer' (Siegel 1980: 275). In the 1978 feature-length pilot, a rag-tag fleet of human survivors is lead by the giant battle cruiser Galactica as it searches for a new home on Earth. The surviving colonists were drawn from the original twelve colonies whose only knowledge of Earth was that it supported the legendary paradise world of the thirteenth colony, Kobol. Along their way, the fleet of space pilgrims were continually attacked by Cylons, man-made machines created as slaves, who 'hate the human love for freedom and independence, and the human need to feel, to question, to affirm, and to rebel against oppression' (275). The colonists' endeavours were morally and ideologically juxtaposed against the Cylons' inhuman and alien savagery. This *space opera* role-play replicated the American colonial experience as played out between Puritan settlers and Indian inhabitants, yet it also alluded to the Mormon faith's particular belief in a plural God. Similarities between the twelve colonies' search for Kobol and the journey of Joseph Smith to re-establish Eden in America recounted in the Book of Mormon may not have been coincidental, as Glen A. Larson (creator and writer of the original series) was a Mormon (Ford 1983: 87).

Space opera series like *Battlestar Galactica* replicated the stereotypical method of demonising the Indian as the savage warrior under control of the devil. For Gregory Pfitzer (1995: 52), 'The destruction of the Indians in particular symbolized in an extreme form the American... attitude toward Nature,' as nature stood as a metaphorical obstruction that had to be overcome, 'since the Indians came to represent "red savages" or "red devils" placed on this Earth as punishment for sins committed and as barriers to resurrection and renewal'. Thematically and ideologically, *Star Trek* also recreated the dichotomous relationship between pioneer and savage in the later spin-off series *Star Trek: Voyager* (1995–2001). In this the Kazon, resident bad guys for the first two seasons, mirror representations of Native Americans in American culture from colonial contact to the nineteenth century. Furthermore, the ship's

Indian first officer, Chakotay, was continually positioned as exotic native other in relation to the white female captain Janeway (Geraghty 2003c). More recent examples of the western myth played out on the final frontier, including the battle between settler and savage, come in Joss Whedon's *Firefly* (2002–2003). As well as playing with established stereotypes of femininity, depicting strong women at work and play on the frontier, Whedon subverts the western genre by further complicating the representation of the series' resident bad guys, the Reavers. According to Robert L. Lively (2009: 194–5), the Reavers 'share many stereotypical similarities with descriptions of Indians': bodily mutilation, war paint and scalping; however, Whedon 'makes them innocent victims of governmental meddling' by revealing that they were the result of chemical experiments performed on an innocent group of settlers.

The British Are Coming

James Chapman acknowledges the impact that American film and television series such as *Star Wars, Battlestar Galactica* and *Buck Rogers* were having on the BBC and its attempts to modernise the look of British series such as *Doctor Who* (1963–1989). Producer Graham Williams had to comply with the BBC's tight budgetary requirements and entertain an audience becoming familiar with and attracted to big-budget cinema and television from across the Atlantic (Chapman 2006: 123). However, the 1970s was a boom time for the genre in the UK, and many of the best productions made their way back across the Atlantic and created a solid fan base of American viewers. Along with the ever-present *Doctor Who,* there was *Blake's 7* (1978–1981), *Survivors* (1975–1977), *Doomwatch* (1970–1972), *UFO* (1970–1971) and *Space: 1999* (1975–1977), to name just a select few. Both the BBC and ITV were keen to cash in on the sci-fi craze, therefore *Blake's 7* was created by the BBC for the sole purpose of holding its own 'in a post-*Star Wars* era' (Bould 2008b: 221). ITV funded its own productions as well as importing big-budget American series.

The third and fourth incarnations of the Doctor took the series into new territory. Jon Pertwee's flamboyant interpretation (1970–1974), with Edwardian ruffles, a debonair smile for the ladies and high speed chases in yellow roadster Bessie, 'coincided with a switch from black-and-white to color transmission' (Booker 2004: 68) that gave the series a renewed youthful air. Tom Baker's fourth Doctor (1974–1981) became the most popular and memorable version; with his wild curly hair, toothy grin and mischievous sense of humour, the fourth Doctor appeared the most superhuman of the incarnations: 'he was a particularly youthful doctor [sic], a figure of individualist rebellion against the normally conservative practices of the powers that be among the time lords of Gallifrey' (Booker 2004: 70). Alongside the renaissance of the Doctor, his enemies got a face lift too, with the Daleks and Cybermen both getting revamped looks. The more modern versions of the Cybermen, with the silver jumpsuit, subdivided helmet and booming deep voice, were more like Darth

Vader than the synthetic human in a knitted mask seen in the 1960s. Piers Britton and Simon Barker (2003: 172–3) see this development as a sign of *Doctor Who*'s intention in the 1970s to accommodate designs from contemporary American science fiction films.

As the decade drew to a close, science fiction on both film and television had undergone remarkable change. Consolidating the position it held as a popular genre in Cold War America, it tackled divisive and difficult issues affecting the nation. More often than not it depicted the future as a dystopian nightmare that contemporary society may find hard to avoid if immediate changes to the economy and politics were not put into effect. Yet, also, the genre was able to survive this downturn and offer spectacular, big-budget adventures that entertained audiences and cemented its position as one of Hollywood's most reliable genres. Although film seemed more concerned with warning than wonder, both American and UK television offered an alternative outlet for more traditional forms of action adventure and space opera that had typified the genre in the 1950s and 1960s. Many of the themes and tropes that emerged in the cinema of the 1970s, however, would resurface in the following decade, and as a result the genre would go from strength to strength as studios and networks realised the money-making potential of the science fiction blockbuster.

—4—

Hopes and Fears
Aliens, Cyborgs and
the Science Fiction Blockbuster

After a sustained period of negativity, science fiction film in the 1980s returned to its extraterrestrial roots, with films such as Spielberg's *ET* (1982) and *batteries not included* (1987) offering light relief to the concerns of the 1970s. These films once again looked to the stars, offering visions of wonder and hope through the relationship between friendly, benevolent aliens and the young and elderly. Whereas films of the 1950s depicted aliens as a monstrous threat to America in the invasion narrative, Spielberg, Lucas and others showed that America could benefit from extraterrestrial life. The alien threat on the big screen instead rested with the monstrous feminine (see Creed 1993) in space, exemplified by the *Alien* (1979 onwards) quadrilogy, where, allegorically, America's curiosity would be punished if it started to look elsewhere for profit and resources.

Blockbusters aimed at children in this period focused on the relationships shared between children, the elderly and the alien visitor—such a focus can be seen as representative of, and a response to, America's changing political landscape. As Ronald Reagan tried to promote a political ideology centred on revitalising the economy by tapping into the nation's patriotism (through speeches reminding citizens of America's exceptional past), science fiction films depicting alien/child/senior relations also promoted ideas of human exceptionalism and progress. Themes of nostalgia, yearning for past times, youthful optimism and childhood innocence came to epitomise the science fiction film at this time, while also borrowing and adapting recognizable generic tropes and paradigms familiar to other film genres in the 1980s such as the action adventure, feature-length animation, fantasy, horror, romantic comedy, western, and the road movie.

Some academics and film critics saw this nostalgic return to established genres as part of a conservative backlash to the political radicalism of the 1970s (Ryan and Kellner 1988). Andrew Britton (2009: 113), in his seminal article of 1986, 'Blissing Out: The Politics of Reaganite Entertainment', stated that 'the banality of the films derives from the undialectical conception of Good and Evil and the reduction to the level of routine of the contest between them'. However, it should be stressed that many of the key examples of cinematic radicalism in the late 1960s and early 1970s were themselves examples of the nostalgic film: *The Wild Bunch* (1969), *Bonnie and Clyde* (1967), *Chinatown* (1974) and *The Godfather* (1972), and even *2001,* were revisionist interpretations of the Hollywood western, noir, gangster and science fiction film. In addition, so-called nostalgic films shared much of the political paranoia of the early 1970s: the Empire in *Star Wars* represents bureaucratic, ruthless, imperialism; and *Close Encounters of the Third Kind* (1977) clearly plays on anxieties about the relationship between the state and the individual citizen.

The Benevolent Alien

Between 1977 and 1988, there is a clear historical period in which enlightened alien beings bring salvation to America after the 1970s and its rash of dystopian science fiction films. Many films in the 1980s concentrated not simply on the relationship between the human and the alien but specifically on the relationship between children and aliens. *The Last Starfighter* (1984), *Explorers* (1985), and *Flight of the Navigator* (1986) all featured encounters between adolescents and aliens, in which it was suggested that the young are simply more open to wonder and therefore more able to accept the otherness of alien life forms. In fact, being young was integral to the plot of these movies; as the young male human protagonist would encounter the aliens (in the case of *Explorers* the aliens were children too), his open-mindedness was key to the successful completion of a particular mission. Children were both empowered by and entrusted with the huge responsibility of representing Earth and defending it from hostile others. This common narrative in family film and children's cinema can be related to Robin Wood's (2003: 145) observation that Hollywood had tended to construct the viewer as child-like and therefore receptive to the wonder of the cinematic illusion, a construction that is clearly related to the commercial success of Lucas's *Star Wars* sequels *The Empire Strikes Back* (1980) and *Return of the Jedi* (1983) and Spielberg's *Close Encounters* and *E.T. The Extra-Terrestrial* (see also Bazalgette and Staples 1995; Krämer 1998). However, the prevalence and popularity of children's film also signals, according to Estella Tincknell (2005: 88), 'one of the central concerns of the post-war moment' in 'that the future of post-war society depended on the inclusion of children within its conception of the social'.

For example, *E.T.* not only features a benevolent and enlightened alien, who is willing to exchange ideas with others, but the child that he encounters also shares these same qualities. In the process, E.T. not only builds a close relationship with the child, Elliott, but is also able to heal Elliott's troubled family. Furthermore, E.T.'s willingness to exchange ideas with Elliott is contrasted with the ignorance of the adult work of masculine authorities: the threat and menace within the film do not come from anything malevolent within the alien himself, but rather from the fear that he inspires in narrow-minded *adult* humans. The masked invader that comes to take him away becomes the real alien for Elliott and his family, not unlike his absent father who is alienated from the family and now lives in Mexico, far from his native land (see also Heung 1983).

In the exemplary *Close Encounters,* the aliens are also associated with children and child-like adults, but the film also suggests that human communion with the enlightened and amicable aliens will bring about social cohesion. Whilst an elite group of scientists aim to conceal the truth about the UFOs that have been witnessed around the world, power repairman Roy Neary represents the everyman who succeeds in reaching the aliens and proving that such information cannot be kept hidden. Drawing on the theme of the messianic alien, the aliens of *Close Encounters,* who are absent from the majority of the film, appear to be almost heavenly beings when they are finally revealed at the end and offer a technological salvation to humanity, which is presented as having lost its way. As Hugh Ruppersburg (1990: 33) posits, the aliens of the film 'offer solace and inspiration to a humanity threatened by technology and the banality of modern life'. The religious connotations of the arrival of these aliens is also emphasised by scenes of mass worship that follow early sightings of the alien in the heavens and suggest that the aliens are a 'cosmic incarnation of Christian myth and doctrine' (36).

The actions of the naive Neary also involve a journey of self-discovery that is not only implied to be a personal narrative but also one that suggests humanity's passing from childhood into maturity: 'The film suggests that Neary and, by extension, the rest of humankind, might grow to a new maturity, one in which he will be able to maintain a sense of that child within... necessary for opening up to and understanding the human place in the universe' (Telotte 2001: 151). This journey is facilitated by the appearance of the child-like aliens, who, as J. P. Telotte points out, exhibit the same sense of wonder in their encounter with humanity as humanity exhibits in its encounter with the alien (153). Imagery of the child pervades the entire narrative, and an abiding symbol of the film continues to be the image of the young child, Barry Guiler, standing in front of an open door to symbolically welcome the aliens. In this scene, Spielberg builds up suspense using a medley of sounds and a vivid orange glow to herald the arrival of the alien who had finally returned to cinemas after a ten-year absence. The optimism of this scene, and of the whole film, demonstrates Spielberg's desire to suggest a new beginning for post-Vietnam America and to open the door to a new era.

In *Cocoon* (1985), *Cocoon: The Return* (1988) and **batteries not included* (see boxed text) aliens are also presented as bringing harmony and peace to humanity, but in this case the encounter is not with children but senior citizens. If on the one level children represent a positive response to alien visitations because of their innocence and open-hearted acceptance of the fantastic, senior citizens represent a knowing wisdom and a lack of prejudice. Furthermore, in these films, the alien effectively brings out the child in them. In *Cocoon* and **batteries not included* an elderly or mature group of friends refuse to give up on life by helping the aliens return home and, in return for their help, they receive a new lease of life: in *Cocoon,* they even journey home with the aliens where they will have the chance to live forever; in *batteries not included* the elderly protagonists—with the help of their alien friends—succeed in stopping developers who want to tear down their old apartment building and build a modern office block for the younger generation in its place.

In these films, the alien visitor allows humans to recover or discover their essential humanity: it is not only able to preserve or resurrect human life, but also to enable those who feel estranged from society to rediscover the joys of life. Thus, while the aliens in *Cocoon* enable the elderly to live forever, they also 'change a swimming pool into a fountain of youth' and so 'make children of senior citizens' (Grant 1999: 25). Furthermore, the story also concerns the grandson of one of the elderly. Although an adult, this grandson not only helps the aliens to return home but, in so doing, demonstrates a child-like open-mindedness that is contrasted to the attitudes of his parents who believe that both he and his grandfather are suffering from delusions. In other words, this grandson embodies all the qualities that these films associate with children—youthful exuberance, enthusiasm and curious innocence. Steve Guttenberg's character, Jack Bonner, is the first human to be contacted by the aliens to help recover their companions from the bottom of the ocean not only because he owns the boat necessary for a deep-sea rescue, but also because he too embodies all the indispensable qualities of a child needed to go along with their plan and ultimately believe in it—Jack is tirelessly optimistic and enthusiastic. Guttenberg's role in both *Cocoon* films is clearly informed by his other major roles in films such as *Short Circuit* (1985), *Three Men and a Baby* (1987) and even the four *Police Academy* (1984, 1985, 1986, 1987) films, in which he played the eternal prankster, Mahoney. Guttenberg's youthful exuberance, like Roy Neary's in *Close Encounters,* provides an intertextual link between all these films regardless of their genre; from science fiction including alien encounters and road movie robotic hi-jinx to gentle romantic comedy and slapstick police farce, he represents the eternal child struggling to live the way he has always lived amid the militaristic and bureaucratic constraints foisted upon him by the aggressive conservatism of the decade.

---

*BATTERIES NOT INCLUDED (1987)

batteries not included, produced by Steven Spielberg and direct by Matthew Robbins, is an overlooked film that clearly depicts the conflict between the aggressive capitalism of Reaganite America and the new era utopianism called upon in the late 1970s. It tells the story of a small group of New Yorkers living in a soon-to-be demolished apartment block in the Lower East Side of Manhattan. Under constant threat from the bulldozers, suited slimeballs, and hired heavies of the Lacey Corp., the residents of the building find it increasingly hard to resist taking the money and moving out so that Mr Lacey can build his new business and leisure complex, Lacey Plaza. Two of the oldest residents are retired couple Frank and Faye Riley, who used to own the once successful and popular Riley's Café on the ground floor of the building. Throughout the opening credits sequence of the film we are introduced to them via old black and white photos of their family living and working in the neighbourhood—a neighbourhood that once thronged with people living together in a close-knit community centred on Riley's Café. This is their story, a story of community seen through a nostalgic lens. Not only is the building under threat from big business, but so too is the Rileys' way of life. Now living amongst the squalor and depravation of an underdeveloped area of New York, the Rileys are also haunted by the death of their only son, Bobby, and Faye's increasing senility. In the first few scenes we see that even though they are not the only ones living in the building—there is the struggling artist Mason, the heavily pregnant Marisa and the tall but simple superintendent Harry—the sense of community once so important has long since died. The old way of life, so loved by Frank and Faye and even lamented by the younger residents, is passing—to be replaced by a cold, harsh, metallic edifice of Reaganite economics. It is perhaps no coincidence that while Reagan was trying to inspire big business by reminding Americans that 'the chief business of the American people is business' Gordon Gekko in *Wall Street* (1987) was proclaiming 'greed is good' to young executives keen to rise up the corporate ladder and make their mark (Troy 2005: 52). The 1980s represented the merging of Reagan's optimistic vision for American society and a nostalgic return to the heroism of the past.

Like *E.T., Close Encounters* and the other life-affirming family films of the 1980s, the residents of the apartment block are helped by visiting extraterrestrials. Two small flying spaceships that are robotic sentient life forms in themselves arrive one night and begin to fix the old and broken household furnishings. These alien spaceships (iconographically linked to the bright and shiny blinking lights of the UFO in *Close Encounters*) have come to Earth to seek refuge while the female (made symbolically female with big blue eyes and a smaller, smoother outer hull) prepares to give birth to their children. The seemingly uninhabited apartment building is a perfect place to recharge and collect construction material in preparation for the birth. After first contact with the spaceships Frank and the other residents begin to believe that they have come to help them on purpose, because their individual predicaments had called for some form of divine intervention. Frank and Mason both see the arrival of the spaceships as a sign: for Frank they are there to help himself and Faye stay in the building, perhaps filling the gap left by the death of their son; for Mason they are there to provide inspiration for his ailing painting career (if he can't make it as an artist then perhaps he can benefit from their unique technology and sell them to make millions). The women of the building see the visitors as people; both Marisa and Faye talk to them as friends and in particular feel affinity with the female spaceship as she draws nearer to giving birth. Marisa has been left alone by her travelling musician husband, Hector, throughout her entire pregnancy and feels isolated and unworthy of motherhood; Faye sympathises with the spaceship as she relives her own time as a mother looking after Bobby. Harry, an ex-boxer and self-imposed mute, keeps himself busy by tinkering with electrical gadgets and trying to fix the tile floor in the lobby. The spaceships, in particular the third stillborn offspring he brings back to life, inspire him to take on a more active role in the building—he literally throws out Lacey's chief heavy Carlos and is instrumental in finding the baby spaceships when they go missing toward the end of the film.

The spaceships create life from broken coffee pots and stolen toasters; their children are made up from electrical goods and Pepsi cans. They can fix broken appliances, picture frames, and watches, making new what once was old—literally making life out of the consumer goods that continued to drive the American economy through recession. The aliens' technological mastery and mechanical ingenuity are symbolic of the rejuvenating processes each of the residents undergo. As well as coming together as a community to fight Carlos and the Lacey Corp., each person begins to see life in a positive way, and their individual talents and personal strengths prove invaluable when trying to save their building: Frank comes to terms with his wife's senility and understands that what is important is that they live the rest of their lives in happiness together; Faye finally accepts her son is dead and begins to look forward to moving from the building with Frank; Mason realises that he needs to give up his fascination for the old and depressing and that the inspiration for his art comes from his new relationship with Marisa, who in return recognizes that Hector can never be a good father to her baby and that she loves Mason; for Harry, the close bond formed with the littlest spaceship forces him to speak for the first time since hanging up his boxing gloves. Even Carlos is redeemed from his life of petty crime when he dives into the burning apartment block to save Faye at the end of the film. The personal and emotional transformations experienced by the residents are sparked by the arrival of the alien spaceships and the birth of the three alien children, however their continued self-improvement is driven by the growing sense of community exemplified by the fact that after the building is burnt down they remain close friends. The nostalgia felt for the building by Mason and Harry and the good old days by Frank and Faye are still important to all of them, yet the prospect of moving on also plays a key part in their eventual rehabilitation. The final compromise is reached when the family of spaceships with the help of millions of others rebuild the burnt-out apartment building, restoring it to its former glory, thus saving it from being demolished and replaced by Lacey Plaza. The last scene of the film shows Lacey Plaza built but the apartment building still standing right in the middle of the tall office blocks; the shot of busy downtown New York shows that the old and new can exist side by side, each benefiting from the other to survive in an increasingly economically hostile and materialistic modern America.

As Gil Troy asserts, while Reagan repeated 'his antistatist, pro-capitalist mantra', creating a society of free enterprise, he also affirmed 'America's traditional ambivalence about excess', applauding the virtues of family life, neighbourhood community and religion (2005: 294). These seemingly polar opposite political viewpoints come together in the movie; big business is necessary for America to prosper and progress, but only if that prosperity is founded on a bedrock of community and family cohesion. The metallic aliens, representative of this combination of capitalism and community (a family of robots made up from Pepsi cans), provide the impetuous for the residents to build a stronger community that could survive in the 1980s—after all, progress was inevitable if America wanted to continue as a world superpower. Film and television in the 1980s continually offered viewers a dichotomous picture of America: 'The confusion, the despair, the agonizing decline of liberalism, the empty and hypocritical promise of conservatism' (Troy, 2005: 113). Neither could exist without the other, yet *batteries not included* belies their inevitability through the visit of extraterrestrial life.

batteries not included can be seen as an elegiac representation of an America quickly being demolished in favour of big business and aggressive capitalism, the destruction of the 1950s-style Riley's Café emblematic of the failed dreams of an older generation being replaced. However, the film also offers a vision of compromise where Frank, Faye, and all the residents benefit from modern technology represented by the magical and benevolent alien spaceships. The trappings of modern American society seen in the electrical name-brand goods used by the aliens to reproduce and the plethora of neon signs flashing in Times Square are not only the end products of the consumerist regimen espoused by the Lacey Corp., but they are also the building blocks of the physical and mental rehabilitation undergone by the residents. As a group of individuals they fail to deal with what life throws at them, yet as a community (brought together by the alien's technological interventions and inspired by memories of past times) they have the strength to resist change. However old or alone Faye and Marisa are they are eternally optimistic about the future, even though they look to the past for comfort. The youthful enthusiasm and knowing wisdom shared by all in *batteries not included* is indicative of Spielberg's and science fiction's utopian preoccupation in the 1980s, a far departure from what preceded it in the 1970s and what was to come in the following decade.

The Monstrous Alien

If Spielberg opened the door to the alien, Ridley Scott's *Alien* nearly ripped it from its hinges. The threat posed by the individual alien monster can be seen as a response to the political climate of the time. In one sense, it could be argued, the alien's attack on humans was related to American fears of Soviet aggression, while the reason that the alien threat came in the form of an lone individual can be related to Reagan's one-man mission to rid the world of the so-called evil empire. However, lone killing machines were not only a feature of the alien monster movie but also of the psychotic knife-wielding aggressor of the slasher films of the late 1970s and early 1980s. Furthermore, this was also a generic feature that can be traced back to the 1970s: to Yul Brynner's android in *Westworld,* Michael Myers in *Halloween* (1978) and the shark in *Jaws* (1975). Not only was the alien or pursing monster determined to survive at the expense of others in these films, but we also see in *Alien* a faceless corporation stopping at nothing to capture the xenomorph and harness its unique potential in the pursuit of profit. In *Aliens* (1986) Ripley suggests that it is the yuppie greed of Burke rather than the xenomorph's aggression which is most despicable and dangerous: 'I don't know which species is worse. You don't see them fucking each other over for a goddamn percentage.'

In these films, the child-like curiosity of Neary in *Close Encounters* is castigated as myopic and dangerous. From *Alien* to *Species* (1995), science fiction horror hybrid films have created and recreated ever-more-terrifying extraterrestrials to play on our fear of the unknown. The eponymous alien has epitomised our idea of the alien ever since the first film, spawning three sequels and a number of imitations. In *Close Encounters,* humanity's curiosity about the alien visitors is rewarded; the extraterrestrial visitors share their galactic knowledge with Roy Neary as he ascends with them in their spaceship. In *Alien,* the crew's curiosity of the extraterrestrial egg chamber is severely punished as John Hurt's character Kane plays host to the monster's embryo. The film combines elements of both the horror and science fiction genre to create a dark and menacing environment that is as alien to the human crew as the xenomorph. For Telotte (2001: 9), science fiction and horror are distinguished from one another by their different attitudes towards curiosity. In horror, curiosity is dangerous, while in science fiction curiosity is the means by which the characters grow and humanity's intellectual capacity is expanded. In alien horror, 'there are things we are better off not knowing', and this rejects the unquenchable thirst for answers that characterised Spielberg's films. Ridley Scott's film even stresses *Alien*'s connections with gothic horror through Lovecraft's claim that 'the oldest and strongest emotion of mankind is fear, and the oldest and strongest kind of fear is fear of the unknown' (1927: 423).

The now notorious scene at the end of *Alien* where Ripley meets the beast face to face in her underwear emphasises the attitude to curiosity within the film. As she sits and waits with her back turned toward the creature, trying to press the right button in her overly large gloves to coax it out of its hiding place, one is struck by her courage to remain still and not turn to face it. Even as the alien struggles from its alcove and looms over Ripley, she waits until the last second to release the airlock and fire the thing out into space. It is her own curiosity that warns her of the creature's proximity, as she dares to turn around she immediately presses the button. Only this time her curiosity is rewarded: instead of being punished like the rest of her crewmates for trying to seek out the alien—always looking around one too many corners—Ripley's curiosity saves the day. Her 'fear of the unknown' spurs on her actions and, in the process, Ripley begins to realise the nature of the beast's tenacity, which will become a recurring theme in the three *Alien* sequels. In *Predator* (1987), the horrific alien is transferred onto Earth with Sigourney Weaver's Ripley transformed into a muscle-bound *Rambo*-style hero played by Arnold Schwarzenegger.

The Cyborg

Studies on the cyborg in popular culture remain transfixed on the products of the big screen. Cinema is the focus for many works that continue to examine the cyborg as a predominantly American reality. Fear of technology, or fear of the automaton, is largely understood as an inherently American phenomenon. J. P. Telotte provides a coherent reading of the cyborg through an examination of *RoboCop* (1987). Sean Redmond's *Liquid Metal* (2004) collects together key texts in science fiction film criticism. Doran Larson's 'Machine as Messiah' (2004) draws specific parallels between the cyborg body in *Terminator 2: Judgement Day* (1991) and the American body politic, the main claim being that the movie signals a shift towards a 'technodemocracy' where the technological body stands as threat to our freedom and thus our power over the machine (Larson 2004: 192). Similarly, Sue Short's *Cyborg Cinema and Contemporary Subjectivity* maintains the hierarchy of film over television as she locates the attraction of the cyborg in its crossing of 'boundaries between the artificial and the organic, revising speculations regarding the nature of subjectivity' (Short 2005: 3). Overall, these titles suggest that the domain for questioning our relationship with technology, and thus our fears of assimilation, is the cinema. Without question, television appears to lack the narrative space in which we as humans can put our fears to the test and investigate the cyborg as a postmodern subject.

As Elaine Graham (2002: 17) notes, 'representations of the post/human' in the '"stories we live by" can be important critical tools in the task of articulating what it means to be human in a digital and bio technological age'. In terms of the genre's presence on film, it is interesting to note at what point in its history Francisco Collado-Rodríguez attributes the birth of the cyborg and the fear of technology taking over humanity. He sees manifestations of the cyborg—the replicants in *Blade Runner* (1982), Seth Brundle's fly in *The Fly* (1986), the artificial reality of the matrix in *The Matrix* (1999) as well as the Borg in *Star Trek*—as being influenced by the cyberpunk genre, including its most notable example: William Gibson's *Neuromancer* (1984).

Cyberpunk's 'emphasis on the controlling power of artificial intelligence systems and its radical views on the process of bodily transgression into the cybernetic are motifs that combine with the importance cyberpunk confers to virtual reality, and with its actual presentation of our metaphoric fear of being fused with and eventually controlled by the machine' (Collado-Rodríguez 2002: 71–2).

Cyborg imagery has not lived up to the ungendered ideal envisioned by Donna Haraway in her seminal article 'A Manifesto for Cyborgs' (1985), later reprinted in her 1991 book *Simians, Cyborgs and Women.* The cyborg was seen as a potential liberator for women; by getting rid of the physical body, one 'could release women from their inequality under patriarchy by making genders obsolete' (Springer 1991: 309). However, due to science fiction cinema's fascination with the hard-bodied male cyborg, personified by Arnold Schwarzenegger's Terminator, notions of gender inequality remain ever present even in the relatively neutral world of cyberspace. Like the numerous highly eroticised and muscle-bound images of the techno-male in films such as *RoboCop* and *The Terminator* (1984) described by Yvonne Tasker (1993) and Susan Jeffords (1994), the cyborg has remained firmly located within the realms of the real world, not cyberspace, and their bodies act as metallic markers of their fragile reliance on human parts and the shifting boundaries between the organic and technological. As with depictions of the robot and technology in the 1970s, the Terminator represents the dual fear of human obsolescence and technology's superiority:

> the machine becomes an image of both pleasure and horror for modern culture. The machine promises to free labor from "machine-like" operations and to open up the possibility of a utopian space beyond the realm of necessity. But it is also one of the main means by which capital has come to degrade the labor process and transforms human activity into a mere mechanistic component. It is for this reason that we find a recurring image of the machine as monster within contemporary culture. (Jancovich 1992: 6)

Equally, the female cyborg body has come to represent the inherent threat posed to established patriarchy. From the first depiction of the inhuman cyborg vamp in *Metropolis,* as discussed previously, to the overtly sexual Borg Queen in *Star Trek: First Contact* (1996) technology has been regularly eroticised and coded as female, and thus the threat posed by new technologies to the freedom of humanity also becomes female. As suburban threat in *The Stepford Wives* and *Demon Seed,* technology is seen as even more threatening when linked with the possibility of female reproduction.

From Bust to Boom

Science fiction on television underwent tremendous change in the 1980s. As the industry evolved to cope with renewed challenges from cinema and new media such as interactive computer games, the science fiction genre was at the forefront of the medium's attempts to maintain a regular and devoted audience. From what is usually considered a lean period in the American television industry during the 1980s, the genre developed two distinct and popular forms through which it continues to attract viewers in today's overcrowded and diverse multichannel climate: the cult series and the quality series. Both have their roots in the 1960s, where series such as the original *Star Trek* and even Britain's *Doctor Who* first attracted devoted fans through reruns and fan conventions. Formats of more expensive television drama such as the series, serial and miniseries were forced to combine with popular genres such as science fiction, crime, horror and medical drama to produce programmes that either maintained a small but hard-core fan base over several seasons or attracted millions of casual viewers through hype and marketing in a relatively short period of one or two seasons.

Both the cult television series and the quality series have evolved dramatically during this period. Science fiction from the late 1980s is representative of what Brian Stableford termed 'The Third Generation' of science fiction, where 'TV has become the principal medium through which' the genre is consumed by fans. This has happened through the merging of niche media such as the science fiction novel and magazine with the wide-spread medium of television (Stableford 1996: 322). What was normally considered cult, in that it was produced for and consumed by a small fan community, was transferred to television. The formula of the long-running, potentially infinite television series proved a highly suitable vehicle through which stories based on common science fiction narratives such as space or time travel, alien invasion or alternate worlds could be screened. The potential to attract devoted followers increases as series grow in narrative complexity and introduce more characters: 'Seriality, textual density, and, perhaps most especially, the nonlinearity of multiple time frames and settings that create the potentially infinitely large metatext of a cult television text create the space for fans to revel' (Gwenllian-Jones and Pearson 2004: xvii). Alongside this development in cult television is the reality that television networks also had to constantly attract new viewers as series that lacked longevity needed replacing. The term *quality television,* usually associated with American television, is bound up with the notion of nonhabitual viewing. Series that cannot rely on established audiences attract viewers through their concentration on high production values, compact narrative, and intense use of marketing and hype to produce a sense of essential viewing or must-see TV (see San Martín 2003) that ensured that would audiences tune in over a shorter period of time: 'These programmes have also been referred to as "date" or "appointment" television, and they are distinguished by the compulsive viewing practices of dedicated audiences who organise their schedules around these shows' (Jancovich and Lyons 2003: 2).

Both the cult and the quality series would appear to share similar characteristics, in that they attract a certain kind of viewer that interacts with the series passionately and regularly. In both cases science fiction is very often always the genre that audiences return to again and again, either through watching reruns of past series or getting engrossed in the latest high-concept, glossy serial. Following the period in television science fiction, discussed in the previous chapter, that harked back to childhood serials of the 1950s such as *Flash Gordon* and *Buck Rogers,* with series from the 1970s such as *The Six Million Dollar Man, The Bionic Woman, Space: 1999, Battlestar Galactica, Blake's 7* and *Buck Rogers in the 25th Century,* the 1980s can be seen as a turning point in the growth and popularisation of the genre. Although long-running series such as *Doctor Who* would eventually die a slow death in 1989, partly due to the fact that British television was experiencing huge financial cutbacks and industrial change, American science fiction was undergoing resurgence. The cult franchise *Star Trek,* no longer just a television phenomenon thanks to a series of successful blockbuster movies, reappeared on American TV with a new ship, cast and crew in *Star Trek: The Next Generation* (1987–1994) (see boxed text). Renewed popularity for a long-lost cult series signalled a change in both television production and science fiction viewing practices. Gene Roddenberry's experiment of not first broadcasting on a network but rather distributing the series through syndication proved to be an important stimulus for other writers and producers to pitch their ideas for new genre television that clearly had a popular following.

STAR TREK: THE NEXT GENERATION (1987–1994)

Star Trek: The Next Generation (TNG) was the embodiment of glossy American science fiction. New ships, sets, uniforms and alien characters breathed life into a well-loved yet marginalised franchise. Its success in maintaining a mainstream audience without the backing of a major network intimated that audiences wanted more series that offered weekly snapshots of distant worlds and intergalactic exploration. Although distinctly *Star Trek* in its ethos, the new series differed in many ways from the original, which was entirely located in a Cold War context and influenced by a distinctive 1960s visual aesthetic. Whereas the original replicated the New Frontier philosophy of John F. Kennedy through the figure of Captain Kirk, *TNG's* Captain Jean-Luc Picard (played by Patrick Stewart) represented a more reserved kind of cosmopolitan diplomacy. Rather than shooting first and asking questions later, Picard would prefer to talk through problems as intergalactic mediator, with the Federation acting as benevolent peacekeepers rather than militaristic police force. Most episodes focused on the relationships between crew members. Over seven seasons, this meant the audience had become very familiar with and attached to individuals, with some characters such as Troi, Riker, Crusher, and Worf also having families introduced in storylines to help flesh out their back stories. The android Data offered huge scope in stories dealing with humanity and notions of mortality; episodes devoted to his character mirrored attempts by Gene Roddenberry to discuss the human condition through Spock, albeit in far more detail: 'The series went from strength to strength as the characters were allowed to develop and interact with others in ways which were denied to the original crew' (Geraghty, 2007: 4).

The spectre of Roddenberry loomed large over the first few seasons of *TNG*. In an interview with *TV Guide* to celebrate the final season in 1994, executive producer Rick Berman explained that he had to become fluent in a language created by Roddenberry in order to continue his vision. Also, rules were in place to keep *Star Trek* on course with its mission to promote liberal humanism in an entertaining but moralistic fashion:

> Gene taught me a new language, and now I have become relatively fluent. We've bent his rules a little, but we haven't broken them. *Star Trek: The Next Generation* is not a series about my vision of the future or Patrick Stewart's or anybody else's. It's a series about Gene's vision of the 24th century. As a result, I will continue to follow his rules as long as I'm connected with *Star Trek* in any way. (Berman 1994: 2)

The Borg, a deadly cyborg race that assimilates people and their technology, were introduced in the two-part season-ending cliff-hanger 'The Best of Both Worlds' (1990). Seen as a departure for the franchise, these new alien villains proved extremely popular with audiences and helped secure *TNG*'s renewal after dwindling ratings during the first two seasons. Lynette Russell and Nathan Wolski (2001) argue that they were *Star Trek*'s first attempt at questioning its own narrative, whereby the Federation was no longer the only colonizing force within the galaxy: The Borg were now 'a post-colonial mirror held up to reflect the nature of colonisation and assimilation'. The Federation's colonialist mission was 'reflected and intensified' by the Borg, who acted as a prism through which ideas of 'self and other, difference and sameness' were 'explored and critiqued' (para. 5). Where the Federation colonises other worlds by implanting their values and laws through trade and political union under the distracting rubric of noninterference, the Borg 'colonize from within, by injecting microscopic nanoprobes into the body of their prey' (para. 17). The popularity of the Borg and their importance in flagging up issues relating to identity, our relationship with technology and the historical consequences of imperialism and colonialism meant that *TNG* continues to attract critical attention more than twenty years after it first aired. Their influence can still be seen as inspiration for the rejuvenated Cybermen in the new *Doctor Who* (2005–present) (see Geraghty, 2008) and *Battlestar Galactica* (2003–2009).

One way of maintaining the vision and creating fresh stories week in and week out, besides building in personal back stories for regular characters, was to write stories that built tension through multilayered narratives. The 'multiform story', described by Janet H. Murray (1997: 30) as a term for 'a written or dramatic narrative that presents a single situation or plotline in multiple versions, versions that would be mutually exclusive in our ordinary experience', was used in episodes such as 'Parallels' (1993). In this episode, Worf shifts through a number of alternative timelines ranging from him having a family with crewmate Deanna Troi to him realising that his friends were all killed in the battle with the Borg from 'The Best of Both Worlds'. 'Yesterday's Enterprise' (1990) also involved a multiform story, only this time it dealt with *Star Trek* lore. The crew of Picard's Enterprise is transported into another time where they are at war with the Klingons—this is because a previous incarnation of the famous ship was somehow not destroyed and henceforth did not go down in history as the catalyst for forging peace between Klingons and humans. Picard decides to sacrifice himself, and the Enterprise that should have made history, in order for the proper timeline to be restored. *TNG* used this method of storytelling because society requires a mode of expression that can accommodate different possibilities. Audiences need a means through which they can exercise their complex and composite imagination; the multiform story provided that because it illustrated various alternative plots and outcomes. As Murray further states:

> [The multiform narrative's] alternate versions of reality are now part of the way we think, part of the way we experience the world. To be alive in the twentieth century is to be aware of the

alternative possible selves, of alternative possible worlds, and of the limitless intersecting stories of the actual world. (Murray 1997: 38)

With *TNG*, the multiform story worked because it had a narrative history which served as the basis for many of its episodes; there was already a narrative framework in place for multiple plots to expand upon and characters to harmonise with. For fans, its 'alternate versions of reality' were part of the way they experienced their own world and, as a result, part of how they identified themselves and wanted to imagine the future. As ever, science fiction succeeded in extrapolating ideas about the future by using contemporary methods of storytelling very much grounded in a literary tradition. Rather than being a twenty-fourth-century tale about the future, *TNG*, ergo *Star Trek*, can and may well always be considered a story about contemporary society and how we deal with our own past and present.

The break up of the established television industry in America in the late 1970s and early 1980s to include independent cable and satellite channels as well as major networks such as NBC, ABC and CBS, meant that stations could offer a wide and diverse range of programming for an increasingly media-savvy and genre-hungry audience (Johnson 2005: 95). Competition meant that networks had to invest in new technologies and new television formats to counter cable and satellite channels, which could afford to cater for more niche audiences: 'New cable and satellite systems mean that general "broadcasting" is not the norm, now we also have niche service "narrowcasting", with special interest groups served by specialist channels' (Johnson-Smith 2005: 3). Furthermore, traditional formats of television such as the series and the serial merged, taking on familiar characteristics from BBC historical dramas and distinctive network serials like ABC's *Roots* (1977) and rebranded itself as the miniseries (Creeber 2004: 9). The 1980s saw the growth in popularity of epic genre miniseries like historical dramas *The Thorn Birds* (1983) and *North and South* (1985) and prime time soap operas such as *Dallas* (1978–1991) and *Dynasty* (1981–1989). These ratings-grabbing series not only influenced the format in which science fiction began to be made but also primed viewers for the repeated pleasures of formula television (see Gripsrud 1995).

Invasion USA

Mark Jancovich and Rayna Denison posit that the shifting representations of the alien/human/technological body in the media can be ascribed to the changing exhibition contexts of commercial television:

As cable and satellite television developed in the 1980s, and was forced to compete with existing channels and networks, one of the key ways in which they could mark themselves out as distinctive was precisely through their ability to provide materials that were taboo on the established television channels. (Denison and Jancovich 2007: para. 10)

One can see how examples of the alien infiltration and invasion narratives seen in series discussed in this chapter, along with later science fiction and crime series the authors mention such as *The X-Files* (1993–2002) and *CSI* (2000–present) becoming popular in the 1990s onwards, can be linked to previous depictions of the human and mysterious body seen in the British *The Quatermass Experiment* (1953) and of course *The Twilight Zone*. The focus on the gory, mutating and exposed body portrayed in 1950s science fiction has evolved to become a crucial component of forensic medical and police dramas that delve deep inside the human body using state-of-the-art computer-generated image effects or detailed and convincing make-up and prosthetics. As I will discuss in the following chapter, niche cable channels started to compete with established networks for viewers and commercial revenues, the result being that science fiction would prove to be a popular genre for reincarnation and adaptation. Not withstanding comedic representations of the alien as seen in *ALF* (1986–1990), the alien invasion series of the late 1980s should be acknowledged for their willingness to debate controversial, and indeed timely, topics in the televisual space such as American race relations, multiculturalism and immigration.

V (1984), followed closely by the sequel *V: The Final Battle* (1985), was symptomatic of the new format of science fiction television. While more a miniseries than a series like *Star Trek*, *V* developed a massive following outside of regular science fiction circles. The story was based on familiar science fiction narratives of the 1950s B-movie; aliens in saucer-like ships come to Earth intent on conquest and the subjugation of humanity. The aliens, or Visitors as they become known, disguised themselves as humans (they were really lizard-like creatures underneath the make-up) and infiltrated the media and world governments in order to bring down society from within. The costume and actions of the Visitors, as discussed by M. Keith Booker, clearly paralleled the Nazis in World War II as the aliens wore military uniforms with jackboots while rounding up humans and interning them in concentration camps (Booker 2004: 91). A human resistance, the heroes of the narrative, continued to outwit and uncover the Visitors through a series of attacks and counter-propaganda that prompted a number of Visitors to swap sides and join the humans.

High-budget effects, sets and location shoots combined with a large cast helped make *V* popular with prime time audiences. Back stories started to develop (the birth of an alien/human hybrid for example) that enabled audiences to interact with characters on a weekly basis, becoming more sympathetic with the minutiae of their daily lives and not just with the overall invasion narrative. A seemingly direct influence on the epic miniseries was *Dynasty:* the Visitors were commanded by a power-hungry, super-bitch called Diana (played by Jane Badler) who was the spitting image in both demeanour and attitude to the villainous Alexis Carrington played by Joan Collins, who is described by Christine Geraghty as a 'scheming manipulator' (Geraghty 1991: 17) and was clearly evocative of Margaret Thatcher's Iron Lady persona in the 1980s. Jane Feuer (1995: 1) acknowledges that *Dynasty* can be viewed as a symptom of the Reagan age—with its 'obsession with the supply-side aristocracy' and fascination with insights into the lives of the rich and powerful. Likewise, episodes of *V* often focused on the relationships between Diana and her elite entourage, showing the power struggles within the upper echelons of the invading alien army.

War of the Worlds (1988–1990) was adapted for TV and, along with the reimagined *The Twilight Zone* (1985–1989), reflected a growing sense of cultural paranoia that would eventually be fully realised by *The X-Files* a few years later. Although it evoked 'a heritage in Orson Welles's 1938 radio broadcast and the 1953 film of the same title', suggesting that its events followed the developments of the earlier narrative, J. P. Telotte (2008a: 21) sees the television adaptation as simply an homage to H. G. Wells's story—using the alien invasion premise as a pretext for depicting a gritty, urban society in decay. *Alien Nation* (1989–1991), based on the 1988 film of the same name starring James Caan, carried on television's proclivity for urban crime narratives with its story about the crash landing of an alien slave ship in Los Angeles. The 'newcomers', as they are labelled by the media, have to assimilate into American life and cope with inevitable human prejudice. One newcomer, George Francisco (the aliens take human names based on famous cities, media celebrities or sports stars), joins the LA police force and is partnered with Matthew Sikes, a hard-nosed veteran cop, on some of the city's more arduous and undesirable cases. Both a science fiction and cop show, this genre hybrid touched on topical issues related to racial politics, poverty, prejudice and gender, and the buddy relationship between Francisco and Sikes allowed for instances of humour and sentiment. Furthermore, references and allusions to the contemporary experiences of nonwhite and ethnic communities living in America can clearly be seen and in fact offered a bleak forewarning of the real social and racial problems that were to hit poorer parts of inner-city Los Angeles in the immediate years to come.

In 1991, attempts to convince nonwhite residents in Los Angeles that the police force was reforming and becoming more sensitive to race and ethnic community issues were quite literally dealt a serious blow when video images showing LAPD officers beating and kicking a young black motorist were beamed across the world's television screens. The brutal attack on Rodney King confirmed Civil Rights groups' beliefs that prejudice and violent racism still existed in America's criminal justice system. The riots that were to follow the acquittal of the four white officers originally charged for police brutality in 1992 were the most serious in the city's history. Images of arson, looting, shootings and beatings in predominantly black and Hispanic areas of Los Angeles inundated the news and media for days as the city struggled to maintain social order. Whether it was seen as a lawless riot or an uprising against racial tyranny, the events in Los Angeles showed America that racism toward the nation's racial and ethnic minorities still existed—no matter to what lengths the government went to promote a multicultural society (Schaller, Scharff and Schulz-inger 1996: 548–9).

'The 1990s shift toward nonwhite minorities was the sharpest of the twentieth century', and, coupled with the nation's move to becoming a predominately urban society at the same time, there was clearly going to be pressure put upon poorer inner-city communities to cope with the increase in population and cultural diversity (Schaller, Scharff and Schulzinger 1996: 543). Immigration was high and the al-ready overstretched community infrastructures of urban America were struggling to cope with the influx of newcomers. Inaccurate media stories stating that immigrants were a threat to the economy and community clearly contributed to the arguments of some who thought the LA riots were instigated by poor (nonwhite) immigrants out to make a quick buck. The breakdown in social order, the focus on urban street life and tense race relations were part of *Alien Nation*'s representation of modern-day Los Angeles; the fact that it would be on American television only a few months before the King case and LA riots shows how the science fiction genre continues to prophesise the future and offer comment on humanity's ongoing failures through allegory and metaphor.

–5–

Beyond Truth and Reason
Politics and Identity in Science Fiction

America headed toward the turn of the century as the leading global superpower following the collapse of the Berlin Wall in 1989 and the end of the Cold War. No longer having an enemy on which to focus the nation's attention, America appeared disillusioned and rudderless. Ronald Reagan had offered a sense of false optimism and prosperity that had united the nation in the face of communist Russia, but focus naturally turned inward and many Americans were unhappy with what they saw: a deep and widening gap between the rich and poor, the white middles classes and the nation's racial and ethnic minorities. Inspired by the capitalist mantras of the 1980s that stressed 'greed is good' and 'the business of America is business,' the economic boom in America in the 1990s created global conglomerates owned by a mega-rich elite who had untold power over industry, finance and the media—and this would only increase as the end of the century approached: 'The buoyant economy of the 1990s created not simply two classes in the United States but two nations, a tendency that has accelerated in the new millennium during the presidency of George W. Bush' (Levine and Papasotiriou 2005: 214). For many social commentators this economic divide was having a noticeable effect on the family and community life at the heart of many American cities and rural areas.

In his monumental work *Bowling Alone: The Collapse and Revival of American Community* (2000), Putnam saw America as having become less community orientated and Americans more disconnected and isolated from society at the end of the twentieth century. Where once Americans went bowling in organised leagues, part of a structured local community, within the last decade more and more Americans are 'bowling alone'—symbolising the fragmentation of community life and lack of social connectedness (Putnam 1995: 70). Securing a democracy means having a 'strong and active civil society' where members of that society contribute to their local community; consequently, the creation of sound social networks is crucial to getting on in daily life (1995: 65–6). More recently, Putnam saw decline in almost every area of American community life: local politics, clubs, organisation membership, church groups, sport and social societies, parent–teacher associations. The number of people willing to get involved with these kinds of groups and actively participate in local affairs had grown significantly smaller. However, Putnam recorded an increase in mass membership of national organisations, where 'the only act of membership consists of writing a check for dues'. This meant that they may 'root for the same team' and 'share some of the same interests' but ultimately are 'unaware of each other's existence' (1995: 71). These new forms of grouping embody elements of the social connectedness that Putnam laments, but they cannot provide real community because the members do not interact or care for each other as in a real family. However, the American middle-class family was also considered to be on the wane, with cultural commentators lamenting a lack of family values reminiscent of the 1950s.

Likewise, according to Robert Bellah et al. (1992: 261) the trouble with the American family toward the end of the century was that it had become very isolated, both geographically and socially. They posited that the nation had to reverse its idea of the family back to a more traditional time when intercommunity relationships and institutions addressed its needs, even though this would go against the then current trend toward postmodernity:

> A new look at localism, at decentralization, at what Josiah Royce long ago, in a positive sense, called "provincialism," at what Lewis Mumford called "settlement," would be valuable for much more than family life. (Bellah et al. 1992: 262)

Bellah and his coauthors (1992: 263) called for more government support in local areas, creating schemes where there is no support at all. With this help, the communities could be given a 'breath of life' in order for them to regain their own feelings of community spirit. The vitality of new communities could more than make up for the passing of parochial local communities. These calls for a reappraisal of the American family and town community coincided with a subtle shift further to the right after Bill Clinton had taken over in the White House in 1992. William Berman (1998: 187) recognises Clinton's shift: 'For him, the goal was to create a new "vital center" in American political life based on harmony and co-operation'. Clinton's appropriation of fundamental Republican issues into the Democratic platform for both the 1992 and 1996 elections triggered a general appreciation of down-to-earth American family values throughout the country. Fixing problems at home was indeed one of Clinton's main objectives—he was at the forefront of encouraging greater tolerance for minorities and promoting civil liberties during a time of increased immigration—yet he also ensured that America would continue to take a leading role in international affairs and global trade markets (Berman 2001: 125–6). Furthermore, as American lurched from being Cold War superpower to global trade partner and peacekeeper, Clinton continued to proffer American values and freedoms as a model to the world's poorer nations and trouble spots. As a result, America continued to see itself as exemplar to the outside world, which meant that all the anxieties and paranoia associated with combating the threat of communism during the Cold War, such as fear of the other and fear of the unknown, continued to manifest themselves in the national culture. Science fiction on film and television proved to be no different in this respect.

Fear of the Other

Aliens and the continued threat of invasion, contamination and the other were becoming well-worn narratives in film and television science fiction toward the end of the century—*Alien Nation* was testament to that fact. By the time *Pitch Black* (2000) was released, science fiction had appeared to come full circle (not for the first time) and returned to the bug-eyed monster type story typical of the 1950s. In this film a group of misfit humans crash on a desert planet and find they must band together to survive the savage *Alien*esque creatures that prey on them once darkness falls. The arid landscape acts as a potent source of alien horror by forming a starkly disquieting vista of limitless, untamed territory in which these aliens have all the advantages. Such scenery serves to highlight the plight of the humans; they are stranded and defenceless in a truly alien world, one which they cannot hope to master. As Vivian Sobchack (1998: 118) argues, an environment so hostile to humanity is fundamentally horrific because it renders its native 'other' as 'almost always indestructible'—a theme used to similar effect in *Alien*. *Pitch Black* also deals with the concept of otherness in human terms. Ultimately, the group is forced to overcome its fear of the human alien in its midst, embodied by the mysterious Riddick, a dangerous convict in transit.

Alien's own monster finally reached Earth in *Alien: Resurrection* (1997), set several hundred years after the first film, opening up the possibility that it could take over the planet—something which would eventually come to fruition in *AVP: Alien vs. Predator* (2004). Taking a different tack than previous *Alien* features, the monstrous mother of all aliens could give birth to an alien-human hybrid thanks to the cloning of Ripley, whose DNA was fused with that of the Alien Queen. The alien other is literally embodied by her human physicality, its genetic make-up totally entwined with hers. It can no longer burst out of its human host but is now part of her DNA and her psyche. Ripley's perpetual nightmare had become inescapable, she now being one with that which she feared most in her life: the alien. The film is a story of genetic hybridity, which Martin Flanagan (1999: 168) sees as an example of 'generic hybridity' in that the franchised reinvented itself after the less than well received *Alien 3* (1992) by mixing the more traditional space narrative with tropes from the action adventure and disaster movie genres. The most inventive aspect of *Alien: Resurrection,* however, was that Ripley became the biological mother of the new alien hybrid—rather than just becoming a figurative mother to Newt in *Aliens* (1986). The 'structures of identity' in the last film invert those established in previous ones; Ripley is both alien and human, clone and mother: 'the finale of *Alien Resurrection* positions the mother as a subject and presents the killing of the child as painful because it constitutes a part of herself. The Incestuous embrace that precedes the killing emphasizes this closeness, but does not constitute a disintegration of difference' (Constable 1999: 197). This concern with the internalisation of the alien is also a feature of films concerning alien viruses. In many films, there is a recurrent concern with an alien virus that contaminates humanity for the purpose of planetary domination.

In 1971, *The Andromeda Strain* suggested that space might contain alien germs that were harmful to humans, but films such as *virus* (1999) and *The X-Files* movie (1998) develop the idea of threat from an alien virus. For example, in *virus,* the alien travels as part of an electrical signal sent from another planet to invade other worlds, and it takes control of any form of technology with which it makes contact. Furthermore, in a manner reminiscent of *The Thing* (1982), it cannibalises this technology and combines it with human flesh to create cyborgs bent on human annihilation. However, the twist of the film is that the virus of the title does not refer to the alien signal but to the humans that it seeks to wipe out: for the alien invader the humans are a virus that need to be wiped out. Again, the single-mindedness of the entity reflects the horror of the unstoppable creature in the *Alien* series. According to Jack Morgan, 'the possibility of human devolution to some such dumb driveness is a chilling horror image' (2002: 102). The alien monster in *virus* could represent humanity's nightmare, as it takes over and subsumes it into an all-consuming alien-techno entity intent on purifying the human disease. In *The X-Files* movie, an alien germ has lain dormant on Earth for centuries. However, it is resurrected when aliens begin collaborating with a secret economic and political elite who want to rule the world. The germ contaminates the human body, which then becomes the host to a new life form that gestates within until it eventually bursts out of the human shell, a process akin to the famous scene from *Alien.* Once free, the newborn alien then indiscriminately attacks humans, thereby transferring the threat of the alien swarm to the one solitary alien.

With *The Faculty* (1998), alien horror entered the new ground established by the postmodern teen horror movie *Scream* (1996). With knowing textual references to films such as *Invasion of the Body Snatchers* plus the comedic elements that made *Scream* and its sequels so influential, *The Faculty* combines a high school setting with alien possession and ultimately speculates on what might happen if one's teachers really were aliens. This film can be viewed as a collective invasion narrative. However, the film's reliance on traditional generic alien tropes such as the malevolent individual alien connects it to its predecessors. *Men in Black* (1997) satirises a similar theme by suggesting that aliens exist peaceably on Earth in the guise of teachers, politicians, actors and so forth. *The Faculty's* tagline 'Meet the Alien Generation' intimates that the film follows in the new cool cinema tradition of *Scream.* But it also suggests that the main characters in the film—the hip teenage high school students, who are both the film's characters and its target audience—are products of a *new* generation. The group of kids is made up of the geek, the jock, the school hard man, the pretty cheerleader and so forth, yet despite their stereotypical roles and forced interaction, they remain isolated from each other. The alien generation of America today is both a stranger to itself and the older generation.

Fear of the Masses

Between 1990 and 2001 alien invasion narratives focused on the alien swarm, rather than the individual, as threat. Of course, films from the period such as *Species* (1995) still concerned individual aliens, although even these aliens represented the advance guard of a larger invasion. Similarly, *The X-Files* and *The Faculty* concentrated on a solitary alien who was meant to infiltrate society before the swarm arrived to complete the invasion. However, in many alien invasion films the invading collective is all that humans encounter. The entire species is characterised as a pestilential entity, focused on invasion, destruction and consumption of our own planetary resources. All attempts at trying to interact with these aliens as individuals—as achieved with E.T. and the benevolent aliens of the 1980s—is futile since they have no concept of personal relationships or individuality. For Americans to defeat the oncoming swarm, they must assume their own sense of collective responsibility and join together. Paranoia and xenophobic distrust of national differences have to be put aside to successfully combat the alien hive mentality. The films of this premillennial period drew attention to issues such as globalisation and transnationalism that characterised a historical shift between superpower politics of the 1980s and the new political order following the end of the Cold War. Typically, once threatened with such an alien attack, humanity is shown to unite and form a global village to protect its citizens from the onslaught.

In *Independence Day (ID4)* (1996), all races work together to confront the alien invaders, putting aside their differences to ensure the future of the species. An alternative view has been proposed by Jan Mair, who claims that *ID4* represents a shift from alien other as communist back to a much older Western fear—that of Islam as 'the dark Other of Europe—the alien Saracen' (2002: 37). The film's explicit celebration of American resilience, she claims, presents the locust-like invaders in terms defined by the then recent American experiences during the Gulf War. Implicit in the film is the American fear of a popular uprising in Iraq controlled by Saddam Hussein and a subsequent loss of power in the region. Therefore, the 'demonised "vicious Oriental"/Arab is mythologised' into a powerful threat that needs to be eradicated (Mair 2002: 38). However one might furnish a simpler argument. The true horror of the aliens lies in their very uniformity and the concomitant suggestion that our own nationality and even individuality is under threat from globalisation.

ID4's plot appeals to anxieties relating to the effects of accelerating globalisation on nation states: the movement of people, money and information across national boundaries. For example, much can be made of the way in which the remaining air forces from around the world come together to confront the global menace. This point will be addressed with reference to *Mars Attacks!* (1996) later in this chapter. It is important to stress that the film clearly communicates the message that it is the aliens' *lack of humanity* that is their undoing: they are insect-like in appearance and likened to locusts insofar as they favour planned ruthless consumption of resources by occupying fertile planets. It is the individualised humans, united in their emotional response to attack from the alien other, that defeat the militaristic and group-minded aliens. The absence of the Cold War allows for a certain ironic freedom of choice, either remain insular and die, give in willingly to the alien and die or stand and fight as humans. National borders and ideas of the state mean nothing if you have no planet on which to live. The same global network theme is parodied in *ID4's* comedy counterpart *Mars Attacks!*, where the political correctness of the former film's multicultural union is made visible through the tri-colour configuration of the president's family, a black family and a family resigned to a trailer park (Hedgecock 1999: 116).

The parodic *Starship Troopers* (1997) took this theme one step further in depicting an austere view of interplanetary conflict institutionalised and regimented to a high degree. Here, aliens are portrayed solely as savage, destructive monsters bent on human bloodshed and destruction. *Starship Troopers'* view of otherness is a priori evil; its fascistic and imperialistic overtones position the alien as inferior in contrast to the humans, who are enlightened and therefore justified in colonising the aliens' homeworld. Organised alien control leading to extermination is the only means by which humanity can ensure its own survival. However, the film satirises the explicit notion that monstrous aliens can be exterminated only when humanity unites with the implicit suggestion that humanity itself has become one such aggressor. When an asteroid collides catastrophically with Earth, its residents blame the aliens for launching it and then retaliate by travelling millions of light years across the galaxy and conveniently exploiting the aliens' otherness to galvanise citizens into extreme action. Roz Kaveney (2005) derides the director's, Paul Verhoeven, fascination with depicting extreme violence and torture while at the same time pretending to critique it, yet the film must clearly be understood as a parody wherein such extremes are necessary to be shown for the parody to work: the aliens are the humans; they are us! The flip side of this can be seen in *Battlefield Earth* (2000), where a savage race of alien warriors seeks to exterminate humanity and conquer Earth. It is only when the few remaining humans band together, exhibiting typically human qualities of stubbornness and loyalty, that the alien threat can be vanquished.

It is interesting to note the polarised depictions of aliens in film, in which they either appear as intellectually advanced beings or as bestial monsters. For example, the insect-like aliens in *ID4*, whose mastery of technology far outstrips our own, are potentially our superiors. In contrast, aliens in *Men in Black*, *Evolution* (2001), *Men in Black II* (2002) and the monstrous figures of fear in *Alien* and *Pitch Black* are more animal than human. Their sole purpose is simply to hunt down and devour people where they find them, in the manner of dinosaurs or the monsters of 1950s B-movies, rather than planning occupation through organised cooperation. As Heidi Kaye and I. Q. Hunter (1999: 2) have summarised, these films 'identify the inhuman with monstrous, gloopy, insect-like otherness, and leave no doubt that the only good alien is a dead alien'. The alien virus theme as previously discussed can also be seen here.

ID4's swarm of aliens has been likened to the threat AIDS poses to humans, the alien being inside the body. According to Michael Rogin (1998: 65) *ID4* takes the alien virus and turns it against the alien, and at the point 'when David [Jeff Goldblum's character] plants his computer virus, he is entering the field of AIDS'.

The invasion narratives of the late twentieth century appear to also tap into the psyche of an America once again looking for meaning in the heavens. According to Jan Mair, 'an estimated 23 per cent of Americans believe in aliens and 10 per cent actually claim to have been abducted' (2002: 47; see also French, 2001). However, whilst Roy Neary's and Elliott's search for enlightenment in the late 1970s and early 1980s reflects an era where the alien can provide the answers, such quests in later film narratives are ridiculed: they make one victim to extraterrestrial domination. For example, *Communion* (1989) sees author Whitley Strieber struggling with writer's block and retreating for a weekend to his country cabin with family and friends. During the first night away, the cabin is flooded with a blinding white light and its inhabitants sense that they are being watched. The two friends subsequently insist on returning home the next day, and months later Strieber experiences alien abduction and a medical examination. The discovery that his young son has also encountered the aliens reiterates the traditional motif of aliens making contact with open-minded youths, as yet unbiased by a more stringently scientific worldview. This theme is continued later as Strieber's psychiatrist refers him to a group of people with similar experiences of the stereotypical bug-eyed and blue-skinned aliens so common in alien abduction narratives. Several of these abductees describe the aliens' interest in children.

Mars Attacks! shows that the trusting openness of the *Close Encounters* era can hold no longer as the savage Martians destroy their welcoming committee in a bid to conquer Earth and rid it of its human inhabitants. It is an ironic reference to the film's most famous predecessor, *The War of the Worlds,* and Liz Hedgecock (1999: 117) has observed how both films have tried 'to expose the uncertainty of civilisation, and show the aggressive invasiveness of contemporary life as a threat to what civilisation we have'. *Mars Attacks!* not only shares a connection with science fiction of the 1950s but also conveys a sense of foreboding for what lies in store for civilisation in the future. America is destroyed, Las Vegas is in ruins and only a rag-tag group of misfits remain to rebuild society. This film forms a striking parallel to the plot of *Independence Day,* released in the same year, and at the same time parodies it by twisting *ID4's* iconographic and spectacular scenes of destruction into a comic strip representation of disaster. When the aliens topple the Washington Monument to obliterate some boy scouts, the film ridicules the overused shot from the trailer for *Independence Day* in which the White House explodes (Hedgecock 1999: 116). *Mars Attacks!* is a true celebration of individuality in the face of the collective alien enemy: groups such as Congress and the army are destroyed, whilst individuals and impromptu bands of individuals are seen to survive. Whereas *ID4* celebrates conformity and collective identity, this film shows how precarious a stance such blind patriotism can be. With the rise of a global mass media comes a latent technophobia and fear of assimilation (a fear literally embodied by *Star Trek*'s Borg) into a dehumanised collective incapable of individuality or free will. Again, this is a theme familiar to the science fiction movies of the 1950s and elucidated by Vivian Sobchack in her discussion of collective anxiety in *Invasion of the Body Snatchers.*

Special Effects and Science Fiction Spectacle

Part of the renewed success of the alien invasion film during the 1990s was that for the first time aliens, their ships and the destruction wrought through invasion could be imagined and realised on a massive scale using the latest in digital effects technology. Michele Pierson pinpoints 1997 as a turning point in the use of digital effects in the science fiction genre, particularly the re-release of *Star Wars* as a special edition including new and reimagined footage. Large set pieces and galactic vistas put together using effects imagery and big-budget visual and special effects were again popular with audiences. Special effects feature films prior to the release of *ID4, Mars Attacks!,* and *Star Wars,* such as *The Abyss* (1989), *Terminator 2: Judgement Day* (1991) and *The Lawnmower Man* (1992), were characterised by a 'technofuturist aesthetic' and their 'insistence on the centrality of the computer-generated image' rather than using digital effects to imagine complete and fully-formed science fiction worlds. These features tended to put developments in effects technology and the individual skills of the animators that created the images before any pretensions of entertaining the audience. Conversely, 'The big-budget, effects-orientated science fiction films' popular with popular audiences and contemporary cult fan groups 'offered them the opportunity to participate in a popular cultural event that again put the display of a new type of effects imagery at the center of the entertainment experience' (Pierson 2002: 96).

Science fiction film in this period returned to the concept of the 'Cinema of Attractions', cited by Tom Gunning as a period in early film history representative of when the medium was an arena for technical experimentation and artistic expression rather than for narrative storytelling (e.g. the works of George Méliès). The notion of cinema as a form of spectacle was becoming increasingly important as it battled with newer forms of media and entertainment for an audience. Pierson cites many of the ways Hollywood tried to reinvigorate itself, including adapting many of the popular video games of the time such as *Mortal Kombat* (1995) and *Street Fighter* (1994) for the big screen. Taking advantage of its primary assets, the 'temporal privilege' of the blockbuster cinema event and 'the social and public dimension' of theatre exhibition (Pierson 2002: 122) meant that film could still compete with other media especially if it had spectacular, special effects-driven stories and visual panoramas to offer. A film like *The Matrix* (1999) combined both these elements and offered a coherent universe in which to draw the audience. Moreover, the release of the film signalled a shift in American science fiction film as it drew inspiration from the work of Asian directors and actors: Tsui Hark, John Woo, and Jackie Chan. The use of wire work under the training and direction of Yuen Wo Ping contributed to the Asian look of *The Matrix* (see boxed text), along with the use of Asian actors and Japanese Kanji as the so-called digital rain source code of the Matrix, thus appealing to wider international markets as well as America: 'It was the film's appeal to a transnational aesthetic matrix—drawn from Hong Kong action cinema, from Japanese anime, and from the art of American comic artist Frank Miller—that prompted the fan magazine *Cinefantastique* to dub it a science fiction film for "the new millennium"'. (Pierson 2002: 162).

THE MATRIX (1999)

Written and directed by Larry and Andy Wachowski, and produced by Joel Silver, *The Matrix* captured the American Zeitgeist at the turn of the millennium. A film about obscuring and disclosing truth and reality, it heralded a new age in Hollywood narrative, digital effects, and science fiction. Not only did it spawn two sequels, a special animated feature, and a popular video game franchise, its aesthetic look and futuristic lexicon has become part of popular culture: *Bullet time, taking the red pill* and *jacking in* are now familiar terms that they have become synonymous with describing virtual reality, the Internet and the cyberpunk genre. For Adam Roberts (2005: 311), William Gibson's novel *Neuromancer* (1984) 'established many of the premises of cyberpunk', listing the virtual reality environment of *Tron* (1982) and the *noir*-esque city of *Blade Runner* (1982) as antecedents. As *Neuromancer*'s nearest relation, however, *The Matrix* offers a literal filmic translation of Gibson's Net or Matrix. The novel's protagonist, Case, is a computer hacker like Keanu Reeves's Thomas Anderson character in *The Matrix*. When inside the Net/Matrix, Case is disembodied, as is Anderson in *The Matrix;* although, when he enters the Matrix, Anderson becomes Neo—a messianic freedom fighter. It is revealed to Anderson that he is humanity's saviour and that the double life he has been living as a New York office worker and hacker is meaningless. The world in which he lives is a construct, artificial, the Matrix.

The Matrix is a virtual reality world created by artificial intelligence to enslave humans and use their bio-energy as fuel to power their existence. The real world, Earth, has been destroyed as a result of the war between humans and machines. Unable to defeat the originally solar powered machines, humans used nuclear weapons to create a dust cloud so big that it blocked out the sun—little did they know that the machines would evolve so that they did not need sunlight; they could instead run off the combined energies of the human race. Some humans woke up to this reality and extricated themselves from the Matrix, creating a resistance determined to free all of humanity. The captain of the ship that rescues Neo, Morpheus (played by Laurence Fishburne), believes that Neo will save the Earth and lead them to freedom. Trinity, played by Carrie-Anne Moss, is his second-in-command, who follows her destiny and falls in love with Neo—eventually sacrificing her life in *The Matrix Revolutions* (2003) so that Neo can fulfil his own destiny. Waking up from the Matrix, breaking the 'bondage [of] false consciousness', is done when people are shown 'the true workings of the system', and M. Keith Booker (2006: 256) compares this to the Marxist interpretation of overthrowing capitalism: 'the best weapons against capitalism are knowledge and understanding of its true nature'. Yet he also points out that the film's endorsement of individualism (Neo as saviour) in fact supports 'one of the principal tenets of capitalist ideology, thus reinforcing the very system it seems to want to criticize'. Multiple readings of the film are plentiful and highlight the *polysemic* nature of the text and subsequent multimedia franchise. From pop philosophy to literary references, from religion to the Joseph Campbell monomyth, *The Matrix* 'opens itself to a fantastically wide range of possible interpretations and applications' (Doty 2004: 6).

One reading of the film, and in particular the character Neo, offers us an interesting insight into the representational qualities of the science fiction genre and the narrative weakness of the virtual reality story. Adam Frisch (2007: 46) sees Neo as a futuristic Byronic hero, combining '*individual* intellectual acuity, technological skill and emotional self-resolve'. The term *Byronic hero* is a nineteenth-century literary term that Atara Stein has appended to popular film and television icons such as the cyborg in *The Terminator* (1984) and Q in *Star Trek: The Next Generation* (1987–1994): 'He creates his own rules and his own moral code . . . [he] provides his audience with a satisfying vicarious experience of power and empowerment, autonomy, mastery, and defiance of oppressive authority' (Stein 2004: 1–2). This reading is somewhat problematic when we take into consideration the notion of race. Neo is a white man, although played by Reeves, who is of mixed race, and therefore his heroic persona places masculine whiteness as the ultimate saviour of humanity. This is brought to the fore even more when we see that his helpers are a black man and a white woman, who both are willing to sacrifice themselves for Neo. Other subordinate characters in the three films are also of a different race and ethnic origin: the Oracle is an African American woman, Tank and Dozer are African American men, and the Asian character Seraph from *The Matrix Reloaded* (2003) *and Revolutions,* who tests Neo's martial arts skills, represents an idealised image of the oriental other.

While Neo's character suggests an '"in-between" mode of being', thanks to Reeves's own mixed race heritage and Neo's mastery of martial arts (Cornea 2007: 199–200), the racial divide between him and his companions is marked. In *The Matrix* and other virtual reality films of this period such as *Johnny Mnemonic* (1995), *Virtuosity* (1995) and *Strange Days* (1995) African American characters serve as aids or counterpoints to the white protagonist, who holds mastery over the virtual reality space. Morpheus and the Oracle act as spiritual guides for Neo; likewise Ice-T's character J-Bone in *Johnny Mnemonic* is leader of a street gang that fights the technologically superior Pharmakom Corporation:

> Race is a central presence and African-Americans are consistently associated with the 'real'. There is an implicit message that African-Americans have a fundamentally 'grounded' essence that resists electronically induced instability and can 'heal' white people who are careening out of control. (Springer 1999: 215)

Nonwhite characters in *The Matrix* and other science fiction film and television—one can also include Chakotay from *Star Trek: Voyager* (1995–2001) (see Geraghty 2003c)—act as active agents to help the white main protagonist and progress the internal narrative. As such, viewers are only ever given a one-dimensional characterisation of otherness and race. In terms of *The Matrix*, the artificiality of the virtual world is thus emphasised by racial stereotypes and the literal masking of certain characters. Lisa Nakamura (2005: 127) describes the virtual world of *The Matrix* as 'reproducing white masculine privilege', in that the Architect is an old white man with a white beard, and the Agents are white men in suits, yet through the interfaces between humans and computer technology the film also promotes difference. Black identity, represented by some of the crew members and inhabitants of Zion, is 'depicted as singular, "natural" and "authentic"' in opposition to whiteness, which, in conjunction with the machine culture of the film, 'is viral, oppressive and assimilative' (129). This, for Nakamura, is a clear critique of the colonial impulse, racism, white power and even technological change.

Joshua Clover (2004: 35) describes the infamous bullet time effect as 'a visual analogy for privileged moments of consciousness'. A response to the increased popularity and income of the video game industry, Hollywood went all out to wow audiences for fear of losing out in the new media market. As gaming technology and visual effects developed at an exponential rate, Hollywood matched the look and feel of digital gaming—with *The Matrix* this was literally and visually emphasised with action taking place in the digital environment and Neo being uploaded with videogame martial arts skills before his combat training. Moreover, whenever bullet time was used, it signalled to the audience that they were perhaps not watching a movie but were in fact inside a high resolution synthetic world, the Matrix, where anything is possible:

> Looking at, for example, bullet time, we recognise it as an explicit immersion effect. Shot from our point of view, the optical perspective swoops through a three-dimensional space, fully rendered, 360 degrees, without ever revealing the apparatus of film-making. (Clover 2004: 25)

With special effects being so central to the initial design and subsequent success of the first film, it was perhaps not surprising that the two sequels and animated series of shorts that made up *The Animatrix* (2003) upped the ante on digital effects usage. The animated features filled in the narrative back story and timeline of events set before and after the first film, with *Final Flight of the Osiris* being shown as a teaser before *Reloaded* was released. Zion, revealed in the first sequel, is imagined as a cavernous underground city reminiscent of the underground dwellings of the workers in *Metropolis*. The final battle to save Zion in *Revolutions,* with sentinel machines attacking humans manning giant armoured exoskeletons, is a dazzling sequence if only because it sits in stark contrast with many of the fight sequences throughout all three films. The intricacies and intimacies of one-on-one martial arts combat are replaced by huge explosions and wide angle battle scenes. The super-cool aesthetic of Neo's bullet time and wire work duels with Agent Smith are part of the franchise look, and they 'cannot be extricated from the narrative, from the movie's worldview . . . the effects *are* the worldview: there is a digital confabulation' (Clover 2004: 28). Yet the titanic battle between thousands of sentinels and the armoured machines (which takes place outside the Matrix) signifies large-scale spectacle and underlines the notion that this is artificial—these machines and scenes have been rendered by artists trying to impress. Instead of confabulation there is separation.

Paranoia and Plenty

The success of *Star Trek: The Next Generation (TNG)* in reminding networks and television audiences that science fiction was still a marketable genre on the small screen lead to what Booker (2004) describes as an 'Age of Plenty' (111). The 1990s saw a proliferation of new science fiction series hot on the heels of *TNG*'s last season in 1994. As well as concurrent series like *Quantum Leap* (1989–1993), *Star Trek*'s own *Deep Space Nine* (1993–1999) and *Voyager* (1995–2001), there followed *The X-Files* (1993–2002), *Babylon 5* (1994–1998), with its own spin-off *Crusade* (1999), *Sliders* (1995–2000), *Space: Above and Beyond* (1995–1996), *Stargate SG-1* (1997–2007) and spin-off *Stargate: Atlantis* (2004-present), *Lexx* (1997–2002), Roddenberry's *Earth: Final Conflict* (1997–2002) followed by his *Andromeda* (2000–2005), a new version of *The Outer Limits* (1995–2002) that followed the renaissance of *The Twilight Zone,* and one might also include genre hybrids like the teen science fiction/horror series *Roswell* (1999–2002), *Buffy the Vampire Slayer* (1997–2003) and *Angel* (1999–2004).

The impact of these series meant that the concept of prime time quality television was firmly established by the mid-1990s, and their episodic formats also encouraged cable networks such as the Sci-Fi Channel (founded in 1992) to continue investment since they attracted a loyal and relatively affluent audience that could afford to buy into the ever-growing merchandising market. For Derek Kompare (2005: 172), cable networks 'function as television *boutiques:* venues offering a limited array of products for specialized audiences'. Series that started on the major networks would also end up on cable through syndication, adding to the pleasure of the rerun marathon which had become a staple cable marketing tool to attract science fiction fans. Preceding Booker's comment that science fiction television was plentiful, John Ellis (2002: 162) described the entire industry at the start of the new millennium as 'rushing towards an emerging era of plenty' in that it offered new technologies and new challenges to the way we watch television. New programmes on new channels, and new forms of technology on which we watch those channels, have increased choice for the typical television viewer. Plenty of choice has meant that the genre has had to adapt even more quickly to changing and diverse audience tastes. Genre hybrids like *Roswell* signalled a shift in science fiction programming and its intended audiences as it combined elements from the popular teen male melodrama epitomised by its contemporary *Dawson's Creek* (1998–2003) and invasion/conspiracy narratives fundamental to *The X-Files* (see boxed text). According to Miranda Banks (2004: 17), *Roswell* brought 'in a variety of niche audiences with [its] blend of science fiction, action-adventure, young romance and melodrama', while also redefining models of teen masculinity through the characterisation of a sympathetic and sensitive young male hero.

An interesting feature of this period is the rise of the writer/producer, those given more creative control over their own series that have become known as modern television auteurs. J. Michael Straczynski, Chris Carter and Joss Whedon for example assumed tremendous power over the creative directions their series took, and their names were used strategically by the networks to attract new and younger audiences to their schedules. In some respects, the existence of television auteurs is not a new phenomenon. Gene Roddenberry and Rod Serling, perhaps even Irwin Allen, are accepted as visionaries who helped to raise the genre up from its juvenile associations to make television science fiction respectable. However, what characterises the newer auteurs in the late 1990s is the relationship they had with the networks and the freedom the networks gave them in order to increase ratings and audience share. For Roberta Pearson (2005: 17), 'The networks granted this creative control because in the post-classical network system era the names of important hyphenates, the hyphenate brand as it were, proved more attractive to demographically desirable audiences than did the network brand.'

This said then, the success of science fiction on television in the 1990s can be ascribed to the increased media attention on the writer/producer and his/her relationship to a younger and more fragmented audience. How these auteurs have been represented in academic criticism is also important in understanding the influence they had on the genre as a whole. Chris Carter, creator of *The X-Files,* was described as having a plan for how many series and episodes he wanted to make (Lavery, Hague and Cartwright 1996: 4). The inspiration for the show was his fascination with the conspiracy culture surrounding the Watergate scandal, and this was identified most of all in how he did not hesitate 'to register its reverberations in 1990s America on the psyche of his alter ego Fox Mulder, a man similarly haunted by the debacle of 1973' (Graham 1996: 56–7). Similarly, as Rhonda Wilcox and David Lavery (2002: xvii) recount in their analysis of *Buffy the Vampire Slayer,* Joss Whedon 'has often said that the original kernel of an idea for *Buffy* came with the reversal of an image from traditional horror: a fragile-looking young woman walks into a dark place, is attacked—and then turns and destroys her attacker'. This description of the origin story implies that through a moment of individual thought the entire premise for a successful series was mapped out, thereby making the auteurist vision a crucial part of contemporary television programming.

Episodic series such as *Babylon 5 (B5)* and *Deep Space Nine (DS9)*, created long story arcs that fed both the audiences' expectations of science fiction and provided a stable and continuous world through which characters, plots, and personal histories could develop. Sherryl Vint (2008: 262) describes *B5* as an 'epic' series that was more often seen as being downbeat despite creator J. Michael Straczynski's intention that it depict a future where we have obligations to each other and society: '*Babylon 5* is, in fact, at its strongest when it defies epic and science fiction convention, emphasizing moral ambiguity over clear right and wrong, portraying complex and fallible characters instead of grandiose epic heroes' (Vint 2008: 261–2). Both series not only manipulated generic tropes such as critical dystopias, the space station, intergalactic conflict and so on, but also borrowed heavily from genres such as soap opera and serious television drama to help maintain their fictional worlds and create a sense of community:

> [*DS9*'s] stories are linked by continuing "soap opera"-type subplots such as Bashir's ineffectual attempts to romance Jadzia, Sisko's difficulties with his adolescent son, Jake, and Odo's continual pursuit of Quark. It is emphasised that *DS9* is a multicultural community in which . . . relationships between characters will be less bound by their rank and position. (Gregory 2000: 74)

Subsequently, the increasingly complex storylines and character arcs helped perpetuate the cult audience's desire and passion for trivia and history. *DS9* resembled contemporary television series of the 1990s such as *Friends* (1994–2004) and *B5* as it took on more soap opera and melodrama characteristics that emphasised relationships between friends, family, husbands and wives (see Geraghty, 2003a). Entire seasons focussed on the continuing war between the Federation and Dominion, the long story arc eventually culminating in the disappearance of Captain Sisko and the dividing up of the crew—their futures unknown. Viewers who would miss certain episodes risked not knowing what was going on, and episodes often ended on a down note with little sign of resolution.

The week-in-week-out nature of the similar *B5* and *DS9* ensured a popular following for both; however, their narratives saw a marked contrast in outlook for the future of Earth. *DS9* clearly kept to the utopian blueprint offered in previous *Star Trek* series: the location of the space station on the edge of a newly discovered wormhole and in the middle of a tense political situation between the occupying and occupied worlds of Cardassia and Bajor indeed emphasised the positive nature of the series as the bonds of the Starfleet crew grew stronger as they faced further peril together. *B5*, on the other hand, was set in a future where Earth had 'deteriorated relative to the late twentieth century in which the show was produced' (Booker 2004: 133). Earth was a dystopian world where corrupt government after corrupt government had destroyed people's faith in authority and politics. Humans had seen hardship and death in brutal wars with the alien Minbari, and the only way they could ensure survival was to create a space station which would act as intermediate neutral ground, 'our last, best hope for peace.' *B5*'s more realistic and cynical tone was shared by most of the series that would follow in the mid- to late 1990s and indeed can be seen as precursor to the new *Battlestar Galactica* (2003–2009). Out on its own, *Quantum Leap,* the story of Dr. Sam Beckett's whimsical time travelling tour of the twentieth century, was a rather more warm-hearted series that focused on the potentials of individuals to enact change that, however small, could improve other people's lives forever. The series stands in marked contrast to the epic space operas just mentioned yet still garnered a devoted fan base that showed science fiction's continuing capacity to attract a family audience in this period of change and pessimism. After the show's cancellation, the genre would witness a bleak turn where such positivism would give way to deep-seated national paranoia.

THE X-FILES (1993–2002)

Chris Carter's *The X-Files* was mix of detective thriller and science fiction horror, with a dash of postmodern pastiche added for fun. The main protagonists, FBI Agents Fox Mulder and Dana Scully, would be given new missions each week to investigate the strange, paranormal, and alien. In the first few seasons, these missions would often lead them to uncover strange human mutations and freaks of nature; rarely would the prospect of full-scale alien visitation be explored. After the release of *The X-Files* movie in 1998, the alien invasion motif familiar to B-movies of the 1950s was unashamedly used to drive the overall narrative of subsequent seasons on TV. Aliens of insect-like appearance reappeared throughout the remaining four years, depicted as having a sinister interest in human anatomy and often in cahoots with the American government and FBI. Here, the archetypal alien figure of fear and mystery is shown to have invaded Earth with the purpose of exploiting human biology, propagating their race by using unsuspecting humans as incubators. The alien abduction narrative is well established in science fiction, a result of extensive media coverage and a pervasive interest created in the 1940s and 1950s inspired by real life events in Roswell and flying saucers at the movies. Christopher French (2001: 115) quotes Terry Matheson that the 'themes of the abduction "myth" reflect both our fear of being enslaved by technology and bureaucracy and our hope that, in some inscrutable way, technology may be our salvation'.

Early episodes offer a flavour of the series' main themes. In 'Ice' (1993) Mulder and Scully are stranded in an arctic laboratory investigating the suspicious deaths of a team of scientists who were drilling through the ice, collecting prehistoric core samples. Plot and scenes that pay homage to both *The Thing From Another World* (1951) and John Carpenter's remake *The Thing* (1982), themselves based on John W. Campbell Jr's novel *Who Goes There?* (1938), add to the claustrophobic atmosphere. The ice samples contain an extraterrestrial wormlike parasite that feeds off the chemicals that produce anxiety and paranoia in humans. As Mulder, Scully and the rest of the team become ever more nervous and start to accuse each other of being an infected carrier of the parasite, they neglect to find out how and why these alien life forms came to Earth millions of years ago. 'Ice' was a portent to the alien conspiracy arc which would become more pronounced in the second season. The episode finishes with Mulder and Scully being told that the arctic lab had been torched by the military to safeguard the nation, the audience thus being left to speculate on why the government would want to cover up the incident. In 'Humbug' (1995), the duo is sent to investigate the murder of a Florida sideshow performer and is introduced to a community of freaks, weirdoes, geeks, magicians and contortionists. Ruminations on the meaning of difference, physical deformity and social acceptance are interspersed with more gruesome murders as Mulder and Scully dig deeper into the bizarre world of the American sideshow. As a more standalone episode, 'Humbug' plays with audience perceptions of what is deemed normal or unusual; *The X-Files'* mantra of 'The Truth Is Out There' is underscored by frequent references to spotting slight of hand, humbugs, and the famous circus impresario, P. T. Barnum. The murderer turns out to be the conjoined twin of one of the sideshow performers; able to detach himself from the body of his brother, he targets likely new 'hosts,' thus inadvertently killing them as he gouges out their stomachs.

The *X-Files* achieved its cult status by creating a certain style that emphasised a sense of lack. According to Catherine Johnson, this lack was reflected in the dark and moody sets, 'use of darkness and bright lights to obscure rather than reveal' and the series' metanarrative of secrets and concealment (2005: 102). What can easily be read as an extension of the alien invasion narratives of the 1950s—*Invasion of the Body Snatchers* for example—worked to create a sense of paranoia and conspiracy that sat oddly in opposition to the contemporary political climate. The Cold War was over, America was undergoing an economic boom and the optimism of Bill Clinton's administration was influencing both domestic and foreign policy. The fact that *The X-Files,* and other contemporary postmodern series such as *Wild Palms* (1993), *Twin Peaks* (1990–91), *Dark Skies* (1996–1997) and Carter's own *Millennium* (1996–1999) projected a dark vision of the near future is testimony to what M. Keith Booker sees as a rejection of the national optimism at that time. Obvious connections to the impending new millennium, including the Y2K problem's threat to global information systems, can be drawn and are clearly seen in science fiction television's continued fascination with technology and our relationship with it. However, the paranoid invasion narrative of *The X-Files,* according to Booker, was more than just a response to fears of Y2K. The outsider or alien other so often depicted in this period was representative of the growing poorer classes in society, a result of the widening poverty gap between the middle class, who were indeed profiting from the economic boom, and deprived workers worldwide. General mistrust of government and politicians was a mechanism through which the have-nots could manifest their resistance to the haves: 'Thus, the richer Americans became, the more threatened and embattled they felt, and the paranoia of *The X-Files* responded perfectly to this mind-set' (Booker 2004: 147).

According to Ray Pratt, *The X-Files* contained 'images of government activity unlike anything in the history of television' (Pratt 2001: 231). Paranoia and conspiracy provided a strong undercurrent to many of the standalone, monster-of-the-week episodes, but clearly such themes provided the main dramatic impetus for the larger alien abduction/invasion story arcs, known as the mythology episodes. Along with other paranoid science fiction and criminal investigation series such as *Law and Order* (1990–present), *The X-Files* can be considered part of what Michael Barkun (2003: 8–9) sees as America's fascination for 'conspiracy and paranoia'. Conspiracy and intrigue have been important, if not major, players in the country's political and cultural history: Who shot JFK? Is there an Area 51? Was 9/11 a government cover-up? Conspiracy narratives create myths shared by a select few, and networks of people that feed off misinformation and half-truths feel unique in a multimedia age where information and the truth is freely available at the touch of a button. *The X-Files* offered its large cult fan base (fans are known as X-Philes) a mythology in which they could immerse themselves (see Lavery 2004). With little resolution at the end of many episodes, it left the fans wanting more, eager to log onto the Internet to discuss what they thought it all meant. Never revealing the truth, only ever hinting at the bigger picture, created and maintained an air of conspiracy for the select few. Revealing too many secrets or explaining away the mystery could jeopardize 'the potency of conspiratorial themes by depriving them of some of their allure . . . Once intended only for the knowing few, they are now placed before the ignorant many' (Barkun 2003: 35). This was the dilemma faced by the series' creator and writers: reveal too much, and fans would be disappointed with the outcome; reveal too little, and audiences may get bored and turn it off.

Cult, Television and New Media

An interesting parallel might be drawn between the subject matter of *The X-Files* and the large fan base it was attracting at a particular time in American history. John Moffitt (2003) identifies several interesting reasons why alien culture, particularly ufology, continued to dominate American popular culture during the 1990s. First, there was a sense of profitability attached to the UFO industry. Moffitt cites the example of how he received no advanced royalties for writing his book, which focused on analysing aliens and abduction stories as works of fiction, whereas the (in)famous Prof John Mack, professor of psychiatry at the Harvard Medical School, received $250,000 as an advance for his book *Abduction: Human Encounters with Aliens* (1995) because it was seen as a work of nonfiction (Moffitt 2003: 26–7). This is a compelling insight into the so-called alien industry in America at that time. The second reason behind the rise of alien culture could be ascribed to the development of cult in American society. According to Moffitt, those people on the periphery of society turned the UFO experience into a postmodern alternative religion: '"abduction by aliens" stories, and the infotainment industry that supports them, are a *symptom* of a larger syndrome, a general "occultation" of the modernist mentality' (Moffitt 2003: 424). This may be true; there is no doubt that in those communities perceived as being susceptible to the popular and cult entertainment markets, the image of the alien visitor and UFO carries great spiritual worth. In some cases, the aliens have replaced traditional symbols of religious faith, and believers (many of them abductees) gather together to worship the extraterrestrial as a Christ figure. At a fundamental level the alien represents that which we might feel is missing in our lives, whether it is a spiritual void or a physical manifestation of what we interpret as familiar or strange, friendly or dangerous. Intriguingly then, one could argue that the appeal of *The X-Files,* following Moffitt's line of reasoning, rested on the fact it attracted an audience who felt in someway estranged from contemporary life and saw something personal and relevant in a series that dealt with truths, untruths, paranoia and conspiracy episode after episode. Such an audience, in today's terminology, would most definitely be considered cult.

As television networks sought ever-increasing niche audiences in the multichannel age of cable and digital television, science fiction was heavily relied upon to guarantee a market share. *The X-Files'* success, however, was by no means universal. It seemed that in attracting a devoted cult audience, to the extent and magnitude of texts like *Star Trek,* would-be cult series had to utilise new media forms such as the Internet to garner and feed an audience no longer looking for just an hour a week of entertainment. Television, particularly science fiction television, was becoming an increasingly important part of fan culture's daily life. From attending international conventions and auctions to dressing up and creating their own Web pages and blogs, fans had become an essential part of what made science fiction series stick. For a show to catch on it had to appeal to a wide enough fan base, offer a little something for everyone. As we have seen already with series like *The X-Files* and the many versions of *Star Trek,* this was achieved by keeping the show as open as possible—allowing multiple readings and multiple points of entry for the millions of different fans. Television is by its very nature a polysemic text; therefore its popularity, the making or breaking of any particular show, depends on it reaching a wide audience—it must be open.

John Fiske (1986) identified in an earlier examination of network television series that we cannot predict the meanings audiences take but we can identify the polysemic characteristics and theorise the relation between text and social context. The polysemy of meaning is as much a power struggle as that of economics or politics, yet TV fails to control meaning just as social authority attempts and fails to control oppositional voices. Consequently, science fiction television, with its potentially infinite textual readings matched against social and historical contexts, attracted the oppositional cult fan who actively sought to promote his or her own interpretation of the series and sought out like-minded fans first through conventions and newsletters and then through forums, chat rooms, blogs and Web pages on the Internet. At the turn of the millennium, science fiction television was in a healthy state of renaissance as a burgeoning fan culture ensured its renewal. The same was not completely true of Hollywood film, which, with the release of

Star Wars Episode I: The Phantom Menace in 1999, had embarked on a road of monotony and repetition.

One exception to this monotony was *Galaxy Quest* (1999), a hilarious parody of the *Star Trek* franchise and mythos, which portrayed cult fans as strong and competent individuals who are part of a supportive and culturally integrated group. This was of course in contrast to the media stereotype of the geeky or nerdy fan, so often associated with the science fiction genre. In a film about a once-popular science fiction TV series that gets brought back for a new generation of fans (mirroring the death and rebirth of *Star Trek* in the late 1980s) *Galaxy Quest* examined perceptions of the frontier as a both physical and personal boundary. Bizarrely, science fiction film was promoting its television counterpart—using familiar generic tropes and parody to highlight the importance of the genre to contemporary cult audiences. As science fiction television continued to be popular with mainstream networks and cable channels, the representation of fandom in *Galaxy Quest* stands as an interesting gauge of how the genre was perceived by Hollywood and still accepted by television audiences and fans. Indeed, the relationship between cult film and cult TV became even closer during the 1990s through what was termed a dispersal of multimedia platforms (video, TV, CD and later also DVD and the Internet). No longer specifically located in cinema, the term *cult* during this period became just as synonymous with TV, and series like *The X-Files* which 'took on most of the aesthetic properties of cult cinema and quickly became a powerful cult' (Mathijs and Mendik 2008: 169). Equally, just as cult films are made cult through a subcultural ideology existing in fan groups who define themselves in opposition to the mainstream, cult television can be seen as developing out of this opposition and incorporating elements of the popular. This does not necessarily mean the total incorporation of all mainstream television—there is still distinction between genres, series and narrative—but it does indicate that to understand the development of cult science fiction series in the 1990s and their continued growth in the new millennium, one must still acknowledge that '"cult" is largely a matter of the ways in which [it is] classified in consumption' (Jancovich et al. 2003: 1).

–6–

American Science Fiction Post-9/11

The events of September 11, 2001, are now part of history, yet the images of that day are indelibly etched on the minds of millions of people around the world. So dramatic was the effect of this one day on the American psyche that many critics and academics describe history as being divided by a pre-9/11 and post-9/11 age, as if a new era had dawned as soon as the first plane hit the World Trade Center: 'In the United States the new millennium began not on January 1, 2000, but on September 11, 2001...In a matter of minutes, the America sense of reality was abruptly changed' (Levine and Papasotiriou 2005: 259). In a political sense this may be true: the Bush administration's reaction to 9/11 was to immediately retaliate overseas in Afghanistan and Iraq—supposedly targeting Muslim fundamentalist and terrorist groups such as the Taliban and Al Qaeda. At home, too, the government implemented new laws under the auspices of protecting America and its citizens: the Patriot Act changed the nature of civil liberties and freedom of speech in America, all in the name of national security.

In his appraisal of post 9/11 film and television Wheeler Winston Dixon (2004: 2–3) describes how the 'bleak landscape of personal loss, paranoia, and political cynicism' has since inspired Hollywood's output: in the first instance, movies like family films and comedies were made to help America forget about the attacks; this was soon to be replaced, however, by the more typical action blockbusters and films that used 9/11 and its fallout as narrative backdrop. Escapist films and television series, symbolised by texts that ignored the current national anxieties or those that revelled in portraying a triumphant America on the road to recovery, were in abundance as the years went by; old formats and franchises were resurrected in an attempt to go back to a time before 9/11 even happened. The knock-on effect of this trend was that Hollywood started to take less risks on the sorts of film it made. Science fiction would still be a popular genre, but only those stories and features that had a proven track record of success would be continued. Hollywood wanted immediate returns on its movies, as if the potential for seeing what the future might bring proved too scary or unnervingly close to real life, so the more creative and original projects would 'be replaced with an assembly line of factory-tooled genre vehicles that deliver predictable thrills to increasingly unsophisticated audiences' (Dixon 2004: 15). While Dixon's views on the audience may not be to everybody's liking, it is hard not to agree with his assessment of genre film; science fiction film was most definitely entering a period of predictability.

In a rather more sensitive reading of television in America after 9/11, Dana Heller posits that it acted as a cathartic device which aided in the individual and national period of healing and mourning. Alongside the obvious rolling news coverage of the event, television from dramas to chat shows 'intimately directed the sense-making strategies that individuals, coworkers, and communities brought to bear upon the unfolding events' (Heller 2005: 7). Long after the event had been emblazoned on people's memory, becoming a static and moving representation of reality, television continued to mediate a collective memory of sound and image bites, a recycling of 9/11 imagery that stood in for and largely ignored the cultural and political contexts which perhaps brought about the terrorist attacks in the first place. Despite this blanking out of critique and context in mainstream television post-9/11, we might acknowledge the influence that this attention to spectacle and image rather than substance and narrative had on regular genre programming that was to follow. Lynn Spigel (2005: 133–4) talked about 'Event TV', or television 'designed to take on the status and audience shares of media events', which developed in the years after the attacks, filling in the gaps in national television schedules left by the repeated documentaries and telethons centred on 9/11's victims and their relatives. In terms of the plethora of science fiction television texts that proceeded 9/11, I would also consider these part of Spigel's 'Event TV' category, to the extent that many series (*Heroes, Battlestar Galactica, Star Trek: Enterprise*) alluded to the terrorist attacks on 9/11 itself or the political fallout in American society associated with Guantanamo Bay, the torture of terrorist suspects, freedom of information, and the wars in Afghanistan and Iraq. As well as filling the narrative gap by offering references to 9/11 culture, science fiction on both film and television filled the gap left by 9/11 imagery by becoming more and more reliant on special effects and computer generated imagery (CGI)—a point I shall develop later in this chapter—therefore indicating that the American fascination with spectacle as entertainment had returned.

Franchise Fatigue

The *Star Trek* franchise has an uncanny ability to regenerate, evolve, and even rejuvenate, which is unique to television or film. It is this sense of rejuvenation or rebirth that explicitly characterised 2002's *Star Trek Nemesis* and also implicitly encapsulates the three *Next Generation* movies of the previous decade: *Generations* (1994), *First Contact* (1996) and *Insurrection* (1998). In fact, one might see *Nemesis* as the final instalment of a story arc that dealt with issues related to life/death, family/individuality and sacrifice/greed. The plot sees Picard and his crew called to Romulus, the home world of the Romulans, to discuss peace. However, after a detour to investigate what appears to be an abandoned prototype of Data on a desert planet, Picard comes face to face with an aggressive young human called Shinzon who has taken over the leadership of the Romulan senate on behalf of the Remans—inhabitants of Remus, Romulus's sister planet. After centuries of being bred as slaves, the Remans have revolted and taken control with brutal force, making Shinzon their spokesman. Their sense of otherness is made more visible by the fact that they have become vampiric in appearance, not just having pointed Vulcan ears but also needle-like teeth, bat like features, and a strong aversion to bright light. However, Shinzon is human, a clone to be more precise, and the result of an abandoned Romulan experiment to replace Picard and bring down the Federation from within. For Picard, this news is particularly hard to bear because he has always longed for a son, if not a sense of kinship or family, since his brother, sister-in-law and his nephew died in a fire briefly reported in *Generations*. As with previous movies, the notions of family, lineage, and youth resound throughout, particularly in the scenes where Shinzon and Picard connect together like aloof father and troubled son.

In a subplot that sees Data confront an earlier version of himself that Dr. Noonien Soong had created but never revealed, similar concepts of ancestry and origin characterise their relationship. Being a more primitive version of Data, tellingly called B-4, the prototype is like a child in need of parental nurturing; he has no understanding of himself as an individual or of his surroundings. Data literally tries to bring him up to speed by downloading his entire memory into B-4's head in order to make him more of an individual but fails to realise that what made him who he is took years to develop—a development that was an indelible part of *The Next Generation* series. Both father/son relationships accentuate a sense of passing on experience, making their perceived offspring into better people. However, Picard's relationship with Shinzon is ultimately doomed because Picard's unwitting absence from his life has contributed to his desire to seek revenge on humanity. Data's brief experience of fatherhood may at first seem to fail as B-4 shows no sign of cognitive awareness, yet after Data's sacrificial death to save both the ship and his captain, B-4 begins to become aware of who he is and, more importantly for the continuing narrative of the *Star Trek* franchise, in what capacity he fills Data's place.

In her book *Screening Space* Vivian Sobchack (1998: 277) says that 'despite all their "futuristic" gadgetry and special effects...the *Star Trek* films are conservative and nostalgic, imaging the future by looking backward to the imagination of a textual past'. The films referred to were the first three feature films to include the original crew: *The Motion Picture* (1979), *The Wrath of Khan* (1982), and *The Search for Spock* (1984); specifically, their futurism entailed looking back on previous visions of the future in order to 're-enact the nostalgic drama of the television series' own death and resurrection'. Together the three films represent a rebirth, death and resurrection cycle constituted by an 'intertextually grounded pseudo-history' and illustrated through their constant references to 'aging, regret, loss, and death' found at the heart of their narratives (276–7). In keeping with this tradition, *Nemesis* offered references to such emotional incidents through the father–son relationships of Picard and Shinzon and Data and B-4, but more importantly it also had elements of the 'intertextually grounded pseudo-history'. When Data sacrifices himself for his captain, he is revisioning the final moments of *The Wrath of Khan,* where Spock dies saving Kirk and the *Enterprise.* By the end of the film, B-4 becomes the regenerated Data just as Spock was given a second chance in *The Search for Spock;* Riker's promotion to captain of the *Titan* mirrors Sulu's promotion in *The Undiscovered Country* (1991). The *Star Trek* mythic text is rewritten to include Riker and Troi's wedding, Captain Janeway's promotion to admiral, and a brief appearance of *TNG* season regulars Wesley Crusher and Guinan. These examples of *Star Trek* narrative continuity strengthen and update the 'pseudo-history' that Sobchack has identified as key to the original movies.

Along with *Nemesis,* the year 2002 saw a significant amount of sequels that relied on previous incarnations to attract an eager audience. *Die Another Day,* the twentieth Bond film in its fortieth franchise year, was replete with in-jokes and intertextual references that kept fans interested long enough to be fooled that it was any good. Despite its ordinariness, the success of *Star Wars Episode II: Attack of the Clones* indicated just how much audiences preferred to watch something reassuringly familiar rather than risk experiencing reality that was becoming increasingly hard to bear after 9/11. *Nemesis* can be counted amongst these types of film but not because it was responding in any way to recent terrorist attacks or global angst; rather, it was merely continuing a *Star Trek* tradition that pre-dates America's recent turn to nostalgia. The film is very much part of the continuing efforts to create a fictional future history that epitomises *Star Trek*'s view of our utopian destiny. *Star Trek*'s representation of a reality through its fictitious future has not only been entrenched as a possible outcome for society; it has become reality for some die-hard fans who want to believe that it is true, or, as David Gerrold (1996: 228) puts it, 'it represents a future we would like to make real'. Its connections to history only add legitimacy to its figuration of the future; they have both become inseparable from each other, making *Star Trek* a signifier of the future and a signifier of the past (Geraghty 2002: 168–9). Intertextual references mean so much more within the narrative framework of *Nemesis* that they are inseparable from its reception.

Both visually and thematically *Star Trek Nemesis* failed to convince its audience that it had something new to offer alongside existing franchise output: a low box office share ensured that it was the last *TNG* film. Yet it shared many similarities with previous *Star Trek* films and borrowed from contemporary sources: Shinzon's piercing by a metal bulkhead wielded by Picard in the final fight scene is iconographically reminiscent of Aragorn's impaling of Lurtz in *Lord of the Rings: The Fellowship of the Ring* (2001). Since reinvention and rejuvenation were such key themes in the film, it is no surprise that they should come to characterise some of the press coverage before *Nemesis*'s cinema release. Stuart Baird, the director, and John Logan, the screenwriter, were relative newcomers to the franchise, brought in to 'break the mould a little bit without breaking the tea set' (Spelling 2003: 24). Unfortunately,

Nemesis appeared to try and push the reset button one too many times—something of which *Star Trek: Enterprise* can also be accused—and its relative failure at the box office, and even amongst die-hard Trekkies, signalled that the Hollywood science fiction film was entering a period of generic exhaustion.

Looking Backwards

The case of *Nemesis* indicated that science fiction film had indeed reached a dead end; no longer guaranteed a box office hit, the big franchises were encountering some resistance from fans who wanted to see originality rather than repetition. The furore from *Star Wars* fans following *The Phantom Menace*'s release hinted at the underlying frustration they felt over Lucas's decision to reboot the franchise by going back to the beginning. Seen as a cynical manoeuvre on Lucas's part to make more money from fans, the film was met with intense criticism and disapproval. However, putting such personal devotion and frustration aside, these two franchise films were merely emblematic of a genre that has routinely looked back on its generic forebears for inspiration and endorsement. Science fiction film looks both forward and back. As Adam Roberts (2000: 30) describes, it is a form of 'prediction and nostalgia'. M. Keith Booker (2006: 23) identifies this trend in twenty-first century film through his focus on science fiction comedy features such as *Mars Attacks!* and *Men in Black* which 'gained ironic energy from a certain nostalgia for earlier [science fiction] films' at a time when the genre 'seemed in general to look backward more than forward'.

However, to say that the genre 'in general' looked to the past rather than attempting to try something different appears to be an understatement. In fact, since 2001 there have been at least thirty remakes, homages and adaptations of classic science fiction film and television produced by Hollywood, indicating not only a sense of generic exhaustion but perhaps, more ominously, a sense of cultural obsolescence. Take the 2008 *Death Race* as an example. A remake of the 1975 exploitation film *Death Race 2000,* this version purposely distanced itself from the political undertones of the original and instead emphasised the spectacular nature of the supercharged racing cars and their edgy male drivers and sexy female navigators. Whereas the original, in the contexts of the political and economic unrest of the 1970s, used spectacle and violence to critique the power of the media and the notion of celebrity, *Death Race* seemingly ignores the politics and aims for the lowest from of entertainment: blood, boobs and bangs. A diluted storyline about how the organiser of the race needed to frame the best NASCAR driver for murder so that he could race for her in prison and help boost ratings offered little in the way of a searing indictment of the media. Similarly, many of the recent remakes and homages to previous texts have dropped the overt social and political messages of the former only to replace them with more special effects. *Rollerball* of 2002 shares very little with its older relative and instead appears to celebrate and revel in the violence depicted on screen rather than critique it. A remake of *Logan's Run* is currently in production.

Other remakes including *The Day the Earth Stood Still* (2008), *War of the Worlds* (2005), *The Invasion* (2007) (based on *Invasion of the Body Snatchers*), *I Am Legend* (2007) (links to *The Omega Man* as well as the book) and *The Stepford Wives* (2004) seemingly ditch the dark cynicism and negativism of their originals, replacing it in some cases with over-the-top humour and special effects. I would argue that perhaps only *The Stepford Wives* managed to do something original with the text, continuing to offer an assessment of defined gender roles in American society albeit in the differing contexts of George W. Bush's administration and its neoconservative agenda. In the absence of the Cold War contexts, *The Day the Earth Stood Still, The Invasion* and *War of the Worlds* rely heavily on the primacy of the individual and his or her relationship to wider society, the first feature offering a comment on the nature of being human, with a thinly veiled critique of our continued ignorance of environmental issues, and the second two examining the notion of family. One could argue that alien invaders in these films are there only to add a sense of peril, rather than being a metaphor for any specific enemy, race or people. However, press coverage at the time of *War of the Worlds'* release reported that its director, Steven Spielberg, was drawing direct parallels between the events of 9/11 and the marauding alien machines attacking innocent American civilians. As Lester D. Friedman (2006: 158) points out, 'the film incorporates tropes from and direct references to the traumatic event, including Ray [Tom Cruise] being covered in ashes, sleeper units mobilizing, and Rachel's [Dakota Fanning] question, "Is it terrorists?"' Yet Friedman also posits a counter-narrative that still fits within the contexts of a post-9/11 world and acknowledges the continued relevance of both Wells's original critique of imperialism and the genre's power to offer timely comment:

> Spielberg provides dramatic examples of what it must have been like for Iraqi civilians during the American invasion/liberation of their country. The "shock and awe" created by the aliens in *War of the Worlds* resembles the panic generated by the American military more than it does the devastating, but as yet singular, attack on the World Trade Center. In essence, the film asks us to consider what it would feel like to be at war with a country stronger and technologically more advanced than the United States, one bent on our destruction. (Friedman 2006: 159)

Monster movies *Cloverfield* (2008) and *The Mist* (2007) follow in science fiction's nostalgic turn; however, both offer more nihilistic visions of humanity on the brink of destruction. In *Cloverfield* New York is attacked by a gigantic four-legged creature; no human weapons can stop it and nobody knows its origins. A group of young friends celebrating a birthday party attempt to record their journey to the other side of the city to rescue one of their missing number—the whole movie is shot on a digital camera from the point of view of the male protagonist. Instead of providing a happy ending, the film has the reunited friends caught escaping in an army helicopter by the monster, the abandoned camera serving as the last and only record of who they were, what they were trying to do and how they died. Further meditations on the futility of human existence and the loneliness of death can be seen in *The Mist,* based on a Stephen King story, where alien creatures from another dimension enter our world through a portal accidentally opened by the military and overrun a New England town. Trapped in the local supermarket, surrounded by a thick mist that hides the true nature and number of the hideous creatures outside, surviving townsfolk speculate on whether they should attempt an escape or wait for help. As time passes, divisions start to form amongst the group, eventually culminating in a violent and bloody showdown between a few who want to leave and the majority that believes the creatures have been sent by God as a punishment for humanity's sins. The film's shocking final twist sees the group of five moderate survivors run out of fuel when escaping by car on the highway. Not wanting to be eaten by the creatures lurking in the mist they make a suicide pact with the male protagonist agreeing to shoot the other four—including his son—as there are only four bullets left. Immediately after the father has executed the plan the mist clears to reveal that the army had arrived to clear out the creatures and rescue the town. The father's horror at having just shot his son for no reason is intensified as he notices one of the survivors going by on the trucks is a woman he had earlier refused to leave the supermarket with to help find her family. This final scene is replete with irony and as such is reminiscent of the dystopian science fiction films of the 1970s and evocative of the anthology television format of the 1950s and 1960s.

Adaptations and film versions of science fiction literature and television also proved popular, with multiple comic book movies being released over a short space of time. *Get Smart* (2008) and *Transformers* (2007) revelled in 1960s and 1980s nostalgia, turning the spy and children's animated series into special effects blockbusters. With *Transformers* (see boxed text) the fact that it was based on a once maligned and cheaply produced cartoon did not seem to dampen the excitement or anticipation of seeing how giant transforming robots could be realised on the big screen. *The X-Files: I Want to Believe* (2008), a follow-up to the 1998 film, tried to reignite the intrigue surrounding the relationship between Mulder and Scully as they investigate strange occurrences and government cover-ups. *AVP: Alien vs. Predator* (2004) and *AVPR: Alien vs. Predator—Requiem* (2007), based on the popular graphic novel series that brought the two infamous alien monsters together during the 1980s and 1990s, relied heavily on the familiar images of face-huggers and gory set pieces of the original four films to draw the audience's attention, rather than attempt to recreate the atmospheric tension and suspense.

Poor scripts and design choices aside, the budding new franchise of Alien/Predator crossovers shows how important comic books, specifically superhero comics, and graphic novels have been to the continued existence of the genre in the new millennium. *Superman Returns* (2006), the *X-Men* (2000, 2003, 2006) and *Spider-Man*

(2002, 2004, 2007) trilogies, *Fantastic Four* (2005), *Fantastic Four: Rise of the Silver Surfer* (2007), *Hulk* (2003), *The Incredible Hulk* (2008) and *Iron Man* (2008) all signal a renewed interest in the superhero narrative and 'the role of the saviour and the status of atonement in a modern, scientific post-Copernican cosmos' (Roberts 2005: 326). Indeed, the adaptations *The League of Extraordinary Gentlemen* (2003) and *V for Vendetta* (2006) not only bring to life the popular graphic novel texts but also pay homage to classic horror and science fiction literary characters such as Captain Nemo, Dr. Jekyll and Mr. Hyde, the Invisible Man and dystopian novels such as Aldous Huxley's *Brave New World* (1932) and George Orwell's *Nineteen Eighty-Four* (1949).

One way we might begin to understand this shift from narrative to spectacle in Hollywood science fiction film, besides dismissing it as symptomatic of a loss of originality and creativity, is through the work of Alison McMahan. In McMahan's analysis of director Tim Burton and his films, she calls for a reappraisal of Hollywood, stating that we should be aware of the 'pataphysical way' films are now made. Critics are keen to pour scorn on the plethora of remakes, adaptations and sequels that fill the multiplexes, but they forget that films are produced in cycles and the return to a 'cinema of spectacle' (akin to the work done by Tom Gunning on the cinema of attractions) means we must learn a new language to understand the 'new system of meanings' these films contain (McMahan 2005: 2). For McMahan, 'filmic narration is changing, though not in a direction without filmic precedent' (1), therefore we must remember that within the history of film there have been periods when the current status quo in production and style has been questioned and judgements of taste and value have been made on new and developing forms of filmmaking. In the current period of Hollywood production, pataphysical films (films that have lost their meaning and acquired new meanings—shifting from the traditional classical Hollywood narrative) have common characteristics. They 'make fun of established systems of knowledge, especially academic and scientific'; 'follow an alternative narrative logic'; 'use special effects in a "gee whiz," that is, blatant, visible way (as compared to "invisible" effects that stimulate live action, but without real harm to the actors)'; 'feature thin plots and thinly drawn characters, because the narrative relies more on the intertextual, nondiegetic references to be understood' (3). These films make up a new genre, one which precludes notions of judgement and taste and is 'applied retrospectively' to films from the last two decades that have been traditionally derided as 'bad' or 'unoriginal' (15). The CGI-heavy films discussed so far, and yet to come, can all be retrospectively termed *pataphysical* then, in so far as

> the main characteristic of a pataphysical film is its dependence on special effects, whether digital or mechanical…With this reliance on effects usually comes a change in narration and a flattening of the emotional aspects of the characters. It is primarily because of the change in narration and characters that critics deride pataphysical films, with the most common critique being that they are more about style than meaning. (McMahan 2005: 15)

Something to also consider when discussing recent science fiction blockbusters and their concomitant franchises is the notion of cross media convergence—something to which I will return when discussing contemporary television—and the point that McMahan raises about pataphysical films being made specifically with extra nonfilmic media in mind. As outlined already in this book, the history of the cult fan experience can be directly linked to the continued growth and popularity of the genre on both film and television. How science fiction is consumed by its audience is central to how it is understood as a genre and a series of texts and interexts. Pataphysical films, according to McMahan, tap into this sense of intertextuality and audience awareness in that

> few contemporary films are meant to be standalone texts, but rather intermediate texts, drawing meaning from and feeding meaning into other media forms such as commercials, print ads, television shows, previous and later films, comic books, games (both board and computer), novels and other books, magazines, newspapers, the web, paintings, music videos—in other words, whatever is out there. (McMahan 2005: 16)

As the rest of this book will draw out, science fiction film and television can no longer be simply defined as forms unto themselves or each other, but their construction of meaning relies on the multiple intertexts and other media forms with which fans are familiar and regularly use in an ever-changing, technological world (see Jenkins 2006).

Homage and nostalgia for past times continue in the recent *Sky Captain and the World of Tomorrow* (2004) and the B-movie *Eight Legged Freaks* (2002). In both, there is a distinct appreciation for a 1940s and 1950s film aesthetic. *Sky Captain* was filmed entirely using green screen so that a parallel 1940s Earth could be painted in behind the actors. Directly harking back to sci-fi and adventure serials of the 1940s, the film uses CGI technology and digital animation to paint a picture of a retrofuture—even going to the extreme lengths of resurrecting old footage of Laurence Olivier to play the evil mad scientist. *Eight Legged Freaks* plays on the nature run amok motif of the 1950s, with giant mutant spiders rampaging and terrorising small-town America. *Children of Men* (2006), although clearly following in the tradition of British dystopian films such as *1984* (1956, 1984) and *Brazil* (1985), as well as the nihilistic urban features typical of 1970s American science fiction, uses the subtlety of slight CGI changes to the buildings, billboards, television screens, road signs and shop fronts of London in the near future to offer a retrovision of a decaying city. *WALL-E* (2008), the Pixar computer-generated animation feature about the last waste disposal robot left on Earth of the future, goes to great lengths to depict human waste and detritus in minute detail. With knowing references to numerous science fiction films including *2001, Short Circuit, Tron, Soylent Green, The Omega Man* and indeed *I Am Legend,* the film uses effects technology in such a way so as to provide a revisioning of multiple genre texts and tropes. These examples conform to Michele Pierson's (2002: 136) assessment of late twentieth-century science fiction

TRANSFORMERS (2007)

The Steven Spielberg-produced and Michael Bay-directed live-action *Transformers* was a prime example of Hollywood's fascination with resurrecting old franchises to bolster flagging box office returns. Based on a Saturday morning cartoon series which ran from 1984 to 1987, itself based on a Japanese toy line of transforming robots, *Transformers* reimagined old characters using the latest in CGI technology and special effects. Part of the appeal of the original television series for children was its endless production line of new merchandise; Transformers became the toy every boy wanted for Christmas. For Timothy Burke and Kevin Burke, in their nostalgic look back at the Saturday morning TV shows they watched when growing up, the series was just one out of a dozen cartoons that tried to cash in on the merchandising market. For them toy companies like Mattel and Hasbro, through series such as *He-Man and the Masters of the Universe* (1983–1985), *She-Ra: Princess of Power* (1985), *The Care Bears* (1985–1988), and *M.A.S.K* (1985–1986), were merely trying to copy the success of Kenner's *Star Wars* action figures by establishing and sustaining a market where the TV show acted as an extended commercial for the line of figures, robots, plush dolls and toy sets that were being produced cheaply in Asia and being sold in America (Burke and Burke 1999: 57–8). Bay's blockbuster was clearly intended to do the same, attracting a new generation of kids to persuade their parents to buy the latest versions of the transforming robot toys.

Ensuring there would be an audience and merchandising market seemed to be the driving force behind the creative team's decision to go for all out spectacle towards the climax of the film. However, the film can be split thematically into two halves: the first has a narrative familiar to many Spielberg science fiction films: a disaffected teenager befriends a group of friendly extraterrestrials and in helping them becomes a responsible adult; the second half is more definitely in the style of Bay, with explosions and digital effects serving to bedazzle the audience even if they really don't add to the overall narrative. It is this second feature of the film which has attracted most criticism and which leaves Mark Bould (2008a: 167) in no doubt that 'digital filmmaking on this scale has produced a regime in which signification is more important than coherence'. For Bould, *Transformers* is an exemplar of current science fiction film's tendency to overload on digital effects—action is fast and frenetic, metal clashes with metal, in an attempt to show off to the audience just how far digital effects technology has developed. Yet this only serves to illustrate 'there is nothing of substance, merely a mastery of technique' (166). His reading of the story and main characters is not any better: 'Bay brings to the film precisely what one would expect:... [a] shockingly poor taste in soft-rock...an inability to imagine women...homoerotism...concealed homosexual panic...jingoism and cynical patriotism...racist stereotypes" (165), and the list goes on. One might agree with such a severe reading, but doing so ignores the more touching and significant scenes clearly inspired by Steven Spielberg's canon of work.

The main human protagonist is Sam Witwicky (played by Shia LaBeouf), who lives a middle-class existence in the Los Angeles suburbs with his parents. The usual teen angst and trouble with girls occupies Sam, and his relationship with his father is typically tense as he struggles to live up to parental expectations. Sam's life changes when he befriends the first Autobot visitor, Bumblebee, and through their bond Sam learns how to take responsibility for his actions. The changed Sam impresses his father, and the two share a new-found respect for each other by the end of the film. This father–son narrative is a perennial favourite of Spielberg's and connects *Transformers* to his past suburban science fiction films such as *E.T.* and *Close Encounters*. These two films were cathartic projects, made to 're-create Spielberg's boyhood home in suburbia and attempt to overcome the shattering of that idyllic existence caused by his parent's divorce' (Gordon 2008: 267), and in that sense *Transformers* is very much a film that reflects his attention to the personal and sentimental, not just the spectacular. The choice of LaBeouf further underscores this nostalgic picture, as he plays the lead in the suburban thriller *Disturbia* (2007) and by the time *Transformers* was released he had been chosen to play Indiana Jones's son in the fourth feature of the franchise, *Indiana Jones and the Kingdom of the Crystal Skull* (2008). In both films LaBeouf plays a teenage delinquent who grows up and takes on the mantle of responsibility; for the latter role, this means becoming the new Indiana Jones, in itself a character that symbolizes a bygone age of daring-do and heroism. While these intertextual references help us to identify familiar character motifs and narrative themes in Spielberg's films, they also highlight contemporary Hollywood's penchant for returning to tried and tested methods of storytelling. Spielberg's other genre films post-2000—*A.I.: Artificial Intelligence* (2001), *Minority Report* (2002) and *War of the Worlds*—rely on strong parent–child, children in peril narratives.

Leaving Bould's and my own disparate critiques aside, what is more interesting to analyse, and perhaps offers us alternative ways of reading the film, is the reception it received from the audience. Online fan discourses surrounding the authenticity, cultural worth and aesthetics of the movie before its release were both heated and imaginative. Such debate was centred on the premise that a reworking of what was once a favourite childhood cartoon series and toy line challenged the fans' own authentic appreciation of a franchise to which they had remained loyal since the 1980s. As adults, now collecting the merchandise long after it had stopped being made (purchasing toys on eBay, at conventions, through fan clubs), they continued to share in their memorialisation of the mythos surrounding the series by re-watching the cartoons on DVD and participating in online blogs and Web chats that follow similar patterns of induction into an exclusive cult community such as can be seen with fans of *Star Trek* and *Star Wars*.

The cultural and personal value that the cartoon series and toys still held with fans was under threat by what was seen as an unwanted blockbuster version of the Transformers brand. Bay's attempt at revamping their favourite toy for modern mainstream cinema screens was seen as an affront to the cult status Transformers accrues both online and at conventions. In opposition to the film, fans produced and uploaded their own fake trailers and outtake scenes on YouTube, poking fun at the live-action nature of the film and the directorial talents of Bay, who they saw as potentially ruining the film on evidence of his other blockbuster flops such as *Pearl Harbor* (2001) and *The Island* (2005). In one fake trailer, the end of the original teaser trailer seen in cinemas is altered so that after the title and release date come up the words transform into a turd, the slogan underneath saying 'Another piece of shit from Michael Bay'. While some fans appreciated the fact that their much-loved but lampooned series was finally getting the cultural and blockbuster recognition they thought it deserved, such vociferous online fan activity intimates a deeply hierarchical and systematized structure of subcultural taste and political discourse. This discourse is rooted in the personal value fans have attached to the Transformers toy and cartoon series. Bay's *Transformers* posed both as a threat to the values and tastes that had been built up around the franchise and as a sign of Hollywood's continued fascination with resurrecting multimedia franchises. More generally, the debate prompted by Bay's adaptation highlights the persistent power of generic canons, authenticity, and aesthetic value in science fiction fan communities and how they contribute to the creation and fragmentation of fan identity and culture.

features in that the 'computer-generated special effects had ceased to figure…as objects of curiosity and wonder'. They are retrovisions, 'a "vision into or of the past" and [imply] an act of possessing the ability to read the past, in the way that one would possess a prophetic vision' (Neely 2001: 74). For Deborah Cartmell and I. Q. Hunter (2001: 7) retrovisions are 'makeovers of history', and as such these films imagine a future based on intertextual references to their generic predecessors and the visual look of the past.

Television and Intertextuality

Perhaps the relative failure of *The X-Files* spin-off *The Lone Gunmen* (2001) signalled a shift in attitudes at the end of TV's period of paranoia; specific reference to conspiracy and political intrigue directly relating to government cover-ups and corruption proved unpalatable for audiences already on edge at the turn of the millennium. However, the predictive nature of the science fiction genre clearly indicates how even some of the least successful series are still important texts that need consideration if we want to understand the full range of science fiction on television. For example, the pilot episode of *The Lone Gunmen* sees the trio of computer hackers first introduced in *The X-Files* uncover a plot to plant a bomb on a commercial airplane and fly it into the World Trade Center. Such parallels to real life events ultimately proved too hard to watch, and the series was cancelled after thirteen episodes.

Although British science fiction television seemed to have disappeared in the 1990s, American series continued to keep foreign audiences entertained. British science fiction comedy, however, was a favourite in America, with *Red Dwarf* (1988–1999) producing some of its best material in the mid-1990s alongside the American series *3rd Rock from the Sun* (1996–2001). The success of the genre hybrid sci-fi comedy has inspired more recent UK series like *Spaced* (1999–2001) and *Hyperdrive* (2006–present) as well as examples from the world of film such as *Shaun of the Dead* (2004). *Spaced* is clearly on the one hand a traditional sitcom, yet its positioning of science fiction fandom, particularly *Star Wars* fandom, lends it a certain intertextuality that references both the George Lucas text and the enormous fan base surrounding it. Will Brooker discusses Simon Pegg's role as Tim, the archetypal middle-age *Star Wars* fan, in conjunction with the release of *The Phantom Menace* and the mass backlash against the film from those fans who saw it as childish and hollow. Scenes between Tim and his flatmate Daisy, where they talk about how bad the film was, are interwoven with fantasy scenes that depict Tim dressed up as Luke Skywalker burning his *Star Wars* collectibles in a form of silent protest toward Lucas. Brooker calls this an example of the series's 'dual address' whereby it speaks to the popular audience of the time and offers a more subversive reading to those fans who are able to understand the reference within the joke and sympathise with Tim, and also Pegg (Brooker 2002: 79–85). Pegg as intertextual referent occurs in *Shaun of the Dead* too as he reprises the archetypal role of middle-age cult fan and uses his knowledge of zombie horror films to help him and his friends escape hordes of zombies in the streets of London. The trend for knowing, postmodern self-parody is illustrated with aplomb in the animated *Futurama* (1999–2003). The series combined genre and parody while offering a critique of contemporary culture and the technologies that continue to mediate that culture. It reused and reinvented many of the tropes and icons of science fiction but also emulated television's fondness for self-reflection, hybridity and intertextuality.

Futurama played with form and genre for comic effect, yet its intertextual refer-encing of previous science fiction and animation highlighted a fundamental interest in genre history. Genres, by their very nature, 'are related to the processes of remem-bering and forgetting…[they] operate to produce a sense of the past' as they cross between different forms of visual media (Geraghty and Jancovich 2008: 12). In this sense, *Futurama* was not just an 'anicom', to use Nichola Dobson's term (2003: 85), which parodied prior texts and popular culture; it created and contributed to the lin-eage and development of the science fiction genre and drew attention to the cultural processes through which generic definitions and iconic representations are made. As genres develop, according to Dan Harries, they are 'constantly in need of redefini-tion', thus parody 'typically emerges when the dynamic nature of the logonomic system [tradition of previous texts and established conventions]' becomes exhausted (Harries 2000: 37). However, parodies not only serve to reinvigorate genres but also reaffirm them and 'reconstitute as they deflate their targets' (King 2002: 114). This is best exemplified in the episodes that parodied *Star Trek,* such as 'Why Must I Be a Crustacean in Love?' (2000) and 'Where No Fan Has Gone Before' (2002), where in both *Futurama* clearly acknowledged the cultural significance of the venerable sci-ence fiction series but poked fun at its ancestor's repetitive storylines, cardboard sets, unconvincing aliens, and sometimes overzealous fans. 'Why Must I Be a Crustacean in Love?' paid tribute to the famous scene from 'Amok Time' (1967), when Spock challenges Kirk to a duel to the death, by pitting Fry and Dr. Zoidberg against each other. However, instead of using the same music and weapons as in the original, the familiar duel melody is played as Zoidberg's national anthem, and both combatants decide not to use the Vulcan *lirpa* (pugil sticks). In 'Where No Fan Has Gone Before' Fry determines to retrieve the original 79 *Star Trek* episode tapes that were banished to a forbidden planet when the Church of Trek was outlawed in the twenty-third century. In trying to justify why they should break the law, Fry exclaims to Leela that 'The world needs *Star Trek* to give people hope for the future', after which she replies, 'But it's set 800 years in the past!' Of course, *Star Trek* is not the only text that *Futurama* emphasizes or parodies. The series is in itself a hybrid text that draws together intertextual elements from science fiction, comedy, horror, melodrama and wider popular culture.

Hybridity and intertextuality are common features of contemporary television programming. Jason Mittell (2004: xii–xiii) believes 'cases of mixture often fore-ground generic conventions even more than "core" examples of a genre, as often unstated generic assumptions rise to the surface through textual juxtapositions, production decisions, and reception controversies'. Indeed, the medium of tele-vision 'brings intertextuality to us' through its televisual flow of multiple texts: from the actual programmes to the commercial breaks. As different texts jostle to get the viewer's attention, multiplied by the increase in digital and satellite channels, the boundaries between texts and their interpretations remain open and incomplete—leaving room for exploitation, reinflection and parodic subversion (Gray 2006: 78–9).

Futurama's interest in the televisual flow and actual process of watching and inter-acting with multiple television texts—for example the numerous television parodies, Fry continually watching or referring to TV, and the many fake promo-spots that interrupt the before and after credits—is emblematic of contemporary television's hyper-intertextuality. Bogus adverts for products such as Molten Boron, Arachno Spores, Thompson's Teeth or Glagnar's Human Rinds that supposedly sponsor some of the aired episodes not only visually call attention to the genre and futuristic setting but also to the format and processes of television broadcasting and its financing.

The generic hybrid *Smallville* (2001–present), first aired on the youth-orientated WB Network, took the traditional Superman story and turned it into an American teen action drama about Clark Kent's life at high school before he donned the fa-mous blue tights and red cape. Instead of seeing Superman take on super criminals in Metropolis, the audience got to see how he first developed his powers and learned to cope with girls, school and teenage angst. Without his fancy costume *Smallville* showed Superman as a vulnerable and innocent teenager. The series was just as much a teen melodrama as a science fiction or fantasy action serial. Although largely over-looked by critics—many Superman fans saw it as too far a departure from the comic book canon—its similarities to previous teen television like *Dawson's Creek* and *Roswell* endeared the Superman story to a whole new generation of viewers. The set-ting, style, narrative and cast of fresh-faced actors suggested that the Superman story was not only ready for a televisual makeover but also still relevant for a post-9/11 American audience. In a sense, the regression back from the big city (Metropolis) to small-town life (Smallville) attests to the major impact 9/11 had on the Ameri-can psyche. The reinvention of America's most famous superhero was a cathartic act, representative of television's return to innocence in times of political and social uncertainty.

What these recent series all illustrate is the genre's propensity for self-reflexivity. Post-9/11 visual media have undergone a shift in perspective as film and television increasingly look back on the past for a sense of familiarity and reassurance—to an age where political enemies and national threats were clearly identifiable. In today's climate of terrorism and violence perpetrated by a faceless enemy targeting civil-ians as well as the military, audiences are drawn to film and television that offer recognizable visions of the past, present and future. *Smallville,* along with *Star Trek: Enterprise* (2001–2005), *Firefly* (2002–2003), *Heroes* (2006–present), *Battlestar Galactica* (2003–2009), *Mutant X* (2001–2004), *Dark Angel* (2000–2002), *Termina-tor: The Sarah Connor Chronicles* (2008–present), *Bionic Woman* (2007–2008) and UK series such as the animated *Captain Scarlet* (2005), *Doctor Who* (2005–present), *Primeval* (2007–present), *Life on Mars* (2006–2007), *Ashes to Ashes* (2008–2009) and to a certain extent *Farscape* (1999–2003), all have used the notion of the past or revised the narrative history of their predecessors to establish new stories and timelines—reworking familiar cultural myths and implanting them in a post-9/11 landscape. 'Unreality TV', a term used in the British *Radio Times*'s feature on

Heroes, has become 'the defining trend in television today', where established rules of small-screen drama have been 'replaced by flights of fancy, leaps of imagination and a collective suspension of disbelief' (Naughton 2007: 14). Aspects of these new series are familiar, as they are either based on established franchises or follow recognizable formats like those of the superhero comic book or the alien invasion narrative as seen in *Invasion* (2005–2006), yet they are infused with a sense of unease—the audience does not know and cannot guess the outcome of stories, and it is as if the writers and producers don't really know either. *Lost* (2004–present), with twists and turns that keep fans awake all night blogging on the Internet, maintains a feeling beyond the obvious paranoia of *The X-Files.* Indeed, Jason Mittell describes it as 'probably one of the least "generic" shows appearing on commercial television', and as such it attracts fans familiar with many different genres, films and TV and who do not necessarily understand it as one particular genre over another (Mittell 2008: 11). Science fiction has entwined itself further with fantasy to produce television that 'has never been more now...never more real' (McLean 2007).

Starting Over

Battlestar Galactica (*BSG*) (see boxed text) is one of many extinct science fiction series to undergo a refit on twenty-first century television. With a renewed focus on the fundamental nature of what it means to be human, *BSG* peeled back the superficial layers of special effects and techno-babble associated with long-running franchises like *Star Trek* and instead focused on what science fiction does best—offer a window on the human condition. For C. W. Marshall and Tiffany Potter (2008: 6) *BSG* did not offer American audiences a salve for the psychological wounds inflicted after 9/11; rather it commented on 'contemporary culture by imaging dystopic alternatives, and by doing so it invites the viewer to interrogate notions of self, nation, and belief that are often taken to be nonnegotiable both on television and in our living rooms'. As part of the new generation of science fiction television it not only visualised other worlds and alien species but it also managed

> to use those fantastic visions, in one of the abiding traditions of science fiction, to interrogate our own nature and our own condition, particularly as we confront an age in which history seems to have lost much of its relevance, the future is mysterious, and our humanity is often perceived as just a construct of various forces beyond our full understanding and control. (Telotte 2008a: 26)

Similar to *BSG,* the ever-popular *Doctor Who* underwent changes to its traditional narrative that both acknowledged its roots in the old series and reflected developments in British television drama inspired by American series like *24* (2001–present), *CSI: Crime Scene Investigation* (2000–present) as well as *Buffy* and *The X-Files* that

BATTLESTAR GALACTICA (2003–2009)

Battlestar Galactica can be described as a vindication of a series long gone; it is, after all, a remake of the original 1970s series, which was very much a product of its time, both narratively and visually. However, the modern *Battlestar Galactica* is far more a product of modern television programming than it is a throwback to what was called by Ed Siegel of the *Boston Globe* 'the worst science fiction show ever' (Siegel cited in Javna 1987: 85) or, somewhat more harshly by Stephen King, as a 'deep-space turkey' (1993: 273). Although the original series was intended as long-running televisual alternative to the effects-laden spectacle of *Star Wars,* what it actually became was an over-hyped short serial that had to come to a conclusion quickly before cancellation could prematurely call an end to the Galactica's journey to find Earth. By the time Adama and his crew did reach their new home in the spin-off series *Galactica 1980* (1980) audiences were so unconvinced of the plot and cardboard characters that the series died before producers could even finish their episode run—it lasted half a season, six hour-long episodes. Effectively, thanks to production values that promised groundbreaking special effects but instead delivered the same recycled fight sequences week after week and the fact that the whole premise of the story implied a natural end to the series when humans eventually found Earth, the original *Battlestar Galactica* satisfies Glen Creeber's criteria for a serial rather than a long-running series in that it was 'A story set over a number of episodes that…comes to a conclusion in the final instalment (even if a sequel follows)' (Creeber 2004: 8).

In contrast, *Battlestar Galactica* of the present day displayed its serial/mini-series credentials openly. Brought back to our screens in 2003 as a two-part mini-series for Sky TV in the UK and then aired on the Sci Fi channel in America, *Battlestar* was conceived and advertised as a must-see television event that not only breathed life into a so-called TV classic but also catered for domestic satellite and cable networks like Sky and Sci Fi Channel who 'function as television *boutiques:* venues offering a limited array of products for specialized audiences' (Kompare 2005: 172). After attracting a sizeable audience interested once again in the story of humanity on the edge of extinction, producers got the go-ahead to make a limited run of thirteen episodes that allowed for the opportunity to make more, if successful. Not only was *Battlestar Galactica*'s format redesigned for modern television audiences, now familiar with and attracted to the concept of must-see TV, a phrase coined to aid the rebranding of NBC's identity and prime time programming output in the 1990s (see San Martín 2003), it also employed more soap opera techniques such as 'flexi-narrative' (where the overall story takes place within 'a complex exchange of narrative and character' development) and 'experimental techniques' (where 'definitions of social reality can be and are increasingly called into question'), both indicative of 'the breakdown between the traditional series and serial' (Creeber 2004: 12). As Creeber notes,

> Not surprisingly, then, the employment of "soap opera" techniques has become a convenient means by which contemporary social realism attempts to re-articulate and re-examine the "psychological" depiction of character. In this context, the "soap operaisation" of long-form television drama should not be conceived purely as a move away from the "social" and the "political" towards the "personal" and the "trivial", but as a gradual progression towards newer forms of representation which offer an arguably more contemporary articulation of present social experience. (Creeber 2004: 13)

Put another way, *Battlestar Galactica*'s rebirth as a long-form serial, whose narrative structure dictates an eventual end once humans find Earth, means that far more attention is paid to the characterisation and representation of the relationships between humans and Cylons, or political and personal conflicts between the military and government, rather than adhering to a preset narrative history as seen in *Star Trek: Enterprise*. Applying recent work done by Angela Ndalianis on the contemporary television series, I would call *Battlestar Galactica* a 'neo-baroque' series, whereby the narrative draws 'the audience into potentially infinite or, at least, multiple directions that rhythmically recall what Focillon labels the "system of the series", or the "system of the labyrinth"' (Ndalianis 2005: 87). Offering interwoven plots, characters, back stories, spin-offs such as *Razor* (2007) and previously unseen footage (through the cross-media form of the webisodes which fills in back story to bigger plot elements seen in the series), *Battlestar Galactica* fits with contemporary television's tendency to not only rely on the weekly episode but to build narrative suspense and fan loyalty through the multiplication of formats offered by media convergence (TV, Internet, comics, DVD): 'Cross-media narrativisation are, in some instances, becoming important disseminators of story information within the franchise as it disperses its form not only across the series of its own medium, but across multiple media' (Ndalianis 2005: 99).

Other current science fiction series, *Heroes* and *Lost* for example, follow in this trend toward narrative complexity (*Heroes* also had a series of comic book webisodes made) and further locate the genre as postmodern and cult. Charles Tryon (2008: 306) sees this development 'as a sign of realism' which can be linked with quality programming. Furthermore, Glen Creeber (2008: 57), in his short analysis of *Heroes,* posits that because of its very nature as a postmodern series it 'tends to problematise any fixed notion of the real…In a postmodern world, the notion of a fixed and authentic self is called into question, the breakdown of traditional subject positions (based on nationhood, sexuality, race and even gender) becoming increasing [sic] unstable'. In *Battlestar Galactica,* this breakdown is most obvious in the relationship between humans and Cylons, where the Cylons are flesh and blood and their existence questions perceptions of human identity and our relationship with technology.

Returning to realism, reimagined series such as *Battlestar Galactica* are far grittier than their forbearers. For example, it does not hide its allusions to the events of 9/11, America's War on Terror and the military occupation of Afghanistan and Iraq. In the episode '33' (2005) corridors of the ship have become makeshift shrines to the missing and dead of the Twelve Colonies after the Cylon's nuclear attack; the walls of the ship are adorned with messages and pictures resembling the scenes at Ground Zero when people stuck up posters and pictures to help find their loved ones. In the third season episode 'Precipice' (2006), those humans left on occupied New Caprica use guerrilla tactics and suicide bombings to attack and kill the Cylons and their human collaborators. Such actions force the audience to momentarily sympathise with those we would normally consider terrorists, our enemies in America's War on Terror, thus problematising our conceptions of right and wrong, civilised and barbaric.

The series, with its emphasis on the seriality of a compact plot (a fleet of humans search for Earth while being pursued and infiltrated by Cylons that look human), makes direct links to contemporary political events. However, the design and mise en scéne of the series borrows heavily from today, with characters opening hinged doors, listening to popular music on radios, and talking on phones with cords. These visual clues to the show's real-life production contexts are central to *Battlestar Galactica*'s engagement with current political, social and philosophical issues. However, according to Dylan Pank and John Caro (2009: 203), realism in the series not only relies on allusions to our news but 'is suggested by techniques more familiar to the "earthbound" crime genre: handheld cameras, urgent refocusing, whip-pans, tight framing, and the low-key, underexposed lighting suggested by practical sources'. Reality is constructed in such a way that, as the executive producers Ronald D. Moore and David Eick first intended, it is possible for the series to be viewed as a contemporary drama rather than traditional science fiction television associated with space operas such as *Star Trek*.

It is important to note that much is made of the original series, including the familiar Viper fighters, pilots' call-signs, and nostalgic reuse of the old theme tune by Stu Phillips as heard in the episode 'Final Cut' (2005), yet this history does not stand in the way of potential story development and complex characterisation. In fact, even though the series had an inevitable end in sight because of the nature of its narrative, *Galactica* was not constrained by its format. Episodes in the first season start with a recapping of events seen in the 2003 mini series: the destruction of Caprica, the attack on the Galactica and fleet, the rise of the human Cylons; history is routinely repeated in a series of flashbacks, which is typical of most popular television serials. As Sarah Kozloff (1992: 91–2) notes, 'Because serials progress from week to week, they face special dilemmas. First, they must bring up to date viewers who do not usually watch the show or who have missed an episode...Second, serials must generate enough viewer interest and involvement to survive their hiatus.' *Galactica's* cliffhangers and flashforwards worked well to ensure this. *Galactica* uses both—the hype surrounding the coming of season four testified to the immense popularity of the series—yet its use of flash-forwards at the beginning of each episode, after the initial flashbacks to the mini series and previous episodes, also built up audience expectation and contributed to the must-see appeal of the series as a whole. While flashbacks represent history, grounding each episode in a back story (in terms of *Enterprise's* opening credits, the back story was the history of flight), flashforwards created a sense of the 'perpetual return to the present' (Thornham and Purvis 2005: 6) that gave *Galactica* an epic quality: history, politics, life and death all wrapped up in a fast-paced, action montage.

Where *Enterprise's* attention to detail and depiction as holographic recreation transformed the show from futuristic series to somewhat unimposing historical play, *Galactica* was able to make much more of its serial quality by playing with the formats and conventions of modern television programming, as well as offering audiences intertextual references to its historical forbear. History is important to the series but not at the expense of continuing narratives and stories that grab the viewers' attention amidst the continual flow of television and also cater for cult fans' desire for facts and trivia.

'were notable for their self-consciousness, visual stylishness and re-imagining of established genres for a postmodern popular culture' (Chapman 2006: 185). Clearly Russell T. Davies, writer and producer, had to maintain the cult audience by following established norms and keeping favourites such as the TARDIS, but the new Doctor was reborn and his character fleshed out with a concentration on emotions and heroism that has never been seen before (Newman 2005: 115): 'The back story of [the new Doctor] thus locates him within a particular archetype of masculinity: the traumatised war veteran...racked by guilt over his inability to prevent the destruction of the Time Lords and holds himself responsible for what happened to them' (Chapman 2006: 190).

As science fiction television continues to sustain loyal cult fans while Hollywood film remains fixed on attracting an audience keen on spectacular thrills rather than intelligent drama, one might be keen to ask if there is a future for the genre. Television, despite the success of *BSG* and its contemporaries, is also competing with new media formats such as online video and downloads, which threaten to change how audiences watch both film and television at the cinema and at home. However, for the genre to survive on any of these new and increasingly popular formats, there might not be too much need for change while 'it offers the pleasures of excitement, fantasy and escape, [at the same time] grappling with some of the oldest questions about what it is to be human' (King and Krzywinska 2000: 58). Indeed, for as long as America doubts or questions the meaning of everyday life and the events which drive its history science fiction in any medium and on any format will continue to offer sanctuary and solace.

Epilogue
The Repeated Pleasures of
Science Fiction Film and Television

Both series like *Star Trek: Enterprise* and *Battlestar Galactica* offer expansive narrative worlds in which viewers, particularly those defined as cult fans, can engross themselves. The television formats that support their production and reception—the episodic series and serial—provide fans with a template for viewing that helps to construct and map the contexts for their own personal appreciation and enjoyment. As the narrative world grows and the sheer number of episodes increase, the potential for facts and trivia also increases as more plot points, characters and events are introduced. Like Sara Gwenllian-Jones and Roberta Pearson maintain, the segmentisation and repeated formats of science fiction television work alongside the narrative to offer multiple possibilities for the show and viewer: 'Seriality, textual density, and, perhaps most especially, the nonlinerarity of multiple time frames and settings that create the potentially infinitely large metatext of a cult television text create the space for fans to revel' (Gwenllian-Jones and Pearson 2004: xvii). Coupled with this created space for fans is the notion of canonicity that becomes crucial to groups who share a passion for the same text but, within the same space, differ in their level of knowledge and memory of intricate details of plot and characterisation. In a sense, familiarity with the text and the recollection of facts and trivia as a form of power within a particular fan group is entirely bound up with narrative, fictional history and the formats of television that support the series: '[Possession of trivia] is therefore a form of cultural capital through which fandom is able [to] claim special access to, and knowledge of, specific texts and groups of texts and, in so doing, to make claims to ownership of them' (Hunt 2003: 198).

The concepts of trivia, ownership and science fiction television's episodic format are unavoidably affected by the new and developing technologies associated with video recording, collecting, and the DVD box set. While series like *Enterprise* and *Battlestar Galactica* garner cult followings through their original appearances on network and cable television, the potential for studios to capitalise on those growing markets increases through the lure of repeats, marathons and home video. Fans who want to enjoy the repeated pleasures of the series, without waiting for it to be repeated at the behest of the network, can either record the episodes they want to keep or go out and buy the entire series on DVD to watch whenever they want: 'This physical and cultural connection between television and home video enables people to use their sets to create or access programming on their own terms rather than stay locked to the fare and schedule dictated by the broadcasting industry' (Kompare 2006: 339). Separating the science fiction television series from the confines of a weekly episodic format enables viewers to construct their own narrative as they can watch episodes in whatever order they want, as many times as they want, and often with extras, deleted scenes and documentaries that add new readings and contexts to the viewing experience.

Moreover, the entire narrative history that can be created and maintained through the series/serial format, as I have already outlined with regard to *Battlestar Galactica,* is destabilised as the audience assumes control of their viewing contexts. Watching episodes out of order, viewing favourite episodes that bare no relation to the overarching chronological timeline or metanarrative or listening to directors' commentary upsets the flow of regular television that keeps the series locked in the viewer's present. The viewing contexts are changed in that the flow of adverts and network logos associated with the original screening are withdrawn and the series becomes a fixed text that can be accessed whenever required: 'The flow of television is not only measured in time but in physical commodities, as cultural objects placed in the permanent media collection alongside similarly mass-produced media artifacts' (Kompare 2006: 353). However, repeats and the DVD box set also situate the series in the past; the box set is an archive with added extras that locates the series in an altogether new history, a personal history: '[DVD], as a hybrid medium dedicated to reproducing an experience alien to it, standardizes, fragments, commodifies, objectifies, and segments that experience' (Tashiro 1991: 16). As I have already argued, science fiction television post-9/11 used history to tell a story and used the format of television to create a sense of unfolding narrative; the repeated pleasures of watching recorded or bought episodes in box sets creates another historical and narrative space detached from that seen on screen for the first time.

With science fiction television now located in a fixed, personal history attributed to individual fan taste and cultural memory, the collecting of associated merchandise like the DVD box set becomes part of the commodification and historicisation of culture. The episodic nature of science fiction television, and its reliance on and continued playing with pre-established narrative history, makes it an attractive and ideal form of cultural capital in which fans can invest. In her study of the home cinephile and video/DVD collector, Barbara Klinger (2006) intimates that the growth of home film cultures has had a positive effect on the once antagonistic relationship between the cinephile (a person who has a passion for film in its original exhibition contexts: projection in a dark theatre) and domestic viewing (the VCR/DVD on TV). New technologies that improve the quality and range of film and television texts that can be watched domestically have meant that it is possible for cinephiles to enjoy the object of their affection at home. Collecting has become even more important to those with a passion for film and television as more and more of their favourite texts can be bought, traded, and collected on formats that do not deteriorate. In addition, box sets in a fan's collection 'have become decorative additions to the chairs, tables, and carpets which form the familiar backdrop to their unfolding' (Tashiro 1996: 17). The domestic space becomes an archive of science fiction television that represents the accumulated cultural capital of a collector and acts as a historic signifier of the impact and influence of popular science fiction series: 'Ardent TV/video collectors are in many ways self-styled media historians, archivists dedicated to discovering and preserving remnants of television past and present' (Bjarkman 2004: 239).

Collecting science fiction series on DVD and video, plus the protectionism and established hierarchies associated with the acquisition of such media artefacts and trivia in fan communities, alludes to the 'masculinity of cult' as defined by Joanne Hollows (2003: 37) as the ways in which 'many of the key consumption practices that constitute cult fandom' (collecting, viewing, reading fanzines etc.) are natura-lised as masculine in opposition to the gendered femininity of the cultural main-stream (popular film and television). In distancing themselves from the 'feminine shopper' and adopting more 'assertively masculine' attitudes to consumption, those fans who collect box sets and interact with related visual products are participating in a collecting ritual that has historically been 'imagined as masculine' in comparison to the idea that women merely bought objects as part of routine and domesticated consumerism (46). Hollows and Klinger do make the case that 'the collector is [not] an "essentially" masculine figure' (Hollows 2003: 47) and that film and television collectors 'do not constitute a homogenous community' (Klinger 2006: 63); how-ever, the stereotype of the socially maladjusted bachelor still persists in science fic-tion fandom.

Through the ever-developing television market, fixed on niche audiences and qual-ity, short-run productions, science fiction has a solid future. New viewing technolo-gies such as digital television, webisodes, On Demand, TIVO and Sky Plus, where *your* TV can record programmes it feels *you* like, in addition to the fan-orientated DVD box set market, where every cult film or TV series ever produced can be bought and kept by enthusiasts and completists, ensure that the genre has an evolving, cross-generational audience that revels in current and old science fiction. With technology that allows viewers to revisit and relive childhood series from film and TV history, as well as watch new films and series that consistently refer back to the classics, science fiction on film and television continues to do what the genre does best: picture the future by questioning the past.

The various formats of serialised and episodic television not only help sustain the genre's reliance on history but they also amplify this combination by drawing the audience into a close relationship with the narrative. Serial narrative is the key element in science fiction's treatment of history. Over the weeks, months and years, television allows a story to be created, developed and concluded (sometimes left open), which speaks to the viewers' desires to see epic vistas of alien worlds and to become emotionally attached to characters with whom they are familiar. Science fiction film may use history as the background to its narratives, but rarely does it, or can it, address the epic nature of history and science fiction's multiple worlds or alien visions. Television and the innovative technologies associated with it offer new and repeating avenues to explore, new themes to address, and new worlds of which to imagine.

Bibliography

Abbott, Jon (2006), *Irwin Allen Television Productions, 1964–1970: A Critical History,* Jefferson: McFarland Publishers.

Altman, Rick (1999), *Film/Genre,* London: BFI.

Alvey, Mark (2007), ' "Too Many Kids and Old Ladies": Quality Demographics and 1960s U.S. Television', in Horace Newcomb (ed.), *Television: The Critical View,* New York: Oxford University Press.

Anderson, Craig W. (1985), *Science Fiction Film of the Seventies,* Jefferson: McFarland Publishers.

Ashley, Mike (2000), *The Time Machines: The Story of the Science-Fiction Pulp Magazines from the Beginning to 1950,* Liverpool: Liverpool University Press.

Ashley, Mike. (2005), *Transformations: The Story of the Science-Fiction Magazines from 1950 to 1970,* Liverpool: Liverpool University Press.

Baccolini, Raffaella, and Moylan, Tom (2003), 'Introduction: Dystopias and Histories', in Raffaella Baccolini and Tom Moylan (eds.), *Dark Horizons: Science Fiction and the Dystopian Imagination,* New York: Routledge.

Banks, Miranda (2004), 'A Boy for All Planets: *Roswell, Smallville* and the Teen Male Melodrama', In Glyn Davis and Kay Dickinson (eds.), *Teen TV: Genre, Consumption and Identity,* London: BFI.

Barkun, Michael (2003), *A Culture of Conspiracy: Apocalyptic Visions in Contemporary America,* Berkeley: University of California Press.

Baxter, John (1970), *Science Fiction in the Cinema,* New York: A.S. Barnes and Co.

Baxter, John (1972), *Hollywood in the Sixties,* London: The Tantivy Press.

Bazalgette, Cary, and Staples, Terry (1995), 'Unshrinking the Kids: Children's Cinema and the Family Film', in Cary Bazalgette and David Buckingham (eds.), *In Front of the Children: Screen Entertainment and Young Audiences,* London: BFI.

Bellah, Robert N., Madsen, Richard, Tipton, Steven M., Sullivan, William M., and Swidler, Ann (1992), *The Good Society,* New York: Vintage Books.

Bellamy, Edward (1888), *Looking Backward,* Mineola: Dover Publications.

Benshoff, Harry M. (1997), *Monsters in the Closet: Homosexuality and the Horror Film,* Manchester: Manchester University Press.

Benson, Michael (1985), *Vintage Science Fiction Films, 1896–1949,* Jefferson: McFarland Publishers.

Berman, Rick (1994), 'Roddenberry's Vision', in Lee Ann Nicholson (ed.), *Farewell to Star Trek: The Next Generation, TV Guide Collector's Edition,* Toronto: Telemedia Communications Inc.

Berman, William C. (1998, 2nd edition), *America's Right Turn: From Nixon to Clinton,* Baltimore: Johns Hopkins University Press.

Berman, William C. (2001), *From the Center to the Edge: The Politics and Policies of the Clinton Presidency,* Lanham: Rowman and Littlefield Publishers.

Bernardi, Daniel L. (1998), *Star Trek and History: Race-ing Towards a White Future,* New Brunswick: Rutgers University Press.

Biskind, Peter (2000), *Seeing Is Believing: How Hollywood Taught Us to Stop Worrying and Love the Fifties,* London: Bloomsbury.

Bjarkman, Kim (2004), 'To Have and to Hold: The Video Collector's Relationship with an Ethereal Medium', *Television and New Media,* 5/3: 217–46.

Black, Jeremy (2006), *Altered States: America Since the Sixties,* London: Reaktion Books.

Booker, M. Keith (2001), *Monsters, Mushroom Clouds, and the Cold War: American Science Fiction and the Roots of Postmodernism, 1946–1964,* Westport: Greenwood Press.

Booker, M. Keith (2002), *Strange TV: Innovative Television Series from The Twilight Zone to The X-Files,* Westport: Greenwood Press.

Booker, M. Keith (2004), *Science Fiction Television,* Westport: Praeger.

Booker, M. Keith (2006), *Alternate Americas: Science Fiction Film and American Culture,* Westport: Praeger.

Bould, Mark (2008a), '*Transformers*', *Science Fiction Film and Television,* 1/1: 163–7.

Bould, Mark (2008b), 'Science Fiction Television in the United Kingdom', in J. P. Telotte (ed.), *The Essential Science Fiction Television Reader,* Lexington: The University Press of Kentucky.

Boyer, Paul (1994), *By the Bomb's Early Light: American Thought and Culture at the Dawn of the Atomic Age,* Chapel Hill: University of North Carolina Press.

Brereton, Pat (2005), *Hollywood Utopia: Ecology in Contemporary American Cinema,* Bristol: Intellect Books.

Briggs, Asa, and Burke, Peter (2002), *A Social History of the Media: From Gutenberg to the Internet,* Malden: Polity Press.

Britton, Andrew (2009), 'Blissing Out: The Politics of Reaganite Entertainment (1986)', in Barry Keith Grant (ed.), *Britton on Film: The Complete Film Criticism of Andrew Britton,* Detroit: Wayne State University Press.

Britton, Piers D., and Barker, Simon J. (2003), *Reading between Designs: Visual Imagery and the Generation of Meaning in The Avengers, The Prisoner, and Doctor Who,* Austin: University of Texas Press.

Brooker, Will (2002), *Using the Force: Creativity, Community and Star Wars Fans,* London: Continuum.

Brosnan, John (1978), *Future Tense: The Cinema of Science Fiction,* London: Mac-Donald and Jane's Publishers.

Bukatman, Scott (1999), '"The Artificial Infinite: On Special Effects and the Sublime', in Annette Kuhn (ed.), *Alien Zone II: The Spaces of Science Fiction Cinema,* London: Verso.

Burke, Timothy, and Burke, Kevin (1999), *Saturday Morning Fever: Growing Up with Cartoon Culture*, New York: St. Martin's Griffin.

Caputi, Mary (2005), *A Kinder, Gentler America: Melancholia and the Mythical 1950s*, Minneapolis: University of Minnesota Press.

Cartmell, Deborah, and Hunter, I. Q. (2001), 'Introduction: Retrovisions: Historical Makeovers in Film and Literature', in Deborah Cartmell, I. Q. Hunter, and Imelda Whelehan (eds.), *Retrovisions: Reinventing the Past in Film and Fiction.* London: Pluto Press.

Castronovo, David (2004), *Beyond the Gray Flannel Suit: Books from the 1950s That Made American Culture*, New York: Continuum.

Chapman, James (1999), *Licence to Thrill: A Cultural History of the James Bond Films*, London: IB Tauris.

Chapman, James (2002), *Saints and Avengers: British Adventure Series of the 1960s*, London: IB Tauris.

Chapman, James (2006), *Inside the TARDIS: The Worlds of Doctor Who*, London: IB Tauris.

Clover, Joshua (2004), *The Matrix*, London: BFI.

Collado-Rodríguez, Francisco (2002), 'Fear of the Flesh, Fear of the Borg: Narratives of Bodily Transgression in Contemporary U.S. Culture', in Ramón Plo-Alastrué and María Jesús Martínez-Alfaro (eds.), *Beyond Borders: Re-Defining Generic and Ontological Boundaries*, Heidelberg: Universitätsverlag C. Winter.

Constable, Catherine (1999), 'Becoming the Monster's Mother: Morphologies of Identity in the *Alien* Series', in Annette Kuhn (ed.), *Alien Zone II: The Spaces of Science Fiction Cinema*, London: Verso.

Cornea, Christine (2007), *Science Fiction Cinema: Between Fantasy and Reality*, Edinburgh: Edinburgh University Press.

Creeber, Glen (2004), *Serial Television: Big Drama on the Small Screen*, London: BFI.

Creeber, Glen (2008, 2nd ed.), '*Heroes*', in Glen Creeber (ed.), *The Television Genre Book*, London: BFI/Palgrave.

Creed, Barbara (1993), *The Monstrous-Feminine: Film, Feminism, Psychoanalysis*, London: Routledge.

Crowley, David (2008a), *Posters of the Cold War*, London: V&A Publishing.

Crowley, David (2008b), 'Looking Down on Spaceship Earth: Cold War Landscapes', in *Cold War Modern: Design, 1945–1970*, London: V&A Publishing.

Dean, Joan F. (1978), 'Between *2001* and *Star Wars*', *Journal of Popular Film and Television* 7/1: 32–41.

DeForest, Tim (2004), *Storytelling in the Pulps, Comics, and Radio: How Technology Changed Popular Fiction in America*, Jefferson: McFarland Publishers.

De Los Santos, Oscar (2009), 'Irwin Allen's Recycled Monsters and Escapist Voyages', in Lincoln Geraghty (ed.), *Channeling the Future: Essays on Science Fiction and Fantasy Television.* Lanham: The Scarecrow Press.

Denison, Rayna, and Jancovich, Mark (2007), 'Mysterious Bodies: Introduction', *Intensities: The Journal of Cult Media* [online journal], 4 (December), <http://intensities.org/Essays/Jancovich_Intro.pdf> accessed 22 September 2008.

Desser, David (1999), 'Race, Space and Class: The Politics of Cityscapes in Science-Fiction Films', in Annette Kuhn (ed.), *Alien Zone II: The Spaces of Science Fiction Cinema,* London: Verso.

Dixon, Wheeler Winston (2004), 'Introduction: Something Lost—Film after 9/11', in *Film and Television After 9/11,* Carbondale: Southern Illinois University Press.

Dixon, Wheeler Winston (2006), *Visions of Paradise: Images of Eden in the Cinema,* New Brunswick: Rutgers University Press.

Dixon, Wheeler Winston (2008), 'Tomorrowland TV: The Space Opera and Early Science Fiction Television', in J. P. Telotte (ed.), *The Essential Science Fiction Television Reader,* Lexington: The University Press of Kentucky.

Dobson, Nichola (2003), 'Nitpicking "The Simpsons": Critique and Continuity in Constructed Realities', *Animation Journal,* 11: 84–93.

Doty, William G. (2004), 'Introduction: The Deeper We Go, the More Complex and Sophisticated the Franchise Seems, and the Dizzier We Feel', in Matthew Kapell and William G. Doty (eds.), *Jacking in to the Matrix Franchise: Cultural Reception and Interpretation,* New York: Continuum.

Douglas, Susan J. (2004), *Listening In: Radio and the American Imagination,* Minneapolis: University of Minnesota Press.

Duchovnay, Gerald (2008), 'From Big Screen to Small Box: Adapting Science Fiction Film for Television', in J. P. Telotte (ed.), *The Essential Science Fiction Television Reader,* Lexington: The University Press of Kentucky.

Ellis, John (2002), *Seeing Things: Television in the Age of Uncertainty,* London: IB Tauris.

Engelhardt, Tom (1998), *The End of Victory Culture: Cold War America and the Disillusioning of a Generation,* Amherst: University of Massachusetts Press.

Evans, Joyce A. (1998), *Celluloid Mushroom Clouds: Hollywood and the Atomic Bomb,* Boulder: Westview Press.

Feuer, Jane (1995), *Seeing through the Eighties: Television and Reaganism,* London: BFI.

Fiske, John (1986), 'Television: Polysemy and Popularity', *Critical Studies in Mass Communication,* 3/4: 391–408.

Flanagan, Martin (1999), 'The *Alien* Series and Generic Hybridity', in Deborah Cartmell, I. Q. Hunter, Heidi Kaye, and Imelda Whelehan (eds.), *Alien Identities: Exploring Differences in Film and Fiction,* London: Pluto.

Ford, James E. (1983), '*Battlestar Galactica* and Mormon Theology', *Journal of Popular Culture,* 17/2: 83–7.

Frayling, Christopher (2005), *Mad, Bad and Dangerous? The Scientist and the Cinema,* London: Reaktion Books.

French, Christopher C. (2001), 'Alien Abductions', in Ron Roberts and David Groome (eds.), *Parapsychology: The Science of Unusual Experience,* London: Arnold.

Friedman, Lester D. (2006), *Citizen Spielberg,* Urbana: University of Illinois Press.

Frisch, Adam J. (2007), 'The Byronic Hero in Science Fiction Film', in Thomas J. Morrissey and Oscar De Los Santos (eds.), *When Genres Collide: Selected Essay from the 37th Annual Meeting of the Science Fiction Research Association,* Waterbury: Fine Tooth Press.

Gateward, Frances (2007), '1973: Movies and the Legacies of War and Corruption', in Lester D. Friedman (ed.), *American Cinema of the 1970s: Themes and Variations,* New Brunswick: Rutgers University Press.

Geraghty, Christine (1991), *Women and Soap Opera: A Study of Prime Time Soaps,* Cambridge: Polity Press.

Geraghty, Lincoln (2002), '"Carved from the rock experiences of our daily lives": Reality and *Star Trek's* Multiple Histories', *European Journal of American Culture,* 21/3: 160–76.

Geraghty, Lincoln (2003a), '"Homosocial Desire on the Final Frontier": Kinship, the American Romance, and *Deep Space Nine's* "Erotic Triangles"', *Journal of Popular Culture,* 36/3: 441–65.

Geraghty, Lincoln (2003b), 'The American Jeremiad and *Star Trek's* Puritan Legacy', *Journal of the Fantastic in the Arts,* 14/2: 228–45.

Geraghty, Lincoln (2003c), 'Neutralising the Indian: Native American Stereotypes in *Star Trek: Voyager*', *US Studies Online* [online journal], 4 (Autumn), <http://www.baas.ac.uk/resources/usstudiesonline/article.asp?us=4&id=13> accessed 5 May 2009.

Geraghty, Lincoln (2007), *Living with Star Trek: American Culture and the Star Trek Universe,* London: IB Tauris.

Geraghty, Lincoln (2008), 'From Balaclavas to Jumpsuits: The Multiple Histories and Identities of *Doctor Who's* Cybermen', *Atlantis: A Journal of the Spanish Association for Anglo-American Studies,* 30/1: 85–100.

Geraghty, Lincoln, and Jancovich, Mark (2008), 'Introduction: Generic Canons', in Lincoln Geraghty and Mark Jancovich (eds.), *The Shifting Definitions of Genre: Essays on Labeling Films, Television Shows and Media,* Jefferson: McFarland Publishers.

Gerrold, David (1996), *The World of* Star Trek*: The Inside Story of TV's Most Popular Series,* London: Virgin Books.

Gordon, Andrew M. (2008), *Empire of Dreams: The Science Fiction and Fantasy of Films of Steven Spielberg,* Lanham: Rowman and Littlefield Publishers.

Graebner, William (2004), 'America's *Poseidon Adventure:* A Nation in Existential Despair', in Beth Bailey and David Farber (eds.), *America in the Seventies,* Lawrence: University Press of Kansas.

Graham, Allison (1996), '"Are You Now or Have Ever Been?": Conspiracy Theory and *The X-Files*', in David Lavery, Angela Hague, and Marla Cartwright (eds.), *'Deny All Knowledge': Reading The X-Files,* London: Faber and Faber.

Graham, Elaine L. (2002), *Representations of the Post/Human: Monsters, Aliens and Others in Popular Culture,* New Brunswick: Rutgers University Press.

Grant, Barry Keith (1999), '"Sensuous Elaboration": Reason and the Visible in the Science-Fiction Film', in Annette Kuhn (ed.), *Alien Zone II: The Spaces of Science Fiction Cinema,* London: Verso.

Grant, Barry Keith (2005), 'Movies and the Crack of Doom', in Murray Pomerance (ed.), *American Cinema of the 1950s: Themes and Variations,* New Brunswick: Rutgers University Press.

Gray, Ann (2002), 'Television in the Home', in Toby Miller, *Television Studies,* London: BFI.

Gray, Jonathan (2006), *Watching with The Simpsons: Television, Parody, and Intertextuality,* New York: Routledge.

Greene, Eric (1998), *Planet of the Apes as American Myth: Race, Politics, and Popular Culture,* Hanover: Wesleyan University Press.

Gregory, Chris (2000), *Star Trek Parallel Narratives,* London: MacMillan Press.

Gripsrud, Jostein (1995), *The Dynasty Years: Hollywood Television and Critical Media Studies,* London: Routledge.

Gunning, Tom (1990), 'The Cinema of Attractions: Early Film, Its Spectator and the Avant-Garde', in Thomas Elsaesser (ed.), *Early Cinema: Space, Frame, Narrative,* London: BFI.

Gunning, Tom (1996), '"Now You See It, Now You Don't": The Temporality of the Cinema of Attractions', in Richard Abel (ed.), *Silent Film,* London: Athlone.

Gwenllian-Jones, Sara, and Pearson, Roberta E. (2004), 'Introduction', in Sara Gwenllian-Jones and Roberta E. Pearson (eds.), *Cult Television,* Minneapolis: University of Minnesota Press.

Halliwell, Martin (2007), *American Culture in the 1950s,* Edinburgh: Edinburgh University Press.

Hammond, Paul (1974), *Marvellous Méliès,* London: Gordon Fraser.

Haraway, Donna (1985), 'Manifesto for Cyborgs: Science, Technology, and Socialist Feminism in the 1980's', *Socialist Review,* 80: 65–108.

Haraway, Donna (1991), *Simians, Cyborgs and Women: The Reinvention of Nature,* New York: Free Press.

Harries, Dan (2000), *Film Parody,* London: BFI.

Heale, M. J. (1990), *American Anticommunism: Combating the Enemy Within, 1830–1970,* Baltimore: The Johns Hopkins University Press.

Hedgecock, Liz (1999), '"The Martians Are Coming!": Civilisation v. Invasion in *The War of the Worlds* and *Mars Attacks!*', in Deborah Cartmell, I. Q. Hunter, Heidi Kaye, and Imelda Whelehan (eds.), *Alien Identities: Exploring Differences in Film and Fiction,* London: Pluto Press.

Helford, Elyce Rae (2003), '"It's a Rip-Off of the Women's Movement": Second-Wave Feminism and *The Stepford Wives*', in Sherrie A. Inness (ed.), *Disco Divas: Women and Popular Culture in the 1970s,* Philadelphia, PA: University of Pennsylvania Press.

Heller, Dana (2005), 'Introduction: Consuming 9/11', in Dana Heller (ed.), *The Selling of 9/11: How a National Tragedy Became a Commodity,* New York: Palgrave.

Hendershot, Cyndy (1998), 'The Invaded Body: Paranoia and Radiation Anxiety in *Invaders from Mars, It Came from Outer Space,* and *Invasion of the Body Snatchers*', *Extrapolation,* 39/1: 26–39.

Hertenstein, Mike (1998), *The Double Vision of Star Trek: Half-Humans, Evil Twins, and Science Fiction,* Chicago: Cornerstone Press.

Heung, Marina (1983), 'The New Family in American Cinema', *Journal of Popular Film and Television,* 11/2: 79–85.

Highmore, Ben (2005), *Cityscapes: Cultural Readings in the Material and Symbolic City,* London: Palgrave.

Hills, Matt (2004), '*The Twilight Zone*', in Glen Creeber (ed.), *Fifty Key Television Programmes,* London: Arnold.

Hilmes, Michele (2007), 'Introduction to Part Three: NBC and the Classic Network System, 1960–85', in Michele Hilmes (ed.), *NBC: America's Network,* Berkeley: University of California Press.

Hilton-Morrow, Wendy, and McMahan, David T. (2003), '*The Flintstones* to *Futurama:* Networks and Prime Time Animation', in Carol A. Stabile and Mark Harrison (eds.), *Prime Time Animation: Television Animation and American Culture,* London & New York: Routledge.

Hockley, Luke (2008, 2nd ed.), 'Science Fiction', in Glen Creeber (ed.), *The Television Genre Book,* London: BFI/Palgrave.

Holloway, Samantha (2008), 'Space Vehicles and Travelling Companions: Rockets and Living Ships', in J. P. Telotte (ed.), *The Essential Science Fiction Television Reader,* Lexington: The University Press of Kentucky.

Hollows, Joanne (2003), 'The Masculinity of Cult', in Mark Jancovich, Antonio Lázaro Reboll, Julian Stringer, and Andy Willis (eds.), *Defining Cult Movies: The Cultural Politics of Oppositional Taste,* Manchester: Manchester University Press.

Humphries, Reynold (2002), *The American Horror Film: An Introduction,* Edinburgh: Edinburgh University Press.

Hunt, Nathan (2003), 'The Importance of Trivia: Ownership, Exclusion and Authority in Science Fiction Fandom', in Mark Jancovich, Antonio Lázaro Reboll, Julian Stringer, and Andy Willis (eds.), *Defining Cult Movies: The Cultural Politics of Oppositional Taste,* Manchester: Manchester University Press.

Jameson, Fredric (1983), 'Postmodernism and Consumer Society', in Hal Foster (ed.), *The Anti-Aesthetic: Essays on Postmodern Culture,* Port Townsend: Bay Press.

Jancovich, Mark (1992), 'Modernity and Subjectivity in *The Terminator:* The Machine as Monster in Contemporary American Culture', *The Velvet Light Trap,* 30: 3–17.

Jancovich, Mark (1996), *Rational Fears: American Horror in the 1950s,* Manchester: Manchester University Press.

Jancovich, Mark, Lázaro Reboll, Antonio, Stringer, Julian, and Willis, Andy (2003), 'Introduction', in Mark Jancovich, Antonio Lázaro Reboll, Julian Stringer, and Andy Willis (eds.), *Defining Cult Movies: The Cultural Politics of Oppositional Taste,* Manchester: Manchester University Press.

Jancovich, Mark, and Lyons, James (2003), 'Introduction', in Mark Jancovich and James Lyons (eds.), *Quality Popular Television,* London: BFI.

Javna, John (1987), *The Best of Science Fiction TV: The Critics' Choice from Captain Video to Star Trek, from The Jetsons to Robotech,* London: Titan Books.

Jeffords, Susan (1994), *Hard Bodies: Hollywood Masculinity in the Reagan Era,* New Brunswick: Rutgers University Press.

Jenkins, Henry (2006), Convergence Culture: Where Old and New Media Collide, New York: New York University Press.

Johnson, Catherine (2005), *Telefantasy,* London: BFI.

Johnson, Paul E. (1978), *A Shopkeeper's Millennium: Society and Revivals in Rochester, New York, 1815–1837,* New York: Hill and Wang.

Johnson-Smith, Jan (2005), *American Science Fiction TV: Star Trek, Stargate and Beyond,* London: IB Tauris.

Kaminsky, Stuart M. (1976), 'Don Siegel on the Pod Society', in Thomas R. Atkins (ed.), *Science Fiction Films,* New York: Monarch Press.

Kaveney, Roz (2005), *From Alien to The Matrix: Reading Science Fiction Film,* London: IB Tauris.

Kaye, Heidi, and Hunter, I.Q. (1999), 'Introduction—Alien Identities: Exploring Difference in Film and Fiction', in Deborah Cartmell, I. Q. Hunter, Heidi Kaye, and Imelda Whelehan (eds.), *Alien Identities: Exploring Differences in Film and Fiction,* London: Pluto Press.

King, Geoff (2002), *Film Comedy,* London: Wallflower Press.

King, Geoff, and Krzywinska, Tanya (2000), *Science Fiction Cinema: From Outerspace to Cyberspace,* London: Wallflower Press.

King, Stephen (1993), *Danse Macabre,* London: Warner Books.

Klinger, Barbara (2006), *Beyond the Multiplex: Cinema, New Technologies, and the Home,* Berkeley: University of California Press.

Kompare, Derek (2005), *Rerun Nation: How Repeats Invented American Television,* New York: Routledge.

Kompare, Derek (2006), 'Publishing Flow: DVD Box Sets and the Reconception of Television', *Television and New Media,* 7/4: 335–60.

Kozloff, Sarah (1992), 'Narrative Theory and Television', in Robert C. Allen (ed.), *Channels of Discourse, Reassembled: Television and Contemporary Criticism,* London: Routledge.

Krämer, Peter (1998), 'Would you take your child to see this film? The Cultural and Social Work of the Family-Adventure Movie', in Steve Neale and Murray Smith (eds.), *Contemporary Hollywood Cinema,* London: Routledge.

Krämer, Peter (2000), '*Star Wars*', in David W. Ellwood (ed.), *The Movies as History: Visions of the Twentieth Century,* Stroud: Sutton Publishing.

Lacey, Nick (2000), *Narrative and Genre: Key Concepts in Media Studies,* Basingstoke: Palgrave.

Larson, Doran (2004), 'Machine as Messiah: Cyborgs, Morphs and the American Body Politic', in Sean Redmond (ed.), *Liquid Metal: The Science Fiction Film Reader,* London: Wallflower.

Laughey, Dan (2007), *Key Themes in Media Theory,* Maidenhead: Open University Press.

LaValley, Al, ed. (1989), *Invasion of the Body Snatchers: Don Siegel, Director,* New Brunswick: Rutgers University Press.

Lavery, David (2004), '*The X-Files*', in Glen Creeber (ed.), *Fifty Key Television Programmes,* London: Arnold.

Lavery, David, Hague, Angela, and Cartwright, Maria (1996), 'Introduction: Generation X—*The X-Files* and the Cultural Moment', in David Lavery, Angela Hague, and Marla Cartwright (eds.), *'Deny All Knowledge': Reading The X-Files,* London: Faber and Faber.

Levine, Paul, and Papasotiriou, Harry (2005), *American since 1945: The American Moment,* Basingstoke: Palgrave.

Lively, Robert L. (2009), 'Remapping the Feminine in Joss Whedon's *Firefly*', in Lincoln Geraghty (ed.), *Channeling the Future: Essays on Science Fiction and Fantasy Television,* Lanham: The Scarecrow Press.

Livingstone, Sonia (2005), 'Media Audiences, Interpreters and Users', in Marie Gillespie (ed.), *Media Audiences,* Maidenhead: Open University Press.

Lovecraft, H. P. (1927), 'Supernatural Horror in Literature', in *The H.P. Lovecraft Omnibus 2: Dagon and Other Macabre Tales,* London: Voyager.

Lucanio, Patrick (1987), *Them or Us: Archetypal Interpretations of Fifties Alien Invasion Films,* Bloomington: Indiana University Press.

Lucanio, Patrick, and Coville, Gary (1998), *American Science Fiction Television Series of the 1950s: Episode Guides and Casts and Credits for Twenty Shows,* Jefferson: McFarland Publishers.

Mack, John (1995), *Abduction: Human Encounters with Aliens,* New York: Ballantine.

Mair, Jan (2002), 'Rewriting the "American Dream": Postmodernism and Otherness in *Independence Day*', in Ziauddin Sardar and Sean Cubitt (eds.), *Aliens R Us: The Other in Science Fiction Cinema,* London: Pluto Press.

Marc, David, and Thompson, Robert J. (2005), *Television in the Antenna Age: A Concise History,* Malden: Blackwell Publishing.

Marling, Karal Ann (1994), *As Seen on TV: The Visual Culture of Everyday Life in the 1950s,* Cambridge: Harvard University Press.

Marshall, C. W., and Potter, Tiffany (2008), '"I See the Patterns": *Battlestar Galactica* and the Things That Matter', in Tiffany Potter and C. W. Marshall (eds.), *Cylons in America: Critical Studies in Battlestar Galactica,* New York: Continuum.

Marx, Leo (1964), *The Machine in the Garden: Technology and the Pastoral Ideal in America,* New York: Oxford University Press.

Mason, Fred (2007), 'Returning to the Coliseum: Science Fiction Visions of Future Sports', in David Mead and Paweł Frelik (eds.), *Playing the Universe: Games and Gaming in Science Fiction,* Lublin: Wydawnictwo UMCS.

Mateas, Michael (2006), 'Reading HAL: Representation and Artificial Intelligence', in Robert Kolker (ed.), *Stanley Kubrick's 2001: A Space Odyssey, New Essays,* New York: Oxford University Press.

Mathijs, Ernest, and Mendik, Xavier (2008), 'Cult Case Studies: Introduction', in Ernest Mathijs and Xavier Mendik (eds.), *The Cult Film Reader,* Maidenhead: Open University Press.

McCurdy, Howard E. (1997), *Space and the American Imagination,* Washington, DC: Smithsonian Institution Press.

McLean, Gareth (2007), 'The New Sci-Fi', *The Guardian* [online], <http://media.guardian.co.uk/site/story/0,2112467,00.html> accessed 5 July 2007.

McMahan, Alison (2005), *The Films of Tim Burton: Animating Live Action in Contemporary Hollywood,* London: Continuum.

May, Elaine Tyler (1999), *Homeward Bound: American Families in the Cold War Era,* New York: Basic Books.

Miller, Mark Crispin (1994), '2001: A Cold Descent', *Sight and Sound,* 4/1: 18–25.

Mittell, Jason (2003), 'The Great Saturday Morning Exile: Scheduling Cartoons on Television's Periphery in the 1960s,' in Carol A. Stabile and Mark Harrison (eds.), *Prime Time Animation: Television Animation and American Culture,* London: Routledge.

Mittell, Jason (2004), *Genre and Television: From Cop Shows to Cartoons in American Culture.* New York: Routledge.

Mittell, Jason (2008, 2nd ed.), '*Lost* (ABC, 2004–)', in Glen Creeber (ed.), *The Television Genre Book,* London: BFI/Palgrave.

Moffitt, John F. (2003), *Picturing Extraterrestrials: Alien Images in Modern Mass Culture,* Amherst: Prometheus Books.

Morgan, Jack (2002), *The Biology of Horror: Gothic Literature and Film,* Carbondale: Southern Illinois University Press.

Moy, Timothy (2004), 'Culture, Technology, and the Cult of Tech in the 1970s', in Beth Bailey and David Farber (ed.), *America in the Seventies,* Lawrence: University Press of Kansas.

Murphy, Graham J. (2009), 'Dystopia', in Mark Bould, Andrew M. Butler, Adam Roberts, and Sherryl Vint (eds.), *The Routledge Companion to Science Fiction,* London: Routledge.

Murray, Janet H. (1997), *Hamlet on the Holodeck: The Future of Narrative in Cyberspace,* Cambridge: MIT Press.

Nakamura, Lisa (2005), 'The Multiplication of Difference in Post-Millennial Cyberpunk Film: The Visual Culture of Race in the *Matrix* Trilogy', in Stacy Gillis (ed.), *The Matrix Trilogy: Cyberpunk Reloaded.* London: Wallflower.

Naughton, John (2007), 'Unreality TV', *Radio Times,* 21–27 July: 12–16.

Ndalianis, Angela (2005), 'Television and the Neo-Baroque', in Michael Hammond and Lucy Mazdon (eds.), *The Contemporary Television Series,* Edinburgh: Edinburgh University Press.

Neale, Steve (2000), *Genre and Hollywood,* London: Routledge.

Neely, Sarah (2001), 'Cool Intentions: The Literary Classic, the Teenpic and the "'Chick Flick"'', in Deborah Cartmell, I. Q. Hunter and Imelda Whelehan (eds.), *Retrovisions: Reinventing the Past in Film and Fiction,* London: Pluto Press.

Newman, Kim (2005), *Doctor Who,* London: BFI.

Noonan, Bonnie (2005), *Women Scientists in Fifties Science Fiction Films,* Jefferson: McFarland Publishers.

Palmer, R. Barton (2006), '*2001:* The Critical Reception and the Generation Gap', in Robert Kolker (ed.), *Stanley Kubrick's 2001: A Space Odyssey, New Essays,* New York: Oxford University Press.

Pank, Dylan, and Caro, John (2009), '"Haven't you heard? They look like us now!": Realism and Metaphor in the New *Battlestar Galactica*', in Lincoln Geraghty (ed.), *Channeling the Future: Essays on Science Fiction and Fantasy Television.* Lanham: The Scarecrow Press.

Pearson, Roberta (2005), 'The Writer/Producer in American Television', in Michael Hammond and Lucy Mazdon (eds.), *The Contemporary Television Series,* Edinburgh: Edinburgh University Press.

Pfitzer, Gregory M. (1995), 'The Only Good Alien is a Dead Alien: Science Fiction and the Metaphysics of Indian-Hating on the High Frontier', *Journal of American Culture,* 18/1: 51–67.

Pierson, Michele (2002), *Special Effects: Still in Search of Wonder,* New York: Columbia University Press.

Pounds, Michael C. (1999), *Race in Space: The Representation of Ethnicity in Star Trek and Star Trek: The Next Generation,* Lanham: Scarecrow Press.

Pratt, Ray (2001), *Projecting Paranoia: Conspiratorial Visions in American Film,* Lawrence: University Press of Kansas.

Putnam, Robert D. (1995), 'Bowling Alone: America's Declining Social Capital', *Journal of Democracy,* 6/1: 65–78.

Putnam, Robert D. (2000), *Bowling Alone: The Collapse and Revival of American Community,* New York: Touchstone.

Quart, Leonard, and Auster, Albert (2002, 3rd ed.), *American Film and Society since 1945,* Westport: Praeger.

Redmond, Sean, ed. (2004), *Liquid Metal: The Science Fiction Film Reader,* London: Wallflower.

Retzinger, Jean P. (2008), 'Speculative Visions and Imaginary Meals: Food and the Environment in (Post-Apocalyptic) Science Fiction Films', *Cultural Studies*, 22/3–4: 369–90.

Roberts, Adam (2000), *Science Fiction*, London: Routledge.

Roberts, Adam (2005), *The History of Science Fiction*, London: Paulgrave.

Rogin, Michael (1998), *Independence Day, or How I Learned to Stop Worrying and Love the Enola Gay*, London: BFI.

Ruppersburg, Hugh (1990), 'The Alien Messiah in Recent Science Fiction Films', in Annette Kuhn (ed.), *Alien Zone: Cultural Theory and Contemporary Science Fiction Cinema*, London: Verso.

Russell, Lynette, and Wolski, Nathan (2001), 'Beyond the Final Frontier: *Star Trek*, the Borg, and the Post-Colonial', *Intensities: The Journal of Cult Media* [online journal], 1 (Spring/Summer), <http://www.cult-media.com/issue1/Aruss.htm> accessed 15 May 2002.

Ryan, Michael, and Kellner, Douglas (1988), *Camera Politica: The Politics and Ideology of Contemporary Hollywood Film*, Bloomington: Indiana University Press.

San Martín, Nancy (2003), '"Must See TV": Programming Identity on NBC Thursdays', in Mark Jancovich and James Lyons (eds.) *Quality Popular Television*, London: BFI.

Schaller, Michael, Scharff, Virginia, and Schulzinger, Robert D. (1996, 2nd ed.), *Present Tense: The United States Since 1945*, Boston: Houghton Mifflin Company.

Schow, David J. (1998), *The Outer Limits Companion*, Hollywood: GNP/Crescendo Records.

Sconce, Jeffrey (1997), 'Science-Fiction Programs', in Horace Newcomb (ed.), *Encyclopaedia of Television*, Chicago: Fitzroy Dearborn.

Seed, David (1999), *American Science Fiction and the Cold War: Literature and Film*, Edinburgh: Edinburgh University Press.

Senn, Bryan (2006), 'The Sport of Violence: *Death Race 2000* and *Rollerball*', in David J. Hogan (ed.), *Science Fiction America: Essays on SF Cinema*, Jefferson: McFarland Publishers.

Shapiro, Jerome F. (2002), *Atomic Bomb Cinema: The Apocalyptic Imagination on Film*, New York: Routledge.

Short, Sue (2005), *Cyborg Cinema and Contemporary Subjectivity*, London: Palgrave.

Siegel, Mark (1980), 'Science Fiction Characterization and TV's Battle for the Stars', *Science Fiction Studies*, 7/3: 270–7.

Silver, Anna Krugovoy (2002), 'The Cyborg Mystique: *The Stepford Wives* and Second Wave Feminism', *Arizona Quarterly*, 58/1: 109–26.

Sobchack, Vivian (1998), *Screening Space: The American Science Fiction Film*, New Brunswick: Rutgers University Press.

Sobchack, Vivian (1999), 'Cities on the Edge of Time: The Urban Science-Fiction Film', in Annette Kuhn (ed.), *Alien Zone II: The Spaces of Science Fiction Cinema*, London: Verso.

Sontag, Susan (2004), 'The Imagination of Disaster', in Sean Redmond (ed.), *Liquid Metal: The Science Fiction Film Reader*, London: Wallflower.

Spelling, Ian (2003), 'Full English, from Darkness into Light ...' *Star Trek: The Official Monthly Magazine,* 100 (January): 24–25.

Spigel, Lynn (1992), *Make Room for TV: Television and the Family Ideal in Postwar America,* Chicago: The University of Chicago Press.

Spigel, Lynn (2005), 'Entertainment Wars: Television Culture after 9/11', in Dana Heller, *The Selling of 9/11: How a National Tragedy Became a Commodity,* New York: Palgrave.

Springer, Claudia (1991), 'The Pleasure of the Interface', *Screen,* 32/3: 303–23.

Springer, Claudia (1999), 'Psycho-Cybernetics in the Films of the 1990s', in Annette Kuhn (ed.), *Alien Zone II: The Spaces of Science Fiction Cinema,* London: Verso.

Stableford, Brian (1996), 'The Third Generation of Genre Science Fiction', *Science Fiction Studies,* 23/3: 321–30.

Stein, Atara (2004), *The Byronic Hero in Film, Fiction, and Television,* Carbondale: Southern Illinois University Press.

Tallack, Douglas (1991), *Twentieth-Century America: The Intellectual and Cultural Context,* London: Longman.

Tallack, Douglas (2005), *New York Sights: Visualizing Old and New New York,* Oxford: Berg.

Tashiro, Charles (1991), 'Videophilia: What Happens When You Wait for It on Video', *Film Quarterly,* 45/1: 7–17.

Tashiro, Charles (1996), 'The Contradictions of Video Collecting', *Film Quarterly,* 50/2: 11–18.

Tasker, Yvonne (1993), *Spectacular Bodies: Gender, Genre and the Action Cinema,* London: Routledge.

Telotte, J. P. (1995), *Replications: A Robotic History of the Science Fiction Film,* Urbana: University of Illinois Press.

Telotte, J. P. (1999), *A Distant Technology: Science Fiction Film and the Machine Age,* Middletown: Wesleyan University Press.

Telotte, J. P. (2001), *Science Fiction Film,* Cambridge: Cambridge University Press.

Telotte, J. P. (2008a), 'Introduction: The Trajectory of Science Fiction Television', in J. P. Telotte (ed.), *The Essential Science Fiction Television Reader,* Lexington: The University Press of Kentucky.

Telotte, J. P. (2008b), 'Lost in Space: Television as Science Fiction Icon', in J. P. Telotte (ed.), *The Essential Science Fiction Television Reader,* Lexington: The University Press of Kentucky.

Thompson, Kristin, and Bordwell, David (2003, 2nd ed.), *Film History: An Introduction,* Boston: McGraw Hill.

Thornham, Sue, and Purvis, Tony (2005), *Television Drama: Theories and Identities,* London: Palgrave.

Tincknell, Estella (2005), *Mediating the Family: Gender, Culture and Representation,* London: Hodder Arnold.

Troy, Gil (2005), *Morning in America: How Ronald Reagan Invented the 1980s,* Princeton: Princeton University Press.

Tryon, Charles (2008), 'TV Time Lords: Fan Cultures, Narrative Complexity, and the Future of Science Fiction Television', in J. P. Telotte (ed.), *The Essential Science Fiction Television Reader,* Lexington: The University Press of Kentucky.

Tudor, Andrew (1989), *Monsters and Mad Scientists: A Cultural History of the Horror Movie,* Oxford: Basil Blackwell.

Turner, Fred (1996), *Echoes of Combat: The Vietnam War in American Memory,* New York: Anchor Books.

Urbanski, Heather (2007), *Plagues, Apocalypses and Bug-Eyed Monsters: How Speculative Fiction Shows Us Our Nightmares.* Jefferson: McFarland Publishers.

Vieth, Errol (2001), *Screening Science: Contexts, Texts, and Science in Fifties Science Fiction Film,* Lanham: Scarecrow Press.

Vint, Sherryl (2008), '*Babylon 5:* Our First, Best Hope for Mature Science Fiction Television', in J. P. Telotte (ed.), *The Essential Science Fiction Television Reader,* Lexington: The University Press of Kentucky.

Walters, Ronald G. (1978), *American Reformers, 1815–1860,* New York: Hill and Wang.

Wagar, W. Warren (2004), *H.G. Wells: Traversing Time,* Middletown: Wesleyan University Press.

Wells, Paul (1993), '*The Invisible Man:* Shrinking Masculinity in the 1950s', in Pat Kirkham and Janet Thumim (eds.), *You Tarzan: Masculinity, Movies and Men,* London: Lawrence and Wishart.

Westfahl, Gary (1998), *The Mechanics of Wonder: The Creation of the Idea of Science Fiction,* Liverpool: Liverpool University Press.

Westfahl, Gary (2007), *Hugo Gernsback and the Century of Science Fiction,* Jefferson: McFarland Publishers.

Whitfield, Stephen J. (1996, 2nd ed.), *The Culture of the Cold War,* Baltimore: The Johns Hopkins University Press.

Wilcox, Rhonda V., and Lavery, David (2002), 'Introduction', in Rhonda V. Wilcox and David Lavery (eds.), *Fighting the Forces: What's at Stake in Buffy the Vampire Slayer,* Lanham: Rowman and Littlefield Publishers.

Wolfe, Peter (1996), *In the Zone: The Twilight World of Rod Sterling,* Bowling Green: Bowling Green State Popular Press.

Wood, Robin (2003), *Hollywood from Vietnam to Reagan . . . and Beyond,* New York: Columbia University Press.

Worland, Rick (1996), 'Sign-Posts Up Ahead: The Twilight Zone, The Outer Limits, and TV Political Fantasy 1959–1965', *Science Fiction Studies,* 23/1: 103–22.

Wyatt, Justin. (1994), *High Concept: Movies and Marketing in Hollywood,* Austin: University of Texas Press.

Zebrowski, George (2009), 'Science Fiction Movies: The Feud of Eye and Idea', in James Gunn, Marleen S. Barr, and Matthew Candelaria (eds.), *Reading Science Fiction,* Basingstoke: Palgrave.

Ziegler, Robert E. (1987), 'Moving Out of Sight: Fantastic Vision in *The Twilight Zone*', *Lamar Journal of the Humanities,* 13/2: 33–40.

Film and Videography

The Abyss (dir. James Cameron, 1989)

Aeon Flux (dir. Karyn Kusama, 2005)

A.I.: Artificial Intelligence (dir. Steven Spielberg, 2001)

ALF (creator Paul Fusco, 1986–1990)

Alien (dir. Ridley Scott, 1979)

Alien 3 (dir. David Fincher, 1992)

Alien Nation (dir. Graham Baker, 1988)

Alien Nation (creator Kenneth Johnson, 1989–1991)

Alien Resurrection (dir. Jean Pierre Jeunet, 1997)

Aliens (dir. James Cameron, 1986)

Andromeda (creators Gene Roddenberry and Robert Hewitt Wolfe, 2000–2005)

The Andromeda Strain (dir. Robert Wise, 1971)

Angel (creators Joss Whedon and David Greenwalt, 1999–2004)

The Animatrix (dir. various, 2003)

Ashes to Ashes (creators Matthew Graham and Ashley Pharoah, 2008–2009)

Attack of the 50 Foot Woman (dir. Nathan H. Juran, 1958)

AVP: Alien vs. Predator (dir. Paul W. S. Anderson, 2004)

AVPR: Alien vs. Predator–Requiem (dir. Colin and Greg Strause, 2007)

Babylon 5 (creator J. Michael Straczynski, 1994–1998)

Barbarella (dir. Roger Vadim, 1968)

*batteries not included (dir. Matthew Robbins, 1987)

Battlefield Earth (dir. Roger Christian, 2000)

Battle for the Planet of the Apes (dir. J. Lee Thompson, 1973)

Battlestar Galactica (creator Glen A. Larson, 1978–1980)

Battlestar Galactica (prod. David Eick and Ronald D. Moore, 2003–2009)

The Beast from 20,000 Fathoms (dir. Eugène Lourié, 1953)

Beneath the Planet of the Apes (dir. Ted Post, 1970)

Ben Hur (dir. William Wyler, 1959)

The Bionic Woman (creator Kenneth Johnson, 1976–1978)

Bionic Woman (creator David Eick, 2007–2008)

Blade Runner (dir. Ridley Scott, 1982)

Blake's 7 (creator Terry Nation, 1978–1981)

Bonnie and Clyde (dir. Arthur Penn, 1967)

A Boy and His Dog (dir. L. Q. Jones, 1975)

Brazil (dir. Terry Gilliam, 1985)

Buck Rogers in the 25th Century (prod. Joseph Cates and Babette Henry, 1950–1951)

Buck Rogers in the 25th Century (creators Glen A. Larson and Leslie Stevens, 1979–1981)

Buffy the Vampire Slayer (creator Joss Whedon, 1997–2003)

Capricorn One (dir. Peter Hyams, 1978)

Captain Scarlet (creator Gerry Anderson, 2005)

Captain Video and His Video Rangers (creators James Caddigan, Frank Telford, and Olga Druce, 1949–1955)

The Care Bears (prod. Michael Hirsh, Patrick Loubert, and Clive A. Smith, 1985–1988)

The Champions (prod. Monty Berman and Denis Spooner, 1969–1970)

Children of Men (dir. Alfonso Cuarón, 2006)

Chinatown (dir. Roman Polanski, 1974)

A Clockwork Orange (dir. Stanley, Kubrick, 1971)

Close Encounters of the Third Kind (dir. Steven Spielberg, 1977)

Cloverfield (dir. Matt Reeves, 2008)

Cocoon (dir. Ron Howard, 1985)

Cocoon: The Return (dir. Daniel Petrie, 1988)

Communion (dir. Philippe Mora, 1989)

The Conquest of Space (dir. Byron Haskin, 1955)

Conquest of the Planet of the Apes (dir. J. Lee Thompson, 1972)

Crusade (creator J. Michael Straczynski, 1999)

CSI: Crime Scene Investigation (creator Anthony E. Zuiker, 2000–present)

Dallas (creator David Jacobs, 1978–1991)

Danger Man (creator Ralph Smart, 1960–1962 and 1964–1968)

Dark Angel (creators James Cameron and Charles H. Eglee, 2000–2002)

Dark Skies (creator Bryce Zabel, 1996–1997)

Dawn of the Dead (dir. George A. Romero, 1978)

Dawson's Creek (creator Kevin Williamson, 1998–2003)

The Day the Earth Stood Still (dir. Robert Wise, 1951)

The Day the Earth Stood Still (dir. Scott Derrickson, 2008)

The Deadly Mantis (dir. Nathan Juran, 1957)

Death Race (dir. Paul W. S. Anderson, 2008)

Death Race 2000 (dir. Paul Bartel, 1975)

Demon Seed (dir. Donald Cammell, 1977)

Destination Moon (dir. Irving Pichel, 1950)

Die Another Day (dir. Lee Tamahori)

Disturbia (dir. D. J. Caruso, 2007)

Doctor Who (creators Sydney Newman, Donald Wilson, and C. E. Webber, 1963–1989, 1996, 2005–present)

Doomwatch (creators Gerry Davis and Kit Pedlar, 1970–192)

Dr. No (dir. Terence Young, 1962)

Dr. Strangelove, Or How I Learned to Stop Worrying and Love the Bomb (dir. Stanley Kubrick, 1964)

Dynasty (creators Richard and Esther Shapiro, 1981–1989)

Earth: Final Conflict (creator Gene Roddenberry, 1997–2002)

Earth vs. the Flying Saucers (dir. Fred F. Sears, 1956)

Eight Legged Freaks (dir. Ellory Elkayem, 2002)

El Cid (dir. Anthony Mann, 1961)

The Empire Strikes Back (dir. Irvin Kershner, 1980)

Escape from the Planet of the Apes (dir. Don Taylor, 1971)

E.T. The Extra-Terrestrial (dir. Steven Spielberg, 1982)

Evolution (dir. Ivan Reitman, 2001)

Explorers (dir. Joe Dante, 1985)

The Faculty (dir. Robert Rodriguez, 1998)

Fail Safe (dir. Sidney Lumet, 1964)

Fantastic Four (dir. Tim Story, 2005)

Fantastic Four: Rise of the Silver Surfer (dir. Tim Story, 2007)

Farscape (creator Rockne S. O'Bannon, 1999–2003)

Father Knows Best (creator Ed James, 1954–1962)

Firefly (creator Joss Whedon, 2002–2003)

Flash Gordon (prod. Wenzel Luedecke and Edward Gruskin, 1954–1955)

Flight of the Navigator (dir. Randal Kleiser, 1986)

The Flintstones (prod. William Hanna and Joseph Barbera, 1960–1966)

The Fly (dir. David Cronenberg, 1986)

Forbidden Planet (dir. Fred McLeod Wilcox, 1956)

Friends (creators David Crane and Marta Kauffman, 1994–2004)

Futurama (creators Matt Groening and David X. Cohen, 1999–2003)

Futureworld (dir. Richard T. Heffron, 1976)

Galaxy Quest (dir. Dean Parisot, 1999)

The Gemini Man (prod. Harve Bennett, 1976)

Get Smart (creators Mel Brooks and Buck Henry, 1965–1970)

Get Smart (dir. Peter Segal, 2008)

Godzilla, King of the Monsters (dir. Ishirō Honda and Terry Morse, 1956)

The Godfather (dir. Francis Ford Coppola, 1972)

Halloween (dir. John Carpenter, 1978)

Happy Days (creator Garry Marshall, 1974–1984)

He-Man and the Masters of the Universe (prod. Lou Scheimer, 1983–1985)

Heroes (creator Tim Kring, 2006–present)

Hulk (dir. Ang Lee, 2003)

Hyperdrive (prod. Jon Plowman, 2006–present)

I Am Legend (dir. Francis Lawrence, 2007)

I Married a Communist (dir. Robert Stevenson, 1950)

I, Robot (dir. Alex Proyas, 2004)

I Was a Communist for the FBI (dir. Gordon Douglas, 1951)

The Incredible Hulk (creator Kenneth Johnson, 1977–1982)

The Incredible Hulk (dir. Louis Leterrier, 2008)

The Incredible Shrinking Man (dir. Jack Arnold, 1957)

Independence Day (dir. Roland Emmerich, 1996)

Indiana Jones and the Kingdom of the Crystal Skull (dir. Steven Spielberg, 2008)

Invaders from Mars (dir. William Cameron Menzies, 1953)

Invasion (creator Shaun Cassidy, 2005–2006)

The Invasion (dir. Oliver Hirschbiegel, 2007)

Invasion of the Body Snatchers (dir. Don Siegel, 1956)

Invasion of the Body Snatchers (dir. Philip Kaufman, 1978)

The Invisible Man (prod. Harve Bennett and Steven Bochco, 1975–1976)

Iron Man (dir. Jon Favreau, 2008)

The Island (dir. Michael Bay, 2005)

It Came from Outer Space (dir. Jack Arnold, 1953)

Jaws (dir. Steven Spielberg, 1975)

The Jetsons (prod. William Hanna and Joseph Barbera, 1962–1963)

Johnny Mnemonic (dir. Robert Longo, 1995)

Journey to the Center of the Earth (dir. Henry Levin, 1959)

Just Imagine (dir. David Butler, 1930)

Land of the Giants (creator Irwin Allen, 1968–1970)

The Last Starfighter (dir. Nick Castle, 1984)

Law and Order (creator Dick Wolfe, 1990–present)

The Lawnmower Man (dir. Brett Leonard, 1992)

The League of Extraordinary Gentlemen (dir. Stephen Norrington, 2003)

Leave It to Beaver (creators Joe Connelly and Bob Mosher, 1957–1963)

Lexx (prod. Paul Donovan and Wolfram Tichy, 1997–2002)

Life on Mars (creators Matthew Graham, Tony Jordan, and Ashley Pharoah, 2006–2007)

Logan's Run (dir. Michael Anderson, 1976)

Logan's Run (prod. Ivan Goff and Ben Roberts, 1977–1978)

Logan's Run (dir. Joseph Kosinski, in production)

The Lone Gunmen (creators Chris Carter, Vince Gilligan, and John Shiban, 2001)

The Lord of the Rings: The Fellowship of the Ring (dir. Peter Jackson, 2001)

Lost (creators J. J. Abrams, Damon Lindelof, and Jeffrey Lieber, 2004–present)

Lost in Space (creator Irwin Allen, 1965–1968)

The Lost World (dir. Irwin Allen, 1960)

The Man from Atlantis (creators Herbert F. Solow and Mayo Simon, 1977–1978)

The Man from U.N.C.L.E. (creator Norman Felton, 1964–1968)

The Man Who Fell To Earth (dir. Nicholas Roeg, 1976)

Mars Attacks! (dir. Tim Burton, 1996)

M.A.S.K (prod. Tetsuo Katayama, 1985–1986)

The Matrix (dir. Andy Wachowski and Larry Wachowski, 1999)

The Matrix Reloaded (dir. Andy Wachowski and Larry Wachowski, 2003)

The Matrix Revolutions (dir. Andy Wachowski and Larry Wachowski, 2003)

Men in Black (dir. Barry Sonnenfeld, 1997)

Men in Black II (dir. Barry Sonnenfeld, 2002)

Metropolis (dir. Fritz Lang, 1926)

Millennium (creator Chris Carter, 1996–1999)

Minority Report (dir. Steven Spielberg, 2002)

Mission: Impossible (creator Bruce Geller, 1966–1973)

The Mist (dir. Frank Darabont, 2007)

Modern Times (dir. Charles Chaplin, 1936)

Mork and Mindy (creators Garry Marshall, Joe Glauberg, and Dale McRaven, 1978–1982)

Mortal Kombat (dir. Paul Anderson, 1995)

Mutant X (creator Avi Arad, 2001–2004)

My Favorite Martian (creator John L. Greene, 1963–1966)

The Mysterious Island (dir. Lucien Hubbard, 1929)

Mysterious Island (dir. Cy Endfield, 1961)

1984 (dir. Michael Anderson, 1956)

1984 (dir. Michael Radford, 1984)

No Blade of Grass (dir. Cornel Wilde, 1970)

North and South (prod. David L. Wolper, 1985)

The Omega Man (dir. Boris Sagal, 1971)

On the Beach (dir. Stanley Kramer, 1959)

The Outer Limits (creator Leslie Stevens 1963–1965)

The Outer Limits (prod. Leslie Stevens, 1995–2002)

Pearl Harbor (dir. Michael Bay, 2001)

Pitch Black (dir. David Twohy, 2000)

Planet of the Apes (dir. Franklin J. Schaffner, 1968)

Planet of the Apes (prod. Herbert Hirshman, 1974–1975)

Planet of the Apes (dir. Tim Burton, 2001)

Police Academy (dir. Hugh Wilson, 1984)

Police Academy: Back in Training (dir. Jerry Paris, 1986)

Police Academy: Citizens on Patrol (dir. Jim Drake, 1987)

Police Academy: Their First Assignment (dir. Jerry Paris, 1985)

The Poseidon Adventure (dir. Ronald Neame, 1972)

Predator (dir. John McTiernan, 1987)

Primeval (creators Adrian Hodges and Tim Haines, 2007–present)

Quantum Leap (creator Donald P. Bellisario, 1989–1993)

The Quatermass Experiment (creator Nigel Neale, 1953)

Razor (prod. David Eick and Ronald D. Moore, 2007)

Red Dwarf (creators Rob Grant and Doug Naylor, 1988–1999)

Return of the Jedi (dir. Richard Marquand, 1983)

RoboCop (dir. Paul Verhoeven, 1987)

RoboCop 2 (dir. Irvin Kershner, 1990)

The Rocky Horror Picture Show (dir. Jom Sharman, 1975)
Rocky Jones, Space Ranger (prod. Roland Reed, 1954)
Rollerball (dir. Norman Jewison, 1975)
Rollerball (dir. John McTiernan, 2002)
Roots (prod. David L. Wolper and Stan Margulies, 1977)
Roswell (creator Jason Katims, 1999–2002)
Science Fiction Theatre (prod. Ivan Tors, 1955–1957)
Scream (dir. Wes Craven, 1996)
Shaun of the Dead (dir. Edgar Wright, 2004)
She-Ra: Princess of Power (prod. Lou Scheimer, 1985)
Short Circuit (dir. John Badham, 1986)
Silent Running (dir. Douglas Trumball, 1972)
The Six Million Dollar Man (prod. Harve Bennett, 1974–1978)
Sky Captain and the World of Tomorrow (dir. Kerry Conran, 2004)
Slaughterhouse-Five (dir. George Roy Hill, 1972)
Sliders (creators Tracy Thorne and Robert Weiss, 1995–2000)
Smallville (creators Alfred Gough and Miles Millar, 2001–present)
Soylent Green (dir. Richard Fleischer, 1973)
Space: Above and Beyond (creators Glen Morgan and James Wong, 1995–1996)
Space: 1999 (creators Gerry Anderson and Sylvia Anderson, 1975–1977)
Spaced (creators Jessica Hynes and Simon Pegg, 1999–2001)
Space Patrol (prod. Mike Moser and Dick Darley, 1950–1955)
Species (dir. Roger Donaldson, 1995)
Spider-Man (dir. Sam Raimi, 2002)
Spider-Man 2 (dir. Sam Raimi, 2004)
Spider-Man 3 (dir. Sam Raimi, 2007)
The Spy Who Loved Me (dir. Lewis Gilbert, 1977)
Star Trek (creator Gene Roddenberry, 1966–1969)
Star Trek (dir. J. J. Abrams, 2009)
Star Trek II: The Wrath of Khan (dir. Nicholas Meyer, 1982)
Star Trek III: The Search for Spock (dir. Leonard Nimoy, 1984)
Star Trek IV: The Voyage Home (dir. Leonard Nimoy, 1986)
Star Trek V: The Final Frontier (dir. William Shatner, 1989)
Star Trek VI: The Undiscovered Country (dir. Nicholas Meyer, 1991)
Star Trek: Deep Space Nine (creator Gene Roddenberry, 1993–1999)
Star Trek: Enterprise (creator Gene Roddenberry, 2001–2005)
Star Trek: First Contact (dir. Jonathan Frakes, 1996)
Star Trek: Generations (dir. David Carson, 1994)
Star Trek: Insurrection (dir. Jonathan Frakes, 1998)
Star Trek: Nemesis (dir. Stuart Baird, 2002)
Star Trek: The Motion Picture (dir. Robert Wise, 1979)
Star Trek: The Next Generation (creator Gene Roddenberry, 1987–1994)
Star Trek: Voyager (creator Gene Roddenberry, 1995–2001)

Star Wars (dir. George Lucas, 1977)
Star Wars: Special Edition (dir. George Lucas, 1997)
Star Wars Episode I: The Phantom Menace (dir. George Lucas, 1999)
Star Wars Episode II: Attack of the Clones (dir. George Lucas, 2002)
Star Wars Episode III: Revenge of the Sith (dir. George Lucas, 2005)
Stargate SG-1 (creators Jonathan Glassner and Brad Wright, 1997–2007)
Stargate: Atlantis (creators Brad Wright and Robert C. Cooper, 2004–present)
The Stepford Wives (dir. Bryan Forbes, 1974)
The Stepford Wives (dir. Frank Oz, 2004)
Strange Days (dir. Kathryn Bigelow, 1995)
Street Fighter (dir. Steven E. De Souza, 1994)
Superman (dir. Richard Donner, 1978)
Superman Returns (dir. Bryan Singer, 2006)
Survivors (creator Terry Nation, 1975–1977)
Tales of Tomorrow (prod. George F. Foley, Mort Abrahams, and Richard Gordon, 1951–1953)
Tarantula (dir. Jack Arnold, 1955)
The Ten Commandments (dir. Cecil B. DeMille, 1956)
The Terminator (dir. James Cameron, 1984)
Terminator: The Sarah Connor Chronicles (creators James Cameron and Josh Friedman, 2008–present)
Terminator 2: Judgment Day (dir. James Cameron, 1992)
Them! (dir. Gordan Douglas, 1954)
The Thing (dir. John Carpenter, 1982)
The Thing from Another World (dir. Christian Nyby, 1951)
Things to Come (dir. William Cameron Menzies, 1936)
3rd Rock from the Sun (creators Bonnie Turner and Terry Turner, 1996–2001)
This Island Earth (dir. Joseph M. Newman and Jack Arnold, 1955)
The Thorn Birds (prod. David L. Wolper, 1983)
Three Men and a Baby (dir. Leonard Nimoy, 1987)
THX-1138 (dir. George Lucas, 1971)
The Time Machine (dir. George Pal, 1960)
The Time Machine (dir. Simon Wells, 2002)
Time Tunnel (creator Irwin Allen, 1966–1967)
Tom Corbett, Space Cadet (creators Allen Ducovny and Albert Aley, 1950–1955)
The Towering Inferno (dir. Irwin Allen and John Guillermin, 1974)
The Transformers (prod. Joe Bacal, Tom Griffin, and Margaret Loesch, 1984–1987)
Transformers (dir. Michael Bay, 2007)
Tron (dir. Steven Lisberger, 1982)
24 (creators Joel Surnow and Robert Cochran, 2001–present)
The Twilight Zone (creator Rod Serling, 1959–1964)
The Twilight Zone (prod. David P. Berman, Michael MacMillan, Mark Shelmerdine, and Philip DeGuere, 1985–1989)

Twin Peaks (creators David Lynch and Mark Frost, 1990–1991)

2001: A Space Odyssey (dir. Stanley Kubrick, 1968)

UFO (creators Gerry Anderson and Sylvia Anderson, 1970–1971)

V (creator Kenneth Johnson, 1984–1985)

V for Vendetta (dir. James McTeigue, 2006)

Virtuosity (dir. Brett Leonard, 1995)

virus (dir. John Bruno, 1999)

Voyage à Travers l'Impossible (dir. George Méliès, 1904)

Voyage dans la Lune (dir. George Méliès, 1902)

Voyage to the Bottom of the Sea (dir. Irwin Allen, 1961)

Voyage to the Bottom of the Sea (creator Irwin Allen, 1964–1968)

WALL-E (dir. Andrew Stanton, 2008)

Wall Street (dir. Oliver Stone, 1987)

War of the Worlds (dir. Byron Haskin, 1953)

War of the Worlds (prod. Greg Strangis, 1988–1990)

War of the Worlds (dir. Steven Spielberg, 2005)

Westworld (dir. Michael Crichton, 1973)

The Wild Bunch (dir. Sam Peckinpah, 1969)

Wild Palms (creator Bruce Wagner, 1993)

The X-Files (creator Chris Carter, 1993–2002)

The X-Files Movie (dir. Rob Bowman, 1998)

The X-Files: I Want to Believe (dir. Chris Carter, 2008)

X-Men (dir. Bryan Singer, 2000)

X-Men: The Last Stand (dir. Brett Ratner, 2006)

X2 (dir. Bryan Singer, 2003)

Zardoz (dir. John Boorman, 1974)

Index